ON THE JEWS AND THEIR LIES

Martin Luther

Edited and Introduced by
Thomas Dalton, PhD

New York, London
CLEMENS & BLAIR, LLC
2020

CLEMENS & BLAIR, LLC

Introduction, Afterword, and Editing copyright © 2020 by Thomas Dalton, PhD

All rights reserved. No part of this publication may be reproduced, stored in a retrieval system, or transmitted, in any form or by any means, electronic, mechanical, photo-copying, recording, or otherwise.

Clemens & Blair, LLC, is a non-profit educational publisher.

Library of Congress Cataloging-in-Publication Data

Luther, Martin (1483-1546)
On the Jews and Their Lies

p. cm.
Includes bibliographical references.

ISBN 978-1732-3532-13 (pbk.: alk. paper)

1. Religion. 2. Christianity. 3. History of

Printing number: 9 8 7 6 5 4 3 2 1

Printed in the United States of America on acid-free paper.

CONTENTS

Introduction, by Thomas Dalton   5

Preface   41

Part I: Jewish Conceit   43
 Descent from "God's Chosen"
 Circumcision
 Conceit and the Law of Moses
 Arrogance regarding the Promised Land

Part II: The Coming of the Messiah   85
 Genesis 49
 2 Samuel 23
 Haggai 2
 Daniel 9
 Ten Lies of the Jews

Part III: Slander Against the Lord   165

Part IV: A Plan of Action   181

Part V: Conclusion   209

Afterword, by Thomas Dalton   225

Bibliography   243

Index   245

ON THE JEWS AND THEIR LIES

INTRODUCTION

THOMAS DALTON

As one of the most notorious works of the Renaissance, Martin Luther's book *On the Jews and Their Lies* (1543) demands a thorough study by anyone concerned with Christianity, Judaism, or the role of Jews in modern society. Unfortunately, the book is so striking in its polemics and so harsh in its condemnation that we can scarcely discuss it in the present day without incurring terrible insults and slander. Like most such books, the only acceptable view is one of total and unconditional repudiation; Luther was wrong, misguided, hate-filled, anti-Semitic, etc. These become the only allowable positions to take on the work. But such simple-minded condemnation belies the sophistication of Luther's argument, and ignores the lengthy, confirmatory history that preceded (and postdated) him. In short, Luther was well-justified in his attacks, both for theological and sociological reasons, and his case is therefore much stronger than many would like to believe.

Here, in this brief introduction, I will outline both the basic themes of his critique and provide something of the important historical context that lends meaning and substance to the book. This work is not merely of historical interest, nor strictly for Christian scholars; it has potent implications for the entire modern world.

On the Jews and Their Lies

In Luther, the Jews could hardly have earned a more formidable opponent. As the founder of the Lutheran Church and originator of Protestantism generally, he is widely regarded as one of the most influential theologians of all time. One source puts him in the "Big 5", along with Augustine, Aquinas, John Calvin, and Karl Barth.[1] His Lutheran Church claims some 75 million members globally, making it one of the largest protestant denominations.[2] As a man, he was known for his absolute commitment to principles, for his rigorous and extensive theological knowledge, and for his moral courage to confront the religious powers of the day, no matter the personal cost. In fact, he fully expected to be put to death for challenging the Catholic hierarchy, though in the end it did not come to that. Today he is known for taking on corruption within Catholicism as much as for his conflict with Judaism. Ultimately, though, it was the latter of these two that turned out to be the more important, as I will show.

Life of a Reformer

Martin Luther was born on 10 November 1483 in Eisleben, Germany—a small town in the center-east of the country, not far from Leipzig. He attended primary school in Magdeburg and Eisenach, and in 1501, at the age of 17, he entered the university at Erfurt to study law, theology, and philosophy; he completed his initial degree four years later. By the summer of 1505, at age 21, he felt his spiritual calling and entered St. Augustine's Monastery in the same city. He followed the Augustinian order of Catholicism and became an ordained priest in 1507. Luther then enrolled in the Wittenberg University to study formal theology, earning a doctorate in 1512. He then began a long career as a member of their faculty.

---

[1] https://globalchristiancenter.com/bible-and-theology/biblical-theology/24545-the-big-5-the-5-most-influential-theologians-in-church-history

[2] Anglicanism, Calvinism, the Baptists, and the Methodists claim similar or somewhat larger figures. The Catholic Church, by comparison, claims around 1.2 billion members.

Introduction

At that time, a variety of corruption issues began to surface within the Catholic Church, one of the most visible being the sale of so-called indulgences—in order to lessen one's time in purgatory, it was said. In a sense, one could buy one's way out of hell. This fund-raising practice was widespread in Europe and had the blessings of the entire church hierarchy, up to Pope Leo X himself. By 1517, at age 34, Luther felt compelled to speak out against such dubious religious practices. Late that year he wrote a short piece articulating his specific grievances against indulgences and other problems with the Church; this itemized list came to be known as his "95 Theses," and it would become the founding document of Protestantism.[3] By early 1518 they had become widely circulated throughout Europe, and Luther acquired both fame and notoriety.

The pope was slow to act, taking a series of gradual measures against Luther over the next three years. But Luther stood fast, confronting him directly. Luther's two main points of theological contention were (a) that faith alone provided salvation, and neither good acts nor indulgences could improve one's standing in the afterlife; and (b) that the pope was not the final arbiter on scripture, and thus was fallible. Luther held that faith in Jesus was the sole means of redemption, and that the Bible was clear and direct, and therefore spoke to each person individually, without the need for an interpreter. But this was too much for the good pope, who excommunicated Luther in January 1521. In May, the Diet of Worms banned his books and issued a warrant for his arrest. They also made it legal for anyone to kill him on sight.

Fortunately, the death warrant and arrest were never enforced. Luther went into hiding for most of the subsequent year, then returned to preach and write at Wittenberg. He got married in 1525, eventually having six children. The late 1520s and 1530s were spent researching, writing, and building his new church. In 1534 he published a full

---

[3] Some of the theses were sharply biting. For example, Number 86 reads, "Why doesn't the pope, whose wealth is today greater than the wealth of the richest Crassus, build this one basilica of St. Peter with his own money, rather than with the money of poor believers?"

German translation of the Bible, now known as the Luther Bible, which proved extremely popular among the German public.

It was also at this time that his health began to deteriorate. Though still a young man—he celebrated his 50th birthday in 1533—he suffered from a variety of ailments including headaches, kidney stones, cataracts, arthritis, and coronary disease. By the 1540s, as he was completing his final major works, his public appearances became ever more infrequent. Into the year 1546 he was still able to give sermons, while becoming increasingly enfeebled. In February of that year he suffered a stroke and died at age 62. His body is buried today in the All Saints' Church in Wittenberg.

A PROPER HISTORICAL CONTEXT

During his lifetime Luther addressed a wide array of theological matters, but the main issue at hand is his treatment of the Jews. When modern commentators tackle this thorny subject, they typically respond in one of two standard ways. First and most commonly, they simply ignore it. Rather than have to discuss and respond to one of the strongest and most consequential anti-Jewish stances in history, they prefer to pass it by. This is by far the easiest course of action, as it raises no troublesome issues. As a case in point, Kolb's important anthology, *The Oxford Handbook of Martin Luther's Theology* (2014), covers some 635 pages, and yet has only a single small chapter on the Jews ("Luther's views of the Jews and Turks"). And even this is split between the two troublesome minorities; thus the entire book allots just three pages to this vitally important matter. A more recent example of this tactic is the 415-page authoritative text *Martin Luther in Context* (2018). Nominally addressing all circumstantial aspects of the man's life, this book scarcely mentions Jews at all. Yes, there is one small dedicated entry on "Jews and Judaism," but it covers all of six pages, and completely avoids Luther's many controversial statements. Only a single page in the entire book so much as mentions the now-

INTRODUCTION

infamous title, *On the Jews and Their Lies* (p. 185). It's almost as if the editor doesn't want the reader to think that there is anything of substance here, in this most-contentious of topics.

Secondly, when compelled to address it, modern writers invariably respond with some variation of three actions: 1) slandering the book, 2) slandering Luther personally, or 3) explaining it away as part of a generally "irrational" anti-Semitic milieu, of a broader anti-Jewish outlook within Christianity that has now been completely repudiated.[4] Such charges, of course, are utterly unsubstantiated, and they furthermore say nothing against the actual arguments presented in the book, or against Luther's many valid insights into the social effect of European Jewry. Suffice to say that Luther has rarely, if ever, received fair treatment on this topic.

Later I will lay out the main points of Luther's critique of the Jews, but first I need to recall the relevant history of anti-Jewish thinking and writing. Though especially harsh, Luther was far from alone in his criticism. There is in fact a long, well-documented, and highly-pedigreed history of such critical language, one that very few people today are aware of. Here I will highlight some of the main individuals in history, as they relate to Luther's writing.[5]

The first independent and objective criticism of Jews dates all the way back to 300 BC, when two Greek writers briefly addressed the Hebrew tribe. Aristotle's student Theophrastus wrote on an alleged

---

[4] For example, we find Rupp (1972: 15-16) calling the book a "terrible tract" and "a boring tract from which all humor has withered." Indeed, amazingly, "it has nothing memorable or quotable." Hillerbrand (1990: 131) declares it "shocking, if not obscene." And for Kaufmann (2017: 123), it is "a hate-filled and obsessive tirade." On Luther himself, Hillerbrand cites approvingly a Danish psychologist who called Luther "a textbook case of manic depressive," one who may also be suffering from "epilepsy" (p. 128). Kaufmann (2006: 104) refers to the "delusions" of a "misguided" theologian, and in his later 2017 book, Kaufmann suggests that Luther suffered from "age-related depression," that he may have been an alcoholic, and that he was merely "an angry old man," one who was "disillusioned, weak and ill, despairing and broken" (pp. 96, 124). Such name-calling is a sure sign of deficient counterarguments.

[5] For a full study of anti-Jewish critiques, see Dalton (2020).

Jewish custom of live sacrifice, both animal and human: "The Syrians, of whom the Jews constitute a part, also now sacrifice live victims... They were the first to institute sacrifices both of other living beings and of themselves." The Greeks, he added, "would have recoiled from the entire business".[6] There is no further comment, but clearly Theophrastus was appalled at this Jewish tradition.

Around that same time, Hecateus of Abdera wrote an entire text (now lost) called *On the Jews*. Only a few fragments of that work survive, including one notable passage on the Exodus: "As a consequence of having been driven out [of Egypt], Moses introduced a way of life which was to a certain extent misanthropic and hostile to foreigners".[7] One can certainly understand the anger of any people who have been driven from their place of residence. But why should this translate into *misanthropy*—that is, hatred of mankind in general? It's as if the Jews took out their anger against the Pharaoh on the rest of humanity.

The Exodus itself was given a different face by an Egyptian high priest, Manetho, around 250 BC. He describes the Jews as a group of "lepers and other polluted persons," 80,000 in number, who were exiled from Egypt and found residence in Judea. There they established Jerusalem and built a large temple. Manetho comments that the Jews kept to themselves, as it was their law "to interact with none save those of their own confederacy." As the story continues, the Jews ("Solymites") returned to Egypt, and temporarily conquered a large territory. When in power they treated the natives "impiously and savagely," "set[ting] towns and villages on fire, pillaging the temples and mutilating images of the gods without restraint".[8] This accords with Old Testament stories of Jewish massacres among the Canaanites. And it anticipates later comments by Luther, as we will see.

In 134 BC, the Seleucid king Antiochus VII Sidetes ruled over a particularly unruly tribe of Jews. He was advised

---

[6] In Stern (1974: 10).

[7] In Gabba (1984: 629).

[8] In Stern (1974: 82-83).

INTRODUCTION

to destroy the Jews, for they alone among all peoples refused all relations with other races, and saw everyone as their enemy; their forbears, impious and cursed by the gods, had been driven out of Egypt. The counselors [cited] the Jews' hatred of all mankind, sanctioned by their very laws, which forbade them to share their table with a Gentile or give any sign of benevolence. (Gabba 1984: 645)

This is a telling statement: If "they alone among all peoples" were so hostile and misanthropic, and that their "hatred of all mankind" was endorsed by their Bible, then the Hebrew tribe was clearly unique; they hated all others, and then naturally they were hated in turn by those who encountered them. Apparently, the famed anti-Semitism found throughout history has its roots in *Jewish* theology and *Jewish* attitudes toward others. This is obviously not the version of history that we hear today, in our politically-correct modern world.

A few decades later, around 75 BC, Apollonius Molon wrote the first true anti-Jewish book, entitled *Against the Jews*. Much of the work is lost, but a few fragments remain, including his biting observation that the Jews are "the very vilest of mankind." The Jewish writer Josephus adds that Molon referred to Jews as "cowards," "atheists," "misanthropes," and "witless barbarians".[9]

Soon thereafter, a momentous event occurred: the Roman conquest of Palestine. In 63 BC, Roman general Pompey moved into the land of Judea and announced that the region would henceforth be under the domain of Rome (then still a republic, not yet an empire). As the local ruling power, the Jews were outraged—once again, a foreign nation was taking control of "their" land, even as they were vastly outnumbered by the indigenous Arabs. Though deeply angered, the Jews could do nothing to oppose Roman rule; most were resigned to wait it out, believing that God would

---
[9] In Stern (1974: 155-156).

yet bring their savior, their Messiah, who would take revenge on the invaders and make Israel into a great worldly power.

Meanwhile, the critics of the Jews continued to write against them. In his prominent work of 50 BC, *Historical Library*, Diodorus Siculus recounted once again the Jewish Exodus story. Upon being driven out of Egypt, he says, "the nation of Jews had made their hatred of mankind into a tradition..." Later he adds that "they alone, of all nations, avoided dealings with any other people and looked upon all men as their enemies".[10] Again we see the striking phrase: "*they alone, of all nations.*" This tells us that there was something uniquely problematic with the tribe of Hebrews. They evidently harbored an intense hatred of others that stunned and shocked the ancient world.

Ptolemy the Historian made an interesting passing remark in his *History of Herod*, circa 25 BC. He examines the various tribes in the region around Palestine, including Jews and 'Idumaeans' (that is, Edomites; Luther makes a relevant observation on them as well). The Idumaeans were defeated by the Jews in 125 BC and forcibly integrated into the Hebrew tribe. The physical sign of their defeat was male genital mutilation, otherwise known as circumcision:

> Jews and Idumaeans differ... Jews are those who are so by origin and nature. The Idumaeans, on the other hand, were not originally Jews, but Phoenicians and Syrians—having been subjugated by the Jews and having been forced to undergo circumcision, so as to be counted among the Jewish nation...[11]

Luther offers an extended and critical discussion on circumcision in Part I of his work, as we will see.

Our final commentator of the pre-Christian era is Lysimachus. Writing circa 20 BC, he remarks that the Jewish exiles were instructed by Moses to "show goodwill to no man," to offer "the worst advice" to others, and to overthrow any temples or sanctuaries they might come

---

[10] HL 34,1. See Stern (1974: 183).
[11] In Stern (1974: 356).

Introduction

upon. Arriving in Judea, "they maltreated the population, and plundered and set fire to the [local] temples." They then built a town called Hierosolyma (Jerusalem), and referred to themselves as Hierosolymites.[12]

The charge of misanthropy, or hatred of mankind, is significant and merits further discussion—not the least because it is an important concept for Luther. It has recurred several times already, in Hecateus, Posidonius, Molon, Diodorus, and now Lysimachus. This is striking because the Romans were notably tolerant of other sects and religions, owing in part to their polytheistic worldview.

In the case of the Jews, though, monotheistic arrogance was combined with racial distinctness and other cultural characteristics, resulting in a deeply-embedded misanthropic streak. They seem to have little concern or true compassion for other races—unless, of course, it served to benefit them. Authentic altruism seems to be all but lacking. Even towards those who have shown them good will, good will is not returned. Rather, Jews have, historically, abused and oppressed anyone, any non-Jews, if it was in their interests. For centuries they have been willing to serve as executors or enforcers of state power (when they had none of their own), with little evident regard for adverse effects on others. In one of the earliest Bible stories, Joseph, son of Jacob, finds favor with the Egyptian pharaoh, only to use his power to exploit the local farmers when a famine strikes.[13] Later we read of the Jews' ruthless slaughter of the Canaanites.

We see this issue recur even through the present day. Others are valued only in an instrumental sense, to serve Jewish ends. Sometimes this appears explicitly, as in the 2010 statement by leading Orthodox Rabbi Yosef, who said, "Goyim [non-Jews] were born only to serve us. Without that, they have no place in the world—only to serve the people of Israel. They will work, they will plow, they will reap. We will

---

[12] Stern (1974: 384-385).

[13] See Genesis 47.

sit like an effendi and eat".[14] It would be difficult to find a cruder statement of Jewish misanthropy.

As Luther realized, there is a Biblical basis for all this. If the Jews consider themselves 'chosen' by God, clearly everyone else is second class, at best. If God gave the Jews dominion, they can feel justified in imposing on others. The Book of Exodus states, "we are distinct...from all other people that are upon the face of the earth" (33:16). Similarly, the Hebrew tribe is "a people dwelling alone, and not reckoning itself among the nations" (Num 23:9). In Deuteronomy (15:6), Moses tells the Jews "you shall rule over many nations"; "they shall be afraid of you" (28:10). Rabbi Yosef could have quoted Genesis: "Let peoples serve you, and nations bow down to you" (27:29); or Deuteronomy, where God promises Jews "houses full of all good things, which [they] did not fill, and cisterns hewn out, which [they] did not hew, and vineyards and olive trees, which [they] did not plant" (6:11). And outside the Pentateuch, we can read in Isaiah: "Foreigners shall build up your walls, and their kings shall minister to you...that men may bring you the wealth of the nations" (60:10-11); or again, "aliens shall stand and feed your flocks, foreigners shall be your plowmen and vinedressers... you shall eat the wealth of the nations" (61:5-6). This is explicit misanthropy, mandated by God and the prophets.

As we will see, Jewish hatred of humanity is not only one of the earliest but also one of the most persistent criticisms. Many prominent commentators over the centuries have observed this especially pernicious trait. And it explains much of Jewish behavior through the present day.

ROMANS AND CHRISTIANS

By the turn of the millennium, Rome had formally become an empire, under their supreme ruler Augustus. Jesus of Nazareth was born, allegedly in 3 BC, and crucified in 30 AD. And the critics continued their attacks. A writer by the name of Apion (35 BC – 45 AD) wrote a

---
[14] *Jerusalem Post*, 18 Oct 2010.

Introduction

popular book, *Against the Jews*, that included a number of specific criticisms, such as Jewish naiveté and foolishness, disrespect for the emperor, "failure to show goodwill to a single alien," and their insistence on cruel circumcision.

In the year 38, Jews in Alexandria (today, Egypt) were agitating and rebelling against Roman rule, causing the local governor, Flaccus, to suppress them. The Jewish writer Philo described the course of events: Flaccus' advisors encouraged random attacks on synagogues and Jewish property, hoping that the pogrom would spread to other lands. Flaccus ended Jewish privilege, reducing them to stateless "foreigners and aliens." He terminated their right to run businesses, and money-lenders lost what they had loaned. His men drove the Jews out of most areas of the city and confined them in one small quarter, effectively forming the first Jewish ghetto in history. Finally, Flaccus "allowed anyone who was inclined to proceed to exterminate the Jews as prisoners of war." Eventually the local populace, who widely despised the Jews, joined in, conducting a variety of attacks, many fatal. The uproar caused then-emperor Claudius to issue a proclamation against the Alexandrian Jews; they "live in a city which is not their own," and they "possess an abundance of all good things," but they must respect the laws and the state. By abusing their status, Claudius said, the Jews could be blamed "for fomenting a general plague which infests the whole world." (Claudius meanwhile had his own problems with the Jews in Rome, and was compelled to banish them from the city in 49 AD.)

Despite all this, the small tribe of Hebrews continued to grow in wealth and influence, as we see in the words of the great Roman philosopher Seneca. In a work from the year 60, he critiqued the Jews' "superstitious" religious beliefs and their laziness, and yet was amazed that this little "accursed race" had attained such importance: "the customs of this accursed race have gained such influence that they are now received throughout all the world. The vanquished have given laws to their victors".[15] For Seneca, this was a clear sign of the impending decay of the mighty Roman Empire.

Then in the year 70, another monumental event: the destruction of Jerusalem. The Jews, it seems, had been agitating and rebelling for decades, even to the point of murdering Roman soldiers; eventually Rome decided to act. They sent in a large military contingent in 66, and after four years of struggle, succeeded in capturing and destroying the famed Jewish temple. Thousands of Jews died, and thousands more were scattered to all parts of the known world. Thus began their "exile," as Luther describes it. By his day, it had been nearly 1,500 years, and still the Jews had not returned to power in Jerusalem. As we know, it would not be until 1948 that they (partially) succeeded.

Into the 2nd century of the new millennium, Romans continued to offer critical remarks. Quintillian (circa 100) condemned their tribe as "a race which is a curse to others." Martial (circa 110) derided, of all things, their personal hygiene, comparing a host of foul-smelling things to "the breath of the fasting Jews." And Plutarch made a number of derisive comments on their various "superstitions."

But the premier critic of that time was the historian Tacitus. In his *Annals* he blasted the Jews as a "disease" and pointedly condemned their misanthropy, or "hatred of the human race." His harshest comments, however, are found in another work, *Histories*. There he offered an extended discussion of "the race of men hateful to the gods." He was appalled at the degraded status of their so-called religion, which was virtually the polar opposite of the noble Roman worldview:

> The Jews regard as profane all that we hold sacred; on the other hand, they permit all that we abhor. ... Whatever their origin, these rites are maintained by their antiquity: the other customs of the Jews are base and abominable, and owe their persistence to their depravity. For the worst rascals among other

---

[15] In Stern (1974: 431).

Introduction

peoples...always kept sending tribute and contributions to Jerusalem, thereby increasing the wealth of the Jews; again, the Jews are extremely loyal toward one another, and always ready to show compassion, but toward every other people they feel only hate and enmity. ... As a race, they are prone to lust, [and have] adopted circumcision to distinguish themselves from other peoples. (Sec. 5.5)

Tacitus closes the section with the comment that "the ways of the Jews are preposterous and mean." He later adds that the Jews are "an obnoxious and superstitious race"—a group who are the "most despised" of subjects and "the basest of peoples."

Back in Jerusalem, the remaining Jews decided to try once more to revolt against Rome, and launched a second effort in 115. Cassius Dio, in his *Roman History*, remarked on the notable cruelty and barbarism of the militant Jews, which included disemboweling their Roman victims and even eating their flesh. After two years, this too ended in failure. Yet a third revolt came in the year 132. This time, wealthy Jews attempted to bribe neighboring peoples into fighting on their side. Dio's comment on this practice is revealing: "many outside nations, too, were joining them through eagerness for gain, and the whole earth, one might almost say, was being stirred up over the matter." But to no avail; as before, the Romans crushed the rebellion.

Even as the Jews were suffering defeat, the Jewish-inspired Christianity was growing in strength. By the late 100s, it had begun to attract critical commentary from both Romans and Greeks. A notable example was the Greek philosopher Celsus, who wrote an important text, *The True Word*, sometime around 178. The book is striking as an extended and scathing critique of the newly-emerging Christian sect, but in the process, he makes a number of negative remarks on the Jews. Beginning with Moses, the Jews "were deluded by clumsy deceits into thinking that there was only one God" (I.23). They were "addicted to sorcery" and thus "fell into error through ignorance and were deceived." Celsus mocks "the race of Jews and Christians," comparing them all "to a cluster of bats or ants coming out of a nest, or frogs holding council round a marsh, or worms assembling in some filthy corner, disagreeing with each other about which of them are the worse sinners" (IV.23). "The Jews," he adds, "were runaway slaves who escaped from Egypt; they never did anything important, nor have they ever been of any significance or prominence." Fate has been justifiably harsh to them, and they are "suffering the penalty of their arrogance" (V.41). Judeo-Christian theology, says Celsus, is a mish-mash of mythology and absurdity. "The God of the Jews is accursed" because he created, or allowed, evil in the world—a classic statement of the Problem of Evil. The cosmogony of Genesis is ridiculous, as is the creation story of mankind; "Moses wrote these stories because he understood nothing... [He] put together utter trash" (VI.49). In the long run Jewry is doomed—"they will presently perish" (VI.80).[16]

Yet other critical voices emerged at that time. The Greek writer Philostratus wrote a history of Rome in which he remarked on their many conflicts with the Hebrews:

> The Jews have long been in revolt not only against the Romans, but against all humanity; and a race that has made its own a life apart and irreconcilable, that cannot share with the rest of mankind in the pleasures of the table nor join in their libations or prayers or sacrifices, are separated from ourselves by a greater gulf than divides us from Susa or Bactra or the more distant Indies. (V.33.4)

Again, we see the infamous Jewish misanthropy: "revolt against all humanity." The Jews, he says, are profoundly different from the rest of mankind—and not in a good way. In the same vein, yet another famed writer, Porphyry, wrote a book in 280 titled *Against the Christians* in

---

[16] The book itself is now lost, but large portions were reproduced in Origen's work *Contra Celsum*.

INTRODUCTION

which he labeled the Jews as "the impious enemies of all nations." The Jews, it seems, simply couldn't buy a friend. This cannot be a coincidence. If one person hates you, it's probably them; if everyone hates you, it's probably *you*.

INTO THE CHRISTIAN ERA

By the 300s, as the power of Rome began to decline, Christianity became increasingly important throughout the Middle East and Europe. Emperor Constantine was the first to convert to the new religion in 312, and Theodosius made it the official religion of Rome in 380. All the while, the theological gulf between Christians and Jews grew, and the Christian emperors found it increasingly necessary to take action against the Hebrews. Constantine, for example, punished anyone attempting to convert to the "deadly" and "nefarious sect" of Judaism. Gratian (383 AD) threatened all who have "polluted themselves with the Jewish contagions." Honorius (409) decreed that no one shall "adopt the abominable and vile name of the Jews," nor accept "the Jewish perversity, which is alien to the Roman Empire." Theodosius II (438) referred to the "blindly senseless Jews" as "monstrous heretics" and "an abominable sect."

Finally, in 476 AD, the classic (western) Roman Empire collapsed, leaving the popes and the Church to fill the void. The Dark Ages thus commenced, and the Christian Church began its rise to power. It was at this time that the theological disputes with Jews came to the fore. Early critiques by the likes of Tertullian and Hippolytus, around the year 200, were quite mild. But by the late 300s, the criticisms became more heated. Gregory of Nyssa, for example, blasted the Jews as the absolute dregs of humanity, deploying an impressive array of adjectives:

> Murderers of the Lord, murderers of prophets, rebels and full of hatred against God, they commit outrage against the law, resist

God's grace, repudiate the faith of their fathers. They are confederates of the devil, offspring of vipers, scandal-mongers, slanderers, darkened in mind, leaven of the Pharisees, Sanhedrin of demons, accursed, utterly vile, quick to abuse, enemies of all that is good. (*In Christi resurr. orat.*, 5).[17]

Such anger must have been grounded in something more than mere theology. There was something deeply personal here. Gregory seems to have found the Jews to be profoundly antisocial, immoral, corrupt, a real danger to the well-being of the public.

Saint Jerome was another harsh critic, attacking the Jews in a number of his many writings. In 407 he predicted that, "by means of intrigue and deception...Jews would persecute the people of Christ [and] rule the world".[18] Later he said of the synagogue, "If you call it a brothel, a den of vice, the Devil's refuge, Satan's fortress, a place to deprave the soul...you are still saying less than it deserves".[19] John Hood (1995: 16) adds that Jerome "accused the Jews of almost every imaginable vice, but avarice, drunkenness, gluttony, and licentiousness were his favorites."

The strongest early critic, however, was undoubtedly John Chrysostom. Of particular note is his work *Adversus Judaeos*, commonly called *Homilies against the Jews* (387 AD).[20] The first homily captures the essence of his attack. He begins with mention of a "very serious illness" that pervades society. "What is this disease? The festivals of the pitiful and miserable Jews" which were soon to commence (I.I.4). "But do not be surprised that I call the Jews pitiable," he adds. "They really are pitiable and miserable" (I.II.1). Citing Biblical precedent, Chrysostom refers to them as dogs, and as "stiff-necked." They are drawn to gluttony and drunkenness (I.II.5), and chiefly characterized by their lust for animal pleasures. Indeed, they are animals,

---

[17] In Simon (1996: 216).

[18] In Jaher (1994: 30).

[19] In Wistrich (2010: 80).

[20] Also known as *Discourses against the Jews*. Following quotations taken from *Fathers of the Church*, vol 68.

INTRODUCTION

though of a worthless kind: "Although such beasts are unfit for work, they are fit for killing" (I.II.6)—a shocking call from this man of God. "And this is what happened to the Jews: while they were making themselves unfit for work, they grew fit for slaughter." He even cites Biblical mandate here, from the Gospel of Luke (19:27): "This is why Christ said, 'But as for these my enemies,... bring them here and slay them'."

Chrysostom disparages the religious rituals of the synagogue: "[The Jews] drag into the synagogue the whole theater, actors and all. For there is no difference between the theater and the synagogue" (I.II.7). "That place is a brothel," he adds. "It is also a den of robbers and a lodging for wild beasts." In fact it has become no less than "the dwelling of demons" (I.III.1)—as "the Jews themselves are demons" (I.VI.3).

He then raises a fundamental metaphysical dispute. The Christian testament speaks of a bifurcated afterlife: either eternal bliss with God in heaven, or eternal damnation. "But the Jews," says Chrysostom,

> neither know nor dream of these things.[21] They live for their bellies, they gape for the things of this world, their condition is no better than that of pigs or goats because of their wanton ways and excessive gluttony. They know but one thing: to fill their bellies and be drunk... (I.IV.1)

Then there are the standard charges of the Jews as Christ-killers, and—presaging Luther—as failing to properly honor the old prophets: "And so it is that we must hate both them and their synagogue all the more because of the offensive treatment of those holy men." On a more practical level, the Jews are to be shunned because of "their plundering, their covetousness, their abandonment of the poor, their thefts, their cheating in trade" (I.VII.1)—charges that relate to fundamental cultural and ethnic traits, rather than religion.

---

[21] In truth, the Old Testament has virtually no mention of either an afterlife with God in heaven, or, astonishingly, of hell. For the Jews, all praise or retribution occurs in the present world. This fact likely explains much of the traditional Jewish obsession with material goods, money, wealth, and power.

For all these reasons, says Chrysostom, we must "turn away from them, since they are the common disgrace and infection of the whole world" (I.VI.7)—recalling Claudius' imagery of a "general plague that infests the whole world." Finally, Chrysostom appeals to his Christian reader to not fear the Jews' sorcery and black powers; "the Jews frighten you as if you were little children, and you do not see it" (I.III.7). Such a sentiment could be repeated in the present day, as many Gentiles seem to act in evident fear of hidden Jewish power of retribution, as if afraid of some evil spell. Overall, Chrysostom's language sounds shockingly harsh to today's sensitive ears, but they merely reflected the prevailing opinion of the time. In light of such talk, Luther's words, coming some 1,000 years later, appear simply as more of the same.

A few years after Chrysostom's death, back in Alexandria, the Jews were once again expelled, in the year 414. Clearly they were a source of endless trouble in the ancient world.

A final, albeit mild critique from those early years of Christianity came from Augustine, who wrote his work *Adversus Judaeos* ('Against the Jews') in 425. Robert Wistrich (2010: 86) describes Augustine's general view of the Jews as "incurably 'carnal,' blind to spiritual meaning, perfidious, faithless, and apostate." In the *Adversus*, Augustine wrote sharply against the Hebrews as the driving force in the crucifixion: "It was the Jews who held [Jesus]; the Jews who insulted him; the Jews who bound him; the Jews who crowned him with thorns; who soiled him with their spit; who whipped him; who ridiculed him; who hung him on the cross; who stabbed his body with their spears." But the harsh personal attacks of his predecessors are absent.

As Europe progressed through the Dark Ages, the Church gradually grew in power, even as learned commentary faded into the background for a few centuries. In the 800s, a French archbishop, Agobard of Lyon, complained vociferously to king Louis the Pious about the "insolence of the Jews." They "daily curse Jesus Christ and the Christians," engage in slave trading of Christians, and pass off their unclean meats to the

Introduction

unsuspecting Gentile public, he said. In general, the Jews are "the detestable enemies of the truth."

By the time of the Fourth Lateran Council of 1215, Pope Innocent III was prepared to reassert control over the Hebrews. New resolutions (canons) were passed, "designed to isolate, restrict, and denigrate Jews".[22] Usury—lending money at interest, and often at exorbitant rates—was a growing problem, especially when it was causing the bankruptcy of church members who were expected to donate generously. Canon 67 reads: "The more the Christians are restrained from the practice of usury, the more are they oppressed in this matter by the treachery of the Jews, so that in a short time they exhaust the resources of the Christians." There was also the problem of identification. Then as now, Jews were able to move largely unnoticed through Gentile society, owing to the lack of obvious ethnic features. This was unacceptable to the Church and hence they mandated a "difference of dress" for Jews (and also Muslims, or "Saracens"): "we decree that such Jews and Saracens of both sexes in every Christian province and at all times shall be marked off in the eyes of the public from other peoples through the character of their dress" (Canon 68). This was no idle declaration; conical caps, badges, and related clothing were instituted in France, Portugal, Spain, and Italy in the following centuries.[23] Finally, Canon 69 states that "Jews are not to be given public offices… [because] it is absurd that a blasphemer of Christ exercise authority over Christians."

This harsher stance was taken up by the preeminent theologian of the day, Thomas Aquinas. In contrast to Augustine, Aquinas preferred to emphasize the fact that the Jews knowingly sinned in first refusing and then later crucifying the Savior. As Hood (1995: 74) writes, "In Aquinas' view, the Jewish leaders had sufficient evidence to know that Jesus was divine, but they willfully refused to draw the conclusion. This increased rather than limited their culpability." This guilt,

---

[22] Carroll (2001: 282).
[23] See Jaher (1994: 70).

Aquinas says, is furthermore perpetually binding on the Jewish people, so long as they refuse Christ and adhere to Mosaic Law: "The blood of Christ binds the children of the Jews insofar as they are imitators of their parents' malice and thus approve of Christ's killing" (*Questiones Disputata de Malo*, 4.8).

Apart from this theological guilt was the practical problem of usury. As he writes in the *Summa Theologica*, "Lending money at interest is intrinsically unjust" (ST_{2-2}, 78.1). All interest is unethical because it entails no effort; it is reward without work, hardly better than sheer theft. That this is a crime is manifestly obvious to Aquinas, and thus he calls for the harshest of punishment. And the Jews come in for special reprimand, as they were most closely identified with that crime. "It seems to me that a Jew, or any other usurer, should be fined more heavily than others who are punished with fines, since they are known to have less title to the money taken from them" (*De Regimine Judaeorum* [On the Government of the Jews], 70-74). Monarchs of Europe would suffer from restrictions on interest, but still they have an obligation to rein in the usurers: "It would be better for [royalty] to compel Jews to work for a living, as is done in parts of Italy, than to allow them to live in idleness and grow rich by usury. If rulers suffer loss, it is only because they have been negligent" (*De Regimine*, 81-88).

The Jews were guilty on both philosophical and pragmatic counts, and thus were to be shunned. For Aquinas, "Jews were profoundly dangerous, and...contact with them should be avoided whenever possible".[24] One should not socialize or eat with them, discuss religion, or marry them; they were indeed the true "enemies" of Christian society (ST_{2-2}, 10.11). Aquinas upheld the Lateran Council's dictate on restricting Jews from public office, and he endorsed the call to mark them with distinctive clothing. On this latter point he wrote, "The response to this question is clear, since, according to the statue of the general [Lateran] council, Jews of each sex in all Christian lands and at

---

[24] Hood (1995: 78).

Introduction

all times should be distinguished from other people by their dress" (*De Regimine*, 244-249). The point is obvious but it bears repeating: the act of identifying one's enemy is the first step in dealing with him.

For theological, sociological, and practical reasons, then, the nations of Europe began to take action, and progressively banished their Jewish populations. Waves of expulsions swept the continent in the 14th and 15th centuries: France (1306 and 1394), Germany (1348), Hungary (1349), Austria (1421), Lithuania (1445), Provence (1490), Spain (1492), Portugal (1497). But these would only be temporary measures, as we know; within two or three centuries the Jews were back, in sufficiently large numbers to cause problems once again.

Luther's Frontal Assault

This brings us to the time of Martin Luther. Recall that it was in 1517, at the age of 34, that he issued his famous 95 Theses against the Catholic Church, largely because of the corrupting sale of indulgences. But even at that age, he had already begun to formulate his critique of the Jews. His lectures on the Psalms, dating to 1513, included many of the main points that he would later raise, as would his *Lectures on Romans* (1515). He back-tracked a bit in a 1523 work, *That Jesus Christ was Born a Jew*, but this seems to have been a minor departure from his generally critical stance.

By the 1540s, his overall position was clear: Jews were a lying, incorrigible people who refused to think sensibly about the Bible, slandered and condemned Christians, stole their money, and refused to believe that a savior had indeed already come to Earth. As such, they posed a mortal (and indeed, immortal!) threat to humanity, and hence the harshest measures were justified. When asked in 1541 about how to go about baptizing a Jew, Luther replied:

> If a Jew, not converted at heart, were to ask baptism at my hands, I would take him on to the bridge, tie a stone round his

neck, and hurl him into the river; for those wretches are wont to make a jest of our religion.[25]

The following year (1542) he became convinced of the need to write a lengthy critique, for reasons that apparently extended beyond mere theology:

> I intend to write against the Jews once again because I hear that some of our lords [nobles] are befriending them. I'll advise them to chase all the Jews out of their land. What reason do they have to slander and insult the dear Virgin Mary as they do? They call her a stinkpot, a hag, a monstrosity. If I were a lord, I'd take them by the throat, or they'd have to show cause [why I shouldn't]. They're wretched people. I know of no stronger argument against them than to ask them why they've been in exile so long.[26]

And write he did. The result was one of the most remarkable books in Western history: *Von den Juden und ihren Lügen*—'On the Jews and Their Lies,' published in 1543. Here, Luther raises two general categories of complaints: (1) theological disputes, and (2) secular (pragmatic or practical) concerns. As befitting a religious man, most of the text—perhaps 90%—is focused on the theological aspect, much of it detailed and arcane. The Jews misread and distort the meaning of the Old Testament, they slander Jesus and Mary, they insult the name of God himself, says Luther. All of this tends to be centered on the key dispute: whether the Messiah has already come or not. Christians, of course, say he came (now) 2,000 years ago, in the person of Jesus. Jews say Jesus was an imposter and fraud, and the real Messiah—the savior of *the Jews*—has yet to come. The Old Testament speaks of a savior who

---

[25] Luther (1902: 165). At that time, many Jews were 'fake' converts, simply to hide their identity.

[26] Luther (1955: 426).

Introduction

would come just prior to the destruction of Jerusalem, in order to save all of humanity, argues Luther; Jews say, by contrast, that it speaks of a still-to-come redeemer of Israel, a commander and general, who will raise it up to become the greatest world power. As we can imagine, both sides are able to cite multiple passages in their own defense, even as Luther displays supreme confidence in his own analysis.

As interesting as Luther's biblical exegesis is, it is the other aspect—the secular and pragmatic dispute—that is of greatest importance for the present day. The main reason, of course, is that modern Western society is, broadly speaking, secular. Governments are formally so, as are corporations, most universities, and most social institutions. Conflicts in modern industrial society are based in politics, economics, or other pragmatic matters; few people are concerned on a day-to-day basis with issues of theology. And many Jews are non-religious, or only mildly so.

Specifically, Luther identifies some eight items of concern, apart from theological matters:

1 Usury: Jews are financiers and money-lenders who exploit and deceive the common people, driving them into bankruptcy, taking their assets, and acquiring vast wealth thereby.

2 Arrogance: For a variety of reasons, Jews see themselves as superior to everyone else, when in fact they are, in many ways, much our inferiors.

3 Lying: Jews lie incessantly, even about the most consequential matters. They are deliberately and maliciously deceitful, in many ways. Hence they can never be trusted, on anything.

4 Stubbornness: Lacking all sense of humility, Jews see no need to modify their behavior or to learn from others.

5 Greedy: Jews have an inordinate love of money, gold, power, and all manifestations of material wealth.

6 Sexist: Male Jews view all females, even their own, as lesser humans.

7 Misanthropic: Jews display a general hatred and contempt toward all other people. They are willing to use and abuse others to any extent, if it serves their benefit.

8 Murderers: Jews will take the most extreme actions, even including mass murder, to gain wealth and power, and to inflict their hatred upon humanity.

We can see from both Luther's remarks and from the long history that preceded him, that such characteristics seem to be endemic to the Jewish people. Not every Jew, of course, exhibits all such vices, and conversely, many other people, many non-Jews, also possess these shortcomings. However, they are disproportionately present in Jews, and they lead to disproportionate harm in the society—or so we may conclude. If Luther had experienced such failings in, say, Turks, he surely would have written a book *On the Turks and Their Lies*. But he did not. And other famous writers before Luther would have written such books. But they did not. Evidence and history point to something uniquely troublesome about the Jewish people—perhaps they are cursed by God, after all.

Both the secular and the religious aspects are amplified today by the outsized and disproportionate role played by Jews in western nations. In the US, for example, Jews number around 6 million, and thus constitute about 2% of the total population. And yet they own or control around half of the total wealth in the country.[27] They own or control all major media corporations. In government, the Jewish Lobby donates between a third and half of all political contributions to Congressmen and presidential candidates, giving them overwhelming influence in governmental policy, both domestic and foreign. And though the percent of Jewish population is smaller in other countries, such as Canada, UK, France, and Australia, a similar situation obtains there. I have documented all these matters elsewhere, and I refer the interested reader to these sources.[28]

---

[27] See the Afterword for further discussion.

Introduction

In sum, considering their numbers, Jews have astoundingly disproportionate power in modern Western nations, and therefore the world. This is most dramatically shown in the United States, the sole global superpower and the nation with more Jews than any other (including Israel). The American Jewish Lobby operates on both right and left of the political spectrum, on both Democrats and Republicans (and minor parties as well). American Jews dictate US economic policy, foreign policy, military policy, and most large spending priorities. Notably, they are the dominant factor when it comes to war. Jews have been central to US involvement in World Wars One and Two, the Vietnam War, both Iraq wars, Afghanistan, and all post-9/11 military actions.[29] In 2003, at the onset of the second Iraq war against Saddam Hussein, US congressman Jim Moran stated, "If it were not for the strong support of the Jewish community for this war with Iraq, we would not be doing this".[30] Later that same year, with the war well underway, Malaysian president Mahathir Mohamad said it best: "Today Jews rule the world by proxy. They get others to fight and die for them".[31] Luther would have been aghast and appalled, to say the least. In fact, these are the very reasons why his analysis is so important today.

Luther's book is organized into five parts, which tend to become increasingly harsh in tone as the work progresses. The main thrust of each is as follows:

Part I: After a few introductory comments, Luther proceeds to address and refute four prime reasons for Jewish conceit and arrogance: (1) they claim descent from God's original "chosen people"; (2) they are circumcised, which is the mark of God's blessing; (3) their

---

[28] See Hitler (2019: 30-40); Dalton (2015: 261-276).
[29] See Dalton (2019).
[30] *Washington Post* (11 Mar 2003).
[31] *FoxNews* (16 Oct 2003).

prophet Moses was the sole recipient of God's "law," i.e. the Ten Commandments; and (4) they were the sole recipients of God's "promised land." Luther challenges each claim in detail, arguing that there is little or no biblical basis for such points, and therefore that Jewish arrogance is completely unfounded.

Part II: The longest of the book, this section addresses the past (or future) coming of the Messiah. In his defense of the coming of Jesus some 1,500 years prior, Luther analyzes four Old Testament passages that are central to his case: (a) Genesis 49:10, (b) 2 Samuel 23:5, (c) Haggai 2:6, and (d) Daniel 9:24. His knowledge of scripture here is truly impressive. However, for those readers less interested in theological minutiae, this part can be skipped without losing the main thrust of the book.

Part III: Here the language becomes harsher, as Luther takes on Jewish insults against Jesus and Mary. Those who could do such things, he says, are capable of the most horrendous acts of abuse and violence against Christian (Gentile) people. Jews have in the past, and would so again, slaughter Christians and Gentiles, given the power to do so. Therefore the Jews must be driven from Christian lands, and perhaps themselves killed, if we are to defend ourselves.

Part IV: The most infamous section of the book, because it lays out in detail Luther's plan of action against the Hebrew tribe. The section opens with seven specific actions: 1) burn down their synagogues and schools, 2) destroy their homes, 3) take away all their holy books, 4) prohibit all rabbis from teaching Jewish theology, 5) abolish their right of free travel, 6) ban all Jewish moneylending ("usury"), and confiscate all Jewish wealth, and 7) put them to hard physical labor. Later he adds an eighth point, that "they must be driven from our country."

Part V: A short concluding section in which Luther reiterates the need to "drive them out like mad dogs." He warns that, through their

INTRODUCTION

vast financial resources, they are on their way to becoming "masters" of the world—a strikingly accurate forecast, unfortunately.

Luther's language, especially in the later parts, is brutal and unforgiving—recalling the harsh earlier words of Gregory, Jerome, and Chrysostom. His frankness and explicitness cannot be overstated. In what follows, we read such astonishing words as these:

- "The sun has never shone on a more bloodthirsty and vengeful people than they are who imagine that they are God's people who have been commissioned and commanded to murder and to slay the Gentiles. In fact, the most important thing that they expect of their Messiah is that he will murder and kill the entire world with their sword." (I)
- "Therefore, be on your guard against the Jews, knowing that wherever they have their synagogues, nothing is found but a den of devils in which sheer self-glory, conceit, lies, blasphemy, and defaming of God and men are practiced most maliciously and vehemently, just as the devils themselves do." (I)
- "They are the circumcised saints who have God's commandments and do not keep them, but are stiff-necked, disobedient, prophet-murderers, arrogant, usurers, and filled with every vice, as the whole of Scripture and their present conduct bear out." (II)
- "Therefore, dear Christian, be on your guard against the Jews, who, as you discover here, are consigned by the wrath of God to the devil, who has not only robbed them of a proper understanding of Scripture, but also of ordinary human reason, shame, and sense, and only works mischief with Holy Scripture through them. Therefore they cannot be trusted and believed in any other matter either, even though a truthful word may occasionally drop from their lips." (II)

- "They alone want to have the Messiah and be masters of the world. The accursed Goyim must be servants, give their desire (that is, their gold and silver) to the Jews, and let themselves be slaughtered like wretched cattle. They would rather remain lost consciously and eternally than give up this view." (II)
- "And these dreary dregs, this stinking scum, this dried-up froth, this moldy leaven and boggy morass of Jewry should merit, on the strength of their repentance and righteousness, the empires of the whole world—that is, the Messiah and the fulfillment of the prophecies—though they possess none of the aforementioned items and are nothing but rotten, stinking, rejected dregs of their fathers' lineage!" (II)
- "Moreover, they are nothing but thieves and robbers who daily eat no morsel and wear no thread of clothing which they have not stolen and pilfered from us by means of their accursed usury. Thus they live from day to day, together with wife and child, by theft and robbery, as arch-thieves and robbers, in the most impenitent security." (II)
- "The Jews have not acquired a perfect mastery of the art of lying; they lie so clumsily and ineptly that anyone who is just a little observant can easily detect it." (II)
- "This is to say that he is to kill and exterminate all of us Goyim through their Messiah, so that they can lay their hands on the land, the goods, and the government of the whole world. And now a storm breaks over us with curses, defamation, and derision that cannot be expressed with words. They wish that sword and war, distress and every misfortune may overtake us accursed Goyim." (III)
- "No one is holding them here now. The country and the roads are open for them to proceed to their land whenever they wish. If they did so, we would be glad to present gifts to them on the occasion; it would be good riddance. They are a heavy

Introduction

burden, a plague, a pestilence, a sheer misfortune for our country." (III)
- "We are at fault in not slaying them." (III)
- "Such a desperate, thoroughly evil, poisonous, and devilish lot are these Jews, who for these 1,400 years have been and still are our plague, our pestilence, and our misfortune." (IV)
- "That they are venomous, bitter, vindictive, tricky serpents, assassins, and children of the devil, who sting and work harm stealthily wherever they cannot do it openly." (IV)
- "Now, let me commend these Jews sincerely to whoever feels the desire to shelter and feed them, to honor them, to be fleeced, robbed, plundered, defamed, vilified, and cursed by them, and to suffer every evil at their hands—these venomous serpents and devil's children, who are the most vehement enemies of Christ our Lord and of us all." (IV)
- "They must be driven from our country." (IV)
- "But since they are loath to quit the country, they will boldly deny everything and will also offer the government money enough for permission to remain here. Woe to those who accept such money, and accursed be that money, which they have stolen from us so damnably through usury. They deny just as brazenly as they lie. And wherever they can secretly curse, poison, or harm us Christians, they do so without any qualms of conscience. If they are caught in the act or charged with something, they are bold enough to deny it impudently, even to the point of death, since they don't regard us worthy of being told the truth. In fact, these holy children of God consider any harm they can wish or inflict on us as a great service to God. Indeed, if they had the power to do to us what we are able to do to them, not one of us would live for an hour." (IV)
- "Therefore, I firmly believe that they say and practice far worse things secretly than the histories and others record about

them, meanwhile relying on their denials and on their money. But even if they could deny all else, they cannot deny that they curse us Christians openly—not because of our evil life, but because we regard Jesus as the Messiah, and because they view themselves as our captives, although they know very well that the latter is a lie, and that they are really the ones who hold us captive in our own country by means of their usury, and that everyone would gladly be rid of them. Because they curse us, they also curse our Lord; and if they curse our Lord, they also curse God the Father, the Creator of heaven and earth. Thus their lying cannot avail them. Their cursing alone convicts them, so that we are indeed compelled to believe all the evil things written about them. Undoubtedly they do more and viler things than those which we know and discover." (IV)

For all this, we must bear in mind that this was no mindless raving, no sheer unrestrained rage. As we will see, Luther had many well-grounded historical, theological, and sociological reasons for his condemnation and for his proposed actions. We may be uncomfortable hearing such words today, but in Luther's time, nothing less would have gotten to the root of the problem.

The question for us now, however, is this: What lessons can we draw for the present day? Many nations around the world have their own versions of a 'Jewish problem.' Israel is perhaps the single most-hated country in the world. Jews are the most disliked, least trusted ethnicity, at least in the Western world and much of the Middle East. The American Jewish Lobby, which distributes more campaign money than any other, is the most corrupting force in US government. Through their manipulation of the American military and NATO, and through Israeli secret services, Jews have much blood on their hands, worldwide. What to do? Or rather, let us ask: What would a present-day Martin Luther recommend to us? In the Afterword to this book, I make a few speculations along this line.

Introduction

To the Main Text

Let me close this introduction by offering a few technical remarks on the text to follow. First, Luther's many Bible citations were originally only partial (book but no verse, for example) or were wrong. In what follows, I have corrected and completed all citations, so that the reader can easily find and confirm all passages. Second, I use the Revised Standard Version (RSV) English Bible. In some cases, the specific translation affects the wording in potentially important ways; in such instances, the reader may want to consult alternate translations for comparison. Third, phrases in parentheses are Luther's original, whereas phrases in square brackets [ ] are my own editorial insertions. Fourth, I have added a significant number of explanatory footnotes throughout, to clarify points, add context, give specific dates, or to supplement Luther's words. Fifth, all cited works are listed in the Bibliography at the end of this book.

Finally, the reader must bear in mind Luther's writing style. He is highly sarcastic, to say the least. Many of his words are dripping with irony and sarcasm, and should probably be set in 'scare quotes' or otherwise highlighted. I have not done this. I trust that the reader will be able to sort this out on his own.

ON THE JEWS
AND
THEIR LIES

PREFACE

I had made up my mind not to write anything more either about the Jews or against them. But since I learned that these miserable and accursed people do not cease to lure even we Christians to themselves, I have published this little book, so that I might be counted among those who opposed such poisonous activities of the Jews and who warned the Christians to be on their guard against them. I would not have believed that a Christian could be duped by the Jews into taking their exile and wretchedness upon himself. The devil, however, is the god of the world, and wherever God's word is absent he has an easy task, not only with the weak but also with the strong. May God help us. Amen.

PART I

JEWISH CONCEIT

Grace and peace in the Lord. Dear sir and good friend, I have received a treatise in which a Jew engages in dialog with a Christian.[1] He dares to pervert the scriptural passages that we cite in testimony to our faith, concerning our Lord Christ and Mary his mother, and to interpret them quite differently. With this argument he thinks he can destroy the basis of our faith.

This is my reply to you and to him. It is not my purpose to quarrel with the Jews, nor to learn from them how they interpret or understand Scripture; I know all of that very well already. Much less do I propose to convert the Jews, for that is impossible. Those two excellent men, Lyra and Burgensis, together with others, truthfully described the Jews' vile interpretation for us 200 and 100 years ago, respectively.[2] In fact, they refuted it thoroughly. However, this was no help at all to the Jews, and they have grown steadily worse.

They have failed to learn any lesson from the terrible distress that has been theirs for over 1,400 years in exile.[3] Nor can they obtain any end or definite conclusion of this, as they suppose, by means of the vehement cries and laments to God. If these blows do not help, it's reasonable to assume that our talking and explaining will help even less.

---

[1] The friend is Count Wolfgang Schlick zu Falkenau, of whom very little is known. The treatise to which Luther refers is likely Münster's work *Messiah of the Christians and Jews* (1539).

[2] Nicholas of Lyra (1270-1349) was a French Franciscan teacher and scholar. Paul of Burgos (1351-1435), aka "Burgensis," was a Spanish Jew who converted to Christianity in 1391. Both men wrote critical analyses of Jews.

[3] That is, since the Roman destruction of Jerusalem in the year 70 AD, when the majority of Jews dispersed throughout the Middle East and Europe.

On the Jews and Their Lies

Therefore, a Christian should be content and not argue with the Jews. But if you must or want to talk with them, don't say any more than this: "Listen, Jew, are you aware that Jerusalem and your sovereignty, together with your temple and priesthood, have been destroyed for over 1,460 years?" This present year, which we Christians write as the year 1542 since the birth of Christ, is exactly 1,468 years, going on 1,500 years, since Vespasian and Titus destroyed Jerusalem and expelled the Jews from the city. Let the Jews chew on this and dispute this question as long as they wish.

The ruthlessness of God's wrath is sufficient evidence that they assuredly have erred and gone astray. Even a child can comprehend this. One dare not regard God as so cruel that he would punish his own people so long, so terribly, and so unmercifully, and in addition keep silent, comforting them neither with words nor deeds, and fixing no time limit and no end to it. Who would have faith, hope, or love toward such a God? Therefore, this wrathful work is proof that the Jews, surely rejected by God, are no longer his people, and neither is he any longer their God. This is in accord with Hosea 1:9, "Call his name Not my people, for you are not my people and I am not your God." Yes, unfortunately, this is their lot, truly a terrible one. They may interpret this as they will; we see the facts before our eyes, and these do not deceive us.

If there were but a spark of reason or understanding in them, they would surely say to themselves: "O Lord God, something has gone wrong with us. Our misery is too great, too long, too severe; God has forgotten us!" etc. To be sure, I am not a Jew, but I really do not like to contemplate God's awful wrath toward this people. It sends a fearful shudder through body and soul, for I ask, What will the eternal wrath of God in hell be like toward false Christians and all unbelievers? Well, let the Jews regard our Lord Jesus as they will. We behold the fulfillment of the words spoken by him in Luke 21:20-23: "But when you see Jerusalem surrounded by armies, then know that its desolation has come near...for these are days of vengeance... For great distress shall be upon the earth and wrath upon this people."

Part I

Thus, as has already been said, don't engage much in debate with Jews about the articles of our faith. From their youth, they have been so nurtured with venom and rancor against our Lord that there is no hope, until they reach the point where their misery finally makes them pliable and they are forced to confess that the Messiah has come, and that he is our Jesus. Until such a time, it's much too early, yes, it's useless to argue with them about how God is triune, how he became man, and how Mary is the mother of God. No human reason nor any human heart will ever grant these things, much less the embittered, venomous, blind heart of the Jews. As has already been said, what God cannot reform with such cruel blows, we will be unable to change with words and works. Moses was unable to reform the Pharaoh by means of plagues, miracles, pleas, or threats; he had to let him drown in the sea.

Descent from "God's Chosen"

Now, in order to strengthen our faith, we want to deal with a few crass follies of the Jews in their belief and their exegesis of the Scriptures, since they so maliciously revile our faith. If this should move any Jew to reform and repent, so much the better. We are now not talking *with* the Jews but *about* the Jews and their dealings, so that our Germans, too, might be informed.[4]

There is one thing about which they boast and pride themselves beyond measure, and that is their descent from the foremost people on earth—from Abraham, Sarah, Isaac, Rebekah, Jacob, and from the twelve patriarchs, and thus from the holy people of Israel. St. Paul[5] himself admits this when he says in Romans 9:5: *Quorum patres*, that is, "To them belong the patriarchs, and of their race...is the Christ," etc. And Christ himself declares in John 4:22, "Salvation is from the Jews."

---

[4] This is the first of four arguments in Part I: Jewish arrogance derives from (1) claimed descent from the "chosen" people, (2) circumcision, (3) Moses' receipt of God's Law, and (4) that they were recipients of a "promised land."

[5] Paul, as Luther well knows, was a converted Jew from Tarsus (present-day Turkey). In Romans, Paul speaks of the Israelites as "my brethren, my kinsmen by race."

Therefore, they boast of being the noblest, yes, the only noble people on earth. In comparison with them and in their eyes, we Gentiles (Goyim) are not human; in fact, we hardly deserve to be considered poor worms by them. We are not of that high and noble blood, lineage, birth, and descent. This is their argument, and indeed I think it is the greatest and strongest reason for their pride and boasting.

Therefore, God has to endure that in their synagogues, their prayers, songs, doctrines, and their whole life, they come and stand before him and plague him grievously—if I may speak of God in such a human fashion. Thus, he must listen to their boasts and their praises to him for setting them apart from the Gentiles, for letting them be descended from the holy patriarchs, and for selecting them to be his holy and peculiar people, etc. And there is no limit and no end to this boasting about their descent and their physical birth from the fathers.

And to fill the measure of their raving, mad, and stupid folly, they boast and they thank God, in the first place, because they were created as human beings and not as animals; in the second place, because they are Israelites and not Goyim (Gentiles); in the third place because they were created as males and not as females. They did not learn such tomfoolery from Israel, but from the Goyim. History records that the Greek Plato daily accorded God such praise and thanksgiving—if such arrogance and blasphemy may be termed praise of God. This man, too, praised his gods for these three items: that he was a human being and not an animal; a male and not a female; a Greek and not a non-Greek or barbarian. This is a fool's boast, the gratitude of a barbarian who blasphemes God! Similarly, the Italians fancy themselves the only human beings; they imagine that all other people in the world are nonhumans, mere ducks or mice by comparison.

No one can take away from them their pride concerning their blood and their descent from Israel. In the Old Testament they lost many a battle in wars over this matter, though no Jew understands this. All the prophets censured them for it, for it betrays an arrogant, carnal presumption devoid of spirit and of faith. They were also slain and perse-

Part I

cuted for this reason. St. John the Baptist took them to task severely because of it, saying, "Do not presume to say to yourselves, 'We have Abraham for our father'; for I tell you, God is able from these stones to raise up children to Abraham" [Matt 3:9]. He did not call them Abraham's children, but a "brood of vipers" [Matt 3:7]. Oh, that was too insulting for the noble blood and race of Israel, and they declared, "He has a demon" [Matt 11:18]. Our Lord also calls them a "brood of vipers"; furthermore, in John 8:39, 44 he states: "If you were Abraham's children, you would do what Abraham did. ... You are of your father the devil." It was intolerable to them to hear that they were not Abraham's but the devil's children, nor can they bear to hear this today. If they should surrender this boast and argument, their whole system built on it would topple and collapse.

I hold that if their Messiah, for whom they hope, should come and do away with their boast and its basis, they would crucify and blaspheme him seven times worse than they did to our Messiah; and they would also say that he was not the true Messiah, but a deceiving devil. They have portrayed their Messiah to themselves as one who would strengthen and increase such carnal and arrogant error regarding nobility of blood and lineage. That's the same as saying that he should assist them in blaspheming God and in viewing his creatures with disdain, including the women, who are also human beings and the image of God as well as we; moreover, they are our own flesh and blood, such as mother, sister, daughter, housewives, etc. In accordance with the aforementioned threefold song of praise, they do not hold Sarah (as a woman) to be as noble as Abraham (as a man). Perhaps they wish to honor themselves for being born half noble—of a noble father—and half ignoble—of an ignoble mother. But enough of this silliness and trickery.

We propose to discuss their argument, and boast and prove convincingly before God and the world—not before the Jews, for, as already said, they would accept this neither from Moses nor from their Messiah himself—that their argument is quite empty and stands condemned. To this end we quote Moses in Genesis 17, whom they surely ought to believe if they are true Israelites. When God instituted circumcision, he said, among other things, "Any uncircumcised male shall be cut off from his people" [Gen 17:14]. With these words, God consigns to condemnation all who are born of flesh, no matter how noble, high, or how low their birth may have been. He does not even exempt from this judgment the seed of Abraham, although Abraham was not merely of high and noble birth from Noah, but was also adjudged holy (Genesis 15) and became Abraham instead of Abram (Genesis 17). Yet none of his children shall be numbered among God's people, but rather shall be rooted out, and God will not be his God, unless he, over and above his birth, is also circumcised and accepted into the covenant of God.

To be sure, before the world, one person is properly accounted nobler than another by reason of his birth, or smarter than another because of his intelligence, or stronger and more handsome than another because of his body, or richer and mightier than another in view of his possessions, or better than another on account of his special virtues. This miserable, sinful, and mortal life must be marked by such differentiation and inequality; the requirements of daily life and the preservation of government make it indispensable.

But to strut before God and boast about being so noble, so exalted, and so rich compared to other people—that is devilish arrogance. Every birth according to the flesh is condemned before him without exception in the aforementioned verse, if his covenant and word do not come to the rescue once again and create a new and different birth, quite different from the old, first birth. So if the Jews boast in their prayer before God and glory in the fact that they are the patriarchs' noble blood, lineage, and children, and that he should regard them and be gracious to them in view of this, while they condemn the Gentiles as ignoble and not of their blood, my dear man, what do you suppose such a prayer will achieve? This is what it will achieve: Even if the Jews were as holy as their fathers Abraham, Isaac, and Jacob themselves—yes, even if they

Part I

were angels in heaven—on account of such a prayer they would have to be hurled into the abyss of hell. How much less will such prayers deliver them from their exile and return them to Jerusalem!

What does such devilish, arrogant prayer do other than to give God's word the lie, for God declares: Whoever is born and not circumcised shall not only be ignoble and worthless but shall also be damned and shall not be a part of my people, and I will not be his God. The Jews rage against this with their blasphemous prayer as if to say: "No, no, Lord God, that is not true; you must hear us, because we are of the noble lineage of the holy fathers. By reason of such noble birth you must establish us as lords over all the earth and in heaven too. If you fail to do this, you break your word and do us an injustice, since you have sworn to our fathers that you will accept their seed as your people forever."

This is just as though a king, a prince, a lord, or a rich, handsome, smart, pious, virtuous person among us Christians were to pray thus to God: "Lord God, see what a great king and lord I am! See how rich, smart, and pious I am! See what a handsome man or woman I am in comparison to others! Be gracious to me, help me, and in view of all of this save me! The other people are not as deserving, because they are not so handsome, rich, smart, pious, noble, and high-born as I am." What, do you suppose, should such a prayer merit? It would merit that thunder and lightning strike down from heaven and that sulfur and hellfire strike from below. That would be just punishment; flesh and blood must not boast before God. As Moses says, whoever is born even from holy patriarchs and from Abraham himself stands condemned before God and must not boast before him. St. Paul says the same thing in Romans 3:27, as does John 3:6.

Such a prayer was also spoken by the Pharisee in the Gospel as he boasted about all his blessings, saying, "I am not like other men." Moreover, his prayer was beautifully adorned, since he said it with thanksgiving and fancied that he was sitting on God's lap as his pet child. But thunder and lightning from heaven cast him down to hell's abyss, as Christ himself declared, saying that the publican was justified but the Pharisee condemned. Oh, what do we poor muck-worms, maggots, stench, and filth presume to boast of before him who is the God and Creator of heaven and earth, who made us out of dirt and out of nothing! And as far as our nature, birth, and essence are concerned, we are but dirt and nothing in his eyes; all that we are and have comes from his grace and his rich mercy.

Abraham was no doubt even nobler than the Jews, since as we pointed out above, he was descended from the noblest patriarch, Noah—who in his day was the greatest and oldest lord, priest, and father of the entire world—and from the other nine succeeding patriarchs. Abraham saw, heard, and lived with all of them, and some of them (such as Shem, Shelah, Eber) outlived him by many years. So Abraham obviously was not lacking in nobility of blood and birth; and yet this did not in the least aid him in being numbered among God's people. No, he was idolatrous, and he would have remained under condemnation if God's word had not called him, as Joshua in chapter 24:2-3 informs us out of God's own mouth: "Your fathers lived of old beyond the Euphrates, Terah, the father of Abraham and of Nahor; and they served other gods. Then I took your father Abraham from beyond the River and led him," etc.

Even later, after he had been called and sanctified through God's word and through faith, according to Genesis 15, Abraham did not boast of his birth or of his virtues. When he spoke with God (Genesis 18) he did not say: "Look how noble I am, born from Noah and the holy patriarchs, and descended from your holy nation," nor did he say, "How pious and holy I am in comparison with other people!" No, he said, "Behold, I have taken upon myself to speak to the Lord, I who am but dust and ashes" [Gen 18:27]. This is, indeed, how a creature must speak to its Creator, not forgetting what it is before him and how it is regarded by him. That is what God said of Adam and of all his children (Genesis 3:19), "You are dust, and to dust you shall return," as death itself persuades us visibly and experientially, to counteract, if need be, any such foolish, vain, and vexatious presumption.

Part I

Now you can see what fine children of Abraham the Jews really are, how well they take after their father, yes, what a fine people of God they are. They boast before God of their physical birth and of the noble blood inherited from their fathers, despising all other people,[6] although God regards them in all these respects as dust and ashes and damned by birth, the same as all other heathen. And yet they give God the lie; they insist on being in the right, and with such blasphemous and damnable prayer they purpose to wrest God's grace from him and to regain Jerusalem.

Furthermore, even if the Jews were seven times blinder than they are—if that were possible—they would still have to see that Esau or Edom, as far as his physical birth is concerned, was as noble as Jacob, since he was not only the son of the same father, Isaac, and of the same mother, Rebekah, but he was also the firstborn; and at that time this conferred the highest nobility over against the other children. But what did his equal birth or even his first-born status—by virtue of which he was far nobler than Jacob—benefit him? He was still not numbered among God's people, although he called Abraham his grandfather and Sarah his grandmother, just as Jacob did; indeed, as has already been said, even more validly than did Jacob. Conversely, Abraham himself as well as Sarah had to regard him as their grandson, the son of Isaac and Rebekah; they even had to regard him as the firstborn and the nobler, and Jacob as the lesser. But tell me, what good did his physical birth and his noble blood inherited from Abraham do him?

One may interpose that Esau forfeited his honor because he became evil, etc. We must rejoin, first of all, that the question at issue is whether nobility of blood in itself is so valid before God that one could thereby be or become God's people. If it's not, why then do the Jews exalt this birth so highly before other children of men? But if it is valid, why then

---

[6] This is the first of a handful of similar comments in which Luther recalls an ancient and long-standing charge of Jewish misanthropy, or hated of mankind. One of the most famous instances was that of the Roman historian Tacitus, who wrote in his *Annals* (circa 110 AD) of the Jews' "hatred of the human race" (*odio humani generis*; XV).

does God not guard it from falling? If God regards physical birth as adequate for making the descendants of the holy patriarchs his people, he dare not let them become evil, thereby losing his people and becoming a non-God. If he does, however, let them become evil, it is certain that he does not regard birth as a means of yielding or producing a people for him.

In the second place, Esau was not ejected from the people of God because he became evil later on, nor was Jacob counted among the people of God in view of his subsequent good life. No—while they were both still in their mother's womb, the word of God distinguished between the two: Jacob was called, Esau was not, in accordance with the words, "The elder shall serve the younger" (Gen 25:23). This was not at all affected by the fact that they were both carried under the same mother's heart; that they were both nourished with the same milk and blood of one and the same mother, Rebekah; that they were born of her at the same time. So one must say that no matter how identical flesh, blood, milk, body, and mother were in this instance, they could not help Esau, nor could they hinder Jacob from acquiring the grace by which people become God's children or his people; decisive here are the word and calling, which ignore the birth.

Ishmael, too, can say that he is equally a true and natural son of Abraham. But what does his physical birth avail him? Despite this, he has to yield up the home and heritage of Abraham and leave it to his brother Isaac. You may say that Ishmael was born of Hagar while Isaac was born of Sarah. If anything, this strengthens our argument. Isaac's birth from Sarah was effected by the word of God and not by flesh and blood, since Sarah was past the natural age for bearing children. To discuss the question of birth a bit further, although Ishmael is Abraham's flesh and blood and his natural son, still the flesh and blood of such a holy father does not help him. It rather harms him, because he has no more than flesh and blood from Abraham and does not also have God's word in his favor. The fact that Isaac is descended from the blood of Abraham does not handicap him—even though it was useless to

Part I

Ishmael—because he has the word of God which distinguishes him from his brother Ishmael, who is of the flesh and blood of the same Abraham.

Why should so much ado be made of this? After all, if birth counts before God, I can claim to be just as noble as any Jew—yes, just as noble as Abraham himself, as David, as all the holy prophets and apostles. Nor will I owe them any thanks if they consider me just as noble as themselves before God by reason of my birth. And if God refuses to acknowledge my nobility and birth as the equal to that of Isaac, Abraham, David, and all the saints, I maintain that he is doing me an injustice and that he is not a fair judge. I will not give it up, and neither Abraham, David, prophets, apostles nor even an angel in heaven, shall deny me the right to boast that Noah, so far as physical birth or flesh and blood is concerned, is my true, natural ancestor, and that his wife (whoever she may have been) is my true, natural ancestress. We are all descended, since the Deluge, from that one Noah. We did not descend from Cain, for his family perished forever in the flood, together with many of the cousins, brothers-in-law, and friends of Noah.

I also boast that Japheth, Noah's firstborn son, is my true, natural ancestor, and his wife (whoever she may have been) is my true, natural ancestress, for as Moses informs us in Genesis 10, he is the progenitor of all of us Gentiles. Thus Shem, the second son of Noah, and all of his descendants have no grounds to boast over against his older brother Japheth because of their birth. Indeed, if birth is to play a role, then Japheth, as the oldest son and the true heir, has reason for boasting over against Shem, his younger brother, and Shem's descendants, whether these be called Jews or Ishmaelites or Edomites. But what does physical first-birth help the good Japheth, our ancestor? Nothing at all. Shem enjoys precedence—not by reason of birth, which would accord precedence to Japheth, but because God's word and calling are the arbiter here.

I could go back to the beginning of the world and trace our common ancestry from Adam and Eve, later from Shem, Enoch, Kenan, Mahalalel, Jared, Enoch, Methuselah, Lamech; for all of these are our ancestors just as well as the Jews', and we share equally in the honor, nobility, and fame of descent from them as do the Jews. We are their flesh and blood, just the same as Abraham and all his seed are. We were in the loins of the same holy fathers in the same measure as they were, and there is no difference whatsoever with regard to birth or flesh and blood, as reason must tell us. Therefore, the blind Jews are truly stupid fools, much more absurd than the Gentiles, to boast so before God of their physical birth, though they are by reason of it no better than the Gentiles; we both partake of one birth, one flesh and blood, from the very first, best, and holiest ancestors. Neither one can reproach or upbraid the other about some peculiarity without implicating himself at the same time.

But let's move on. David lumps us all together nicely and convincingly when he declares in Psalm 51:5: "Behold, I was brought forth in iniquity, and in sin did my mother conceive me." Now go, whether you are Jew or Gentile, born of Adam or Abraham, of Enoch or David, and boast before God of your fine nobility, of your exalted lineage, your ancient ancestry! Here you learn that we all are conceived and born in sin, by father and mother, and no human being is excluded.

But what does it mean to be born in sin other than to be born under God's wrath and condemnation, so that by nature or birth we are unable to be God's people or children, and our birth, glory, and nobility, our honor and praise denote nothing more and can denote nothing else than that, in default of anything to our credit other than our physical birth, we are condemned sinners, enemies of God, and in his disfavor? There, Jew, you have your boast, and we Gentiles have ours together with you, as well as you with us. Now go ahead and pray that God might respect your nobility, your race, your flesh and blood.

This I wanted to say for the strengthening of our faith; the Jews will not give up their pride and boasting about their nobility and lineage. As was said above, their hearts are hardened. Our people, however, must be on their guard against them, lest they be misled by this impenitent, accursed people who give God the lie and haughtily despise all the

Part I

world.⁷ The Jews would like to entice us Christians to their faith, and they do this wherever they can. If God is to become gracious also to them, the Jews, they must first of all banish such blasphemous prayers and songs, that boast so arrogantly about their lineage, from their synagogues, from their hearts, and from their lips, for such prayers ever increase and sharpen God's wrath toward them. However, they won't do this, nor will they humble themselves abjectly, except for a few individuals whom God draws unto himself particularly and delivers from their terrible ruin.

CIRCUMCISION

The other boast and nobility over which the Jews gloat, and because of which they haughtily and vainly despise all mankind, is their circumcision that they received from Abraham.⁸ My God, what we Gentiles have to put up with in their synagogues, prayers, songs, and doctrines! What a stench we poor people are in their nostrils because we are not circumcised! Indeed, God himself must again submit to miserable torment—if I may put it thus—as they confront him with inexpressible presumption, and boast: 'Praised be Thou, King of the world, who singled us out from all the nations and sanctified us by the covenant of circumcision!' And similarly with many other words, the tenor of all of which is that God should esteem them above all the rest of the world because they in compliance with his decree are circumcised, and that he should condemn all other people, just as they do and wish to do.

In this boast of nobility, they glory as much as they do in their physical birth. Consequently I believe that if Moses himself would appear together with Elijah and their Messiah and would try to deprive them of this boast or forbid such prayers and doctrine, they would probably consider all three of them to be the three worst devils in hell, and they

---

⁷ Again recalling Tacitus.

⁸ Circumcision is an ancient tradition, apparently dating back at least to 3000 BC, and perhaps much earlier. The early Egyptians seem to have practiced it by 2400 BC. It was clearly nothing uniquely Jewish.

would be at a loss to know how to curse and damn them adequately, to say nothing of believing them. They have decided among themselves that Moses, together with Elijah and the Messiah, should endorse circumcision—yes, rather that they should help to strengthen and praise such arrogance and pride in circumcision, that these should, like themselves, look upon all Gentiles as awful filth and stench because they are not circumcised. Moses, Elijah, and the Messiah must do all that they prescribe, think, and wish. They insist that they are right, and if God himself were to do other than they think, he would be in the wrong.

Now just behold these miserable, blind, and senseless people. In the first place (as I said previously in regard to physical birth), if I were to concede that circumcision is sufficient to make them a people of God, or to sanctify and set them apart before God from all other nations, then the conclusion would have to be this: Whoever was circumcised could not be evil nor could he be damned. Nor would God permit this to happen, if he regarded circumcision as imbued with such holiness and power. Just as we Christians say: Whoever has faith cannot be evil and cannot be damned so long as faith endures. God regards faith as so precious, valuable, and powerful that it will surely sanctify and prevent him who has faith and retains his faith from being lost or becoming evil. But I shall let this go for now.

In the second place, we note here again how the Jews provoke God's anger more and more with such prayer. There they stand and defame God with a blasphemous, shameful, and impudent lie. They are so blind and stupid that they see neither the words found in Genesis 17 nor the whole of Scripture, which mightily and explicitly condemns this lie. In Genesis 17:12 Moses states that Abraham was ordered to circumcise not only his son Isaac—who at the time was not yet born—but all the males born in his house, whether sons or servants, including the slaves. All of these were circumcised on one day together with Abraham, Ishmael too, who at the time was 13 years of age, as the text informs us. Thus the covenant or decree of circumcision encompasses the entire seed of all the descendants of Abraham, particularly Ishmael,

Part I

who was the first seed of Abraham to be circumcised. Accordingly, Ishmael is not only the equal of his brother Isaac, but he might even—if this were to be esteemed before God—be entitled to boast of his circumcision more than Isaac, since he was circumcised one year sooner. In view of this, the Ishmaelites might well enjoy a higher repute than the Israelites, for their forefather Ishmael was circumcised before Isaac, the progenitor of the Israelites, was born.

Why then do the Jews lie so shamefully before God in their prayer and preaching, as though circumcision were theirs alone, through which they were set apart from all other nations and thus they alone are God's holy people? They should really—if they were capable of it—be a bit ashamed before the Ishmaelites, the Edomites, and other nations when they consider that they were at all times a small nation, scarcely a handful of people in comparison with others who were also Abraham's seed and were also circumcised, and who indubitably transmitted such a command of their father Abraham to their descendants. And that the circumcision transmitted to the one son Isaac is rather insignificant when compared with the circumcision transmitted to Abraham's other sons. Scripture records that Ishmael, Abraham's son, became a great nation, that he begot 12 princes, also that the six sons of Keturah (Genesis 25:1), possessed much greater areas of land than Israel. And undoubtedly these observed the rite of circumcision handed down to them by their fathers.

Now, since circumcision, as decreed by God in Genesis 17, is practiced by so many nations, beginning with Abraham—whose seed they all are the same as Isaac and Jacob—and since there's no difference in this regard between them and the children of Israel, we ask: What are the Jews really doing when they praise and thank God in their prayers for singling them out by circumcision from all other nations, for sanctifying them, and for making them his own people? This is what they are doing: they are blaspheming God and giving him the lie concerning his commandment and his words, where he says (Genesis 17:12) that circumcision shall not be prescribed for Isaac and his descendants alone, but for all the seed of Abraham. The Jews have no favored position exalting them above Ishmael by reason of circumcision, or above Edom, Midian, Ephah, Epher, etc., all of whom are reckoned in Genesis as Abraham's seed. They were all circumcised and made heirs of circumcision, the same as Israel.

Now, what does it benefit Ishmael that he is circumcised? What does it benefit Edom that he is circumcised—Edom who, moreover, is descended from Isaac, who was set apart, and not from Ishmael? What does it benefit Midian and his brothers, born of Keturah, that they are circumcised? They are, for all of that, not God's people; neither their descent from Abraham nor their circumcision, commanded by God, helps them. If circumcision doesn't help them in becoming God's people, how can it help the Jews? It's one and the same circumcision, decreed by one and the same God, and there is one and the same father, flesh and blood or descent that's common to all. There is absolute equality; there is no difference, no distinction among them all so far as circumcision and birth are concerned.

Therefore it's not a clever and ingenious, but a clumsy, foolish, and stupid lie when the Jews boast of their circumcision before God—presuming that God should regard them graciously for that reason, though they should certainly know from Scripture that they are not the only race circumcised in compliance with God's decree, and that they cannot on that account be God's special people. Something more, different, and greater is necessary for that, since the Ishmaelites, the Edomites, the Midianites, and other descendants of Abraham may equally comfort themselves with this glory, even before God himself. With regard to birth and circumcision, these are, as already said, their equals.

Perhaps the Jews will declare that the Ishmaelites and Edomites, etc, don't observe the rite of circumcision as strictly as they do. In addition to cutting off the foreskin of a male child, the Jews force the skin back on the little penis and tear it open with sharp fingernails, as one reads in their books. Thus they cause extraordinary pain to the child, without and against the command of God, so that the father, who should

Part I

really be happy over the circumcision, stands there and weeps as his child's cries pierce his heart. We answer roundly that such an addendum is their own invention—yes, it was inspired by the accursed devil, and is in contradiction to God's command, since Moses says in Deuteronomy 4:2 and 12:32: "You shall not add to the word which I command you, nor take from it." With such a devilish supplement they ruin their circumcision, so that in the sight of God, no other nation practices circumcision less than they, since they append and practice this damnable supplement with such wanton disobedience.

Now let's see what Moses himself says about circumcision. In Deuteronomy 10:16 he says: "Circumcise therefore the foreskin of your heart, and be no longer stubborn," etc. Dear Moses, what do you mean? Does it not suffice that they are circumcised physically? They are set apart from all other nations by this holy circumcision and made a holy people of God. And you rebuke them for stubbornness against God? You belittle their holy circumcision? You revile the holy, circumcised people of God? You should venture to talk like that today in their synagogues! If there were not stones conveniently nearby, they would resort to mud and dirt to drive you from their midst, even if you were worth ten Moseses.

He also chides them in Leviticus 26:41, saying: "If then their uncircumcised heart is humbled," etc. Be careful, Moses! Do you know whom you are speaking to? You are talking to a noble, chosen, holy, circumcised people of God. And you dare to say that they have uncircumcised hearts? That's much worse than having a seven-times-uncircumcised flesh; for an uncircumcised heart can have no God. And to such people, the circumcision of the flesh is of no avail. Only a circumcised heart can produce a people of God, and it can do this even when physical circumcision is absent or is impossible, as it was for the children of Israel during their 40 years in the wilderness.

Thus Jeremiah also takes them to task, saying in chapter 4:4: "Circumcise yourselves to the Lord, remove the foreskin of your hearts, O men of Judah and inhabitants of Jerusalem; lest my wrath go forth like fire, and burn with none to quench it…" Jeremiah, you wretched heretic, you seducer and false prophet, how dare you tell that holy, circumcised people of God to circumcise themselves to the Lord? Do you mean to imply that they were hitherto circumcised physically to the devil, as if God did not esteem their holy, physical circumcision? And are you furthermore threatening them with God's wrath, as an eternal fire, if they don't circumcise their hearts? But they don't mention such circumcision of the heart in their prayer, nor do they praise or thank God for it with as much as a single letter. And you dare to invalidate their holy circumcision of the flesh, making it liable to God's wrath and the eternal fire? I advise you not to enter their synagogue; all devils might dismember and devour you there.

In Jeremiah 6:10 we read, further, "Their ears are uncircumcised, they cannot listen." Well, well, my dear Jeremiah, you are surely dealing roughly and inconsiderately with the noble, chosen, holy, circumcised people of God. Do you mean to say that such a holy nation has uncircumcised ears? And, what's far worse, that they are unable to hear? Is that not tantamount to saying that they are not God's people? He who cannot hear or bear to hear God's word is not of God's people. And if they are not God's people, then they are the devil's people; and then neither circumcising nor skinning nor scraping will avail. For God's sake, Jeremiah, stop talking like that! How can you despise and condemn holy circumcision so horribly that you separate the chosen, circumcised, holy people from God and consign them to the devil as banished and damned? Do they not praise God for having set them apart through circumcision both from the devil and from all the other nations, and for making them a holy and peculiar people? Yea, "He has spoken blasphemy! Crucify him, crucify him!"

In chapter 9:25 Jeremiah says further: "Behold, the days are coming, says the Lord, when I will punish all those who are circumcised but yet uncircumcised—Egypt, Judah, Edom, the sons of Ammon, Moab, and all who dwell in the desert…for all these nations are uncircumcised, and all the house of Israel is uncircumcised in heart…"

Part I

In the face of this, what becomes of the arrogant boast of circumcision, by reason of which the Jews claim to be a holy nation, set apart from other peoples? Here God's word lumps them together with the heathen and uncircumcised, and threatens the same visitation for both. Moreover, the best part of Israel, the noble, royal tribe of Judah, is mentioned here, and after that the entire house of Israel. Worst of all, he declares that the heathen are, to be sure, uncircumcised according to the flesh, but that Judah, Edom, and Israel, who are circumcised according to the flesh, are much viler than the heathen, since they have an uncircumcised heart; and this, as said before, is far worse than uncircumcised flesh.

These and similar passages prove irrefutably that the Jews' arrogance and boast of circumcision over against the uncircumcised Gentiles are null and void, and, unless accompanied by something else, deserves nothing but God's wrath. God says that they have an uncircumcised heart. But the Jews don't pay attention to such a foreskin of the heart; rather they think that God should behold their proud circumcision in the flesh and hear their arrogant boasts over against all Gentiles, who are unable to boast of such circumcision. These blind, miserable people don't see that God condemns their uncircumcised heart so clearly and explicitly in these verses, and thereby condemns their physical circumcision together with their boasting and their prayer. They go their way like fools, making the foreskins of their heart steadily thicker with such haughty boasts before God and their contempt for all other people. By virtue of such futile, arrogant circumcision in the flesh they presume to be God's only people, until the foreskin of their heart has become thicker than an iron mountain and they can no longer hear, see, or feel their own clear Scripture, which they read daily with blind eyes, overgrown with a pelt thicker than the bark of an oak tree.

If God is to give ear to their prayers and praises and accept them, they must surely first purge their synagogues, mouths, and hearts of such blasphemous, shameful, false, and deceitful boasting and arrogance. Otherwise they will only go from bad to worse, arousing God's anger ever more against themselves. He who would pray before God dare not confront him with haughtiness and lying, he dare not praise only himself, condemn all others, claim to be God's only people, and execrate all the others, as they do. As David says in Psalm 5:4: "For thou are not a God who delights in wickedness; evil may not sojourn with thee. The boastful may not stand before thy eyes; thou hatest all evildoers. Thou destroyest those who speak lies; the Lord abhors bloodthirsty and deceitful men." But rather, as verse 7 tells us: "I through the abundance of thy steadfast love will enter thy house, I will worship toward thy holy temple in the fear of thee."

This psalm applies to all men, whether circumcised or not, but particularly and especially to the Jews, for whom it was especially given and composed—as was all the rest of Scripture also. And they are more masterfully portrayed in it than all other heathen. They are the ones who constantly have pursued godless ways, idolatry, false doctrine, and who have had uncircumcised hearts, as Moses himself and all the prophets cry out and lament. But in all this they always claimed to be pleasing to God, and they slay all the prophets on this account. They are the malicious, stiff-necked people that would not be converted from evil to good works by the preaching, reproof, and teaching of the prophets. The Scriptures bear witness to this everywhere. And still they claim to be God's servants and to stand before him. They are the boastful, arrogant rascals who to the present day can do no more than boast of their race and lineage, praise only themselves, and disdain and curse all the world in their synagogues, prayers, and doctrines. Despite this, they imagine that in God's eyes they rank as his dearest children.

They are real liars and bloodhounds who have not only continually perverted and falsified all of Scripture with their mendacious glosses from the beginning until the present day. Their heart's most ardent sighing and yearning and hoping is set on the day on which they can deal with us Gentiles as they did with the Gentiles in Persia at the time of Esther.[9] Oh, how fond they are of the book of Esther, which is so

---

[9] That is, via mass murder. In Esther 9 we read that 75,000 Gentiles were slaughtered

PART I

beautifully attuned to their bloodthirsty, vengeful, murderous yearning and hope. The sun has never shone on a more bloodthirsty and vengeful people than they are who imagine that they are God's people who have been commissioned and commanded to murder and to slay the Gentiles. In fact, the most important thing that they expect of their Messiah is that he will murder and kill the entire world with their sword. They treated us Christians in this manner at the very beginning throughout all the world. They would still like to do this, if they had the power, and often enough have made the attempt, for which they have got their well-deserved beatings.[10]

We can perhaps enlarge on this subject later; but let's now return to their false, lying boast regarding circumcision. These shameful liars are well aware that they are not the exclusive people of God, even if they did possess circumcision to the exclusion of all other nations. They also know that the foreskin is no obstacle to being a people of God. And still they brazenly strut before God, lie and boast about being God's only people by reason of their physical circumcision, unmindful of the circumcision of the heart. Against this there are weighty scriptural examples. In the first place, we adduce Job, who, as they say, descended from Nahor. God did not impose circumcision on him and his heirs. And yet his book shows clearly that there were very few great saints in Israel who were the equal of him and of his people. Nor did the prophet Elisha oblige Naaman of Syria to become circumcised; and yet he was sanctified and became a child of God, and undoubtedly many others with him.

Furthermore, there stands the whole of the prophet Jonah, who converted Nineveh to God and preserved it together with kings, princes, lords, land, and people, yet did not circumcise these people. Similarly, Daniel converted the great kings and peoples of Babylon and Persia, such as Nebuchadnezzar, Cyrus, Darius, etc., and yet they remained

---

by the Jews.

[10] This is an intriguing foreboding of the Jewish-inspired mass murders in World Wars One and Two, and in the Middle East today. See Dalton (2019).

Gentiles, uncircumcised, and did not become Jews. Earlier, Joseph instructed Pharaoh the king, his princes, and his people—as Psalm 105:22 informs us—yet he left them uncircumcised. This, I say, these hardened and inveterate liars know, and yet they stress circumcision so greatly, as though no uncircumcised person could be a child of God. And whenever they seduce a Christian, they try to alarm him so that he will be circumcised. Subsequently they approach God and exult in their prayer that they have brought us to the people of God through circumcision—as though this were a precious deed. They disdain, despise, and curse the foreskin on us as an ugly abomination that prevents us from becoming God's people, while their circumcision, they claim, effects all.

What is God to do with such prayer and praise that they bring forth, together with their coarse, blasphemous lying, contrary to all Scripture (as already stated)? He will indeed hear them and bring them back to their country! I mean that if they were dwelling in heaven, such boasts, prayers, praise, and lies about circumcision alone would hurl them instantly into the abyss of hell. I have already written about this against the Sabbatarians.[11] Therefore, dear Christian, be on your guard against such damnable people whom God has permitted to sink into such profound abominations and lies, for all they do and say must be sheer lying, blasphemy, and malice, however fine it may look.

But you may ask: Of what use then is circumcision? Or why did God command it so strictly? We answer: Let the Jews fret about that! What does that matter to us Gentiles? It was not imposed on us, as you have heard, nor do we stand in need of it, but we can be God's people without it, just as the people in Nineveh, Babylon, Persia, and Egypt were. And no one can prove that God ever commanded a prophet or a Jew to circumcise the Gentiles. Therefore, they shouldn't harass us with their lies and idolatry. If they claim to be so smart and wise as to instruct and circumcise us Gentiles, let them first tell us what purpose circumcision serves, and why God commanded it so strictly. This they owe us; but they won't do it until they return to their home in Jerusalem again—

---

[11] See Luther's treatise *Against the Sabbatarians* (1538).

Part I

that is to say, when the devil ascends into heaven. For when they assert that God enjoined circumcision for the purpose of sanctifying them, saving them, making them God's people, they are lying atrociously, as you have heard. Moses and all the prophets testify that circumcision did not help even those for whom it was commanded, since they were of uncircumcised hearts. How, then, should it help us, for whom it was not commanded?

But to speak for us Christians—we know very well why it was given or what purpose it served. However, no Jew knows this, and even when we tell him, it's just like addressing a stump or a stone. They won't desist from their boasting and their pride, that is, from their lies. They insist that they are in the right; God must be the liar and he must be in error. Therefore, let them go their way and lie as their fathers have done from the beginning. But St. Paul teaches us in Romans 3 that when circumcision is performed as a kind of work, it cannot make holy or save, nor was it meant to do so. Nor does it damn the uncircumcised Gentiles, as the Jews mendaciously and blasphemously say. Rather, he says, "circumcision is of great value in this way—that they were entrusted with the word of God" [Rom 3:1]. That's the point, there it is said, there it is found! Circumcision was given and instituted to enfold and to preserve God's word and his promise. This means that circumcision should not be useful or sufficient as a work in itself, but those who possess circumcision should be bound by this sign, covenant, or sacrament to obey and to believe God in his words and to transmit all this to their descendants.

But where such a final cause or reason for circumcision no longer existed, circumcision as a mere work no longer was to enjoy validity or value—all the more so if the Jews should patch or attach another final cause or explanation to it. This is also borne out by the words in Genesis 17: "I will be your God, and in token of this you shall bear my sign upon your flesh" [Gen 17:8, 11]. This expresses the same thought found in St. Paul's statement that circumcision was given so that one should hear or obey God's word. For when God's word is no longer heard or kept, then he is surely no longer our God, since we in this life must comprehend and have God solely through his word. This wretched life cannot bear and endure him in his brilliant majesty, as he says in Exodus [33:20]: "Man shall not see me and live."

There are innumerable examples throughout all of Scripture which show what cause or purpose the Jews assigned to circumcision. As often as God wanted to speak with them through the prophets—whether about the Ten Commandments, in which he reproved them, or about the promise of future help—they were always obdurate, or as the quoted verses from Moses and Jeremiah testify, they were of uncircumcised heart and ears. They always claimed to do the right and proper thing, while the prophets—that is, God himself whose word they preached—always did the wrong and evil thing. Therefore, the Jews slay them all, and they have never yet allowed any to die unpersecuted and uncondemned, with the exception of a few at the time of David, Hezekiah, and Josiah. The entire course of the history of Israel and Judah is pervaded by blasphemy of God's word, by persecution, derision, and murder of the prophets. Judging them by history, these people [the Jews] must be called wanton murderers of the prophets and enemies of God's word. Whoever reads the Bible cannot draw any other conclusion.

As we said, God did not institute circumcision nor did he accept the Jews as his people in order that they might persecute, mock, and murder his word and his prophets, and thereby render a service to justice and to God. Rather, as Moses says in the words dealing with circumcision in Genesis 17, this was done in order that they might hear God and his word; that is, that they might let him be their God. Apart from this, circumcision in itself would not help them, since it would then no longer be God's circumcision, for it would be without God, contending against his word; it would have become merely a human work. He had bound himself, or his word, to circumcision. Where these two part company, circumcision remains a hollow husk or empty shell devoid of nut or kernel.

Part I

The following is an analogous situation for us Christians: God gave us baptism, the sacrament of his body and blood, and the keys for the ultimate purpose or final cause that we should hear his word in them and exercise our faith therein. That is, he intends to be our God through them, and through them we are to be his people. However, what did we do? We proceeded to separate the word and faith from the sacrament (that is, from God and his ultimate purpose) and converted it into a mere *opus legis*, a work of the law, or as the papists call it, an *opus operatum*—merely a human work, which the priests offered to God and the laity performed as a work of obedience as often as they received it. What's left of the sacrament? Only the empty husk, the mere ceremony, *opus vanum*, divested of everything divine. Yes, it is a hideous abomination in which we perverted God's truth into lies and worshiped the veritable calf of Aaron.[12] Therefore, God also delivered us into all sorts of terrible blindness and innumerable false doctrines, and furthermore, he permitted Muhammad and the pope together with all devils to come upon us.

The people of Israel fared similarly. They always divorced circumcision as an *opus operatum*, their own work, from the word of God, and persecuted all the prophets through whom God wished to speak with them, according to the terms on which circumcision was instituted. Yet despite this, they constantly and proudly boasted of being God's people by virtue of their circumcision. Thus they are in conflict with God. God wants them to hear him and to observe circumcision properly and fully; but they refuse and insist that God respect their work of circumcision, that is, half of circumcision, indeed, the husk of circumcision. God, in turn, refuses to do this; and so they move farther and farther apart, and it's impossible to reunite or reconcile them.

Now, who wishes to accuse God of an injustice? Tell me, anyone who is reasonable, whether it is fitting that God regard the works of those who refuse to hear his word, or if he should consider them to be his people when they don't want to regard him as their God? With all

---

[12] This is the 'golden calf' cited in Exodus 32.

justice and good reason, God may say, as the psalm declares [Ps 81:11]: "Israel would have none of me. So I gave them over to their stubborn hearts, to follow their own counsels." And in Deuteronomy 32:21, Moses states, "They have stirred me to jealously with what is no god. ... So I will stir them to jealousy with those who are no people."

Similarly among us Christians, the papists can no longer pass for the church. They will not let God be their God, because they refuse to listen to his word, but rather persecute it most terribly, then come along with their empty husks, chaff, and refuse, as they hold mass and practice their ceremonies. And God is supposed to recognize them and look upon them as his true church, ignoring the fact that they do not acknowledge him as the true God, that is, they don't want him to speak to them through his preachers. His word must be accounted heresy, the devil, and every evil. This he will indeed do, as they surely will experience, far worse than did the Jews.

Now we can readily gather from all this that circumcision was very useful and good, as St. Paul declares—not indeed on its own account but on account of the word of God. We are convinced, and it is the truth, that the children who were circumcised on the eighth day became children of God, as the words state, "I will be their God" [Gen 17:7], for they received the perfect and full circumcision, the word with the sign, and did not separate the two. God is present, saying to them, "I will be their God"; and this completed the circumcision in them. Similarly, our children receive the complete, true, and full baptism, the word with the sign, and do not separate one from the other; they receive the kernel in the shell. God is present; he baptizes and speaks with them, and thereby saves them.

But now that we have grown old, the pope comes along—and the devil with him—and teaches us to convert this into an *opus legis* or *opus operatum*. He severs word and sign from each other, teaching that we are saved by our own contrition, work, and satisfaction. We share the experience related by St. Peter in 2 Peter 2:22: "The dog turns back to his own vomit, and the sow is washed only to wallow in the mire."

Part I

Thus our sacrament has become a work, and we eat our vomit again. Likewise the Jews, as they grew old, ruined their good circumcision performed on the eighth day, separated the word from the sign, and made a human or even a swinish work out of it. In this way, they lost God and his word and now no longer have any understanding of the Scriptures.

God truly honored them highly by circumcision, speaking to them above all other nations on earth and entrusting his word to them. And in order to preserve this word among them, he gave them a special country; he performed great wonders through them, ordained kings and government, and lavished prophets upon them who not only apprised them of the best things pertaining to the present but also promised them the future Messiah, the Savior of the world. It was for his sake that God accorded them all of this, bidding them look for his coming, to expect him confidently and without delay. God did all of this solely for his sake: for his sake Abraham was called, circumcision was instituted, and the people were thus exalted so that all the world might know from which people, from which country, at which time, yes, from which tribe, family, city, and person, he would come, lest he be reproached by devils and by men for coming from a dark corner or from unknown ancestors. No, his ancestors had to be great patriarchs, excellent kings, and outstanding prophets, who bear witness to him.

We have already stated how the Jews, with few exceptions, viewed such promises and prophets. They were never able to tolerate a prophet, and always persecuted God's word and declined to give ear to God. That is the complaint and lament of all the prophets. And as their fathers did, so they still do today, nor will they ever mend their ways. If Isaiah, Jeremiah, or other prophets went about among them today and proclaimed what they proclaimed in their day, or declared that the Jews' present circumcision and hope for the Messiah are futile, they would again have to die at their hands as happened then. Let him who is endowed with reason, to say nothing of Christian understanding, note how arbitrarily they pervert and twist the prophets' books with their confounded glosses, in violation of their own conscience—of which we can perhaps say more later. Now that they can no longer stone or kill the prophets physically or personally, they torment them spiritually, mutilate, strangle, and maltreat their beautiful verses so that the human heart is vexed and pained. This forces us to see how, because of God's wrath, they are wholly delivered into the devil's hands. In brief, they are a prophet-murdering people; since they can no longer murder the living ones, they must murder and torment the ones that are dead.

Subsequently, after they have scourged, crucified, spat upon, blasphemed, and cursed God in his word—as Isaiah 8 prophesies—they pretentiously trot out their circumcision and other vain, blasphemous, invented, and meaningless works. They presume to be God's only people, to condemn all the world, and they expect that their arrogance and boasting will please God, that he should repay them with a Messiah of their own choosing and prescription. Therefore, dear Christian, be on your guard against such accursed, incorrigible people, from whom you can learn no more than to give God and his word the lie, to blaspheme, to pervert, to murder prophets, and haughtily and proudly to despise all people on earth.[13] Even if God would be willing to disregard all their other sins—which, of course, is impossible—he could not condone such ineffable (although poor and wretched) pride. He is called a God of the humble, as Isaiah 66:2 states: "But this is the man to whom I will look, he that is humble and contrite in spirit, and trembles at my word." I have said enough about the second false boast of the Jews, namely, their false and futile circumcision, which did not avail them when they were taken to task by Moses and by Jeremiah because of their uncircumcised heart. How much less is it useful now when it's nothing more than the devil's trickery with which he mocks and fools them, as he also does the Turks. Wherever God's word is no longer present, circumcision is null and void.

---

[13] Another reference to Jewish misanthropy.

Part I

Conceit and the Law of Moses

In the third place, they are very conceited because God spoke with them and issued them the law of Moses on Mount Sinai. Here we arrive at the right spot, here God really has to let himself be tortured, here he must listen as they tire him with their songs and praises because he hallowed them with his holy law, set them apart from other nations, and led them out of Egypt. Here we poor Goyim are really despised, and are mere ciphers compared to the holy, chosen, noble, and highly exalted people that is in possession of God's word! They state, as I myself heard:[14] "Indeed, what do you have to say to this—that God himself spoke with us on Mount Sinai and that he did this with no other people?" We have nothing with which to refute that, for we cannot deny them this glory. The books of Moses are ready to give proof of it, and David, too, testifies to it, saying in Psalm 147:19: "He declares his word to Jacob, his statutes and ordinances to Israel. He has not dealt thus with any other nation; they do not know his ordinances." And in Psalm 103:7: "He made known his ways to Moses, his acts to the people of Israel."

They relate that the chiefs of the people wore wreaths at Mount Sinai at that time as a symbol that they had contracted a 'marriage' with God through the law, that they had become his bride, and that the two had wedded one another. Later we read in all the prophets how God appears and talks with the children of Israel as a husband with his wife. From this also sprang the peculiar worship of Baal; for "Baal" denotes a man of the house or a master of the house, "Beulah" denotes a housewife. The latter also has taken a German form, as when we say "My dear *Buhle*" [sweetheart], and "I must have a *Buhle*." Formerly this was an inoffensive term, designating a young girl. It was said that a young man courted a young girl with a view to marriage. Now the word has assumed a different connotation.

Now we challenge you, Isaiah, Jeremiah, and all the prophets, and whoever will, to come and to be bold enough to say that such a noble

---

[14] As he explains in Part II, below.

nation with whom God himself converses and with whom he himself enters into marriage through the law, and to whom he joins himself as to a bride, is not God's people. Anyone doing that, I know, would make himself ridiculous and come to grief. In default of any other weapons, they would tear and bite him to pieces with their teeth for trying to dispossess them of such glory, praise, and honor. One can neither express nor understand the obstinate, unbridled, incorrigible arrogance of this people, springing from this advantage—that God himself spoke to them. No prophet has ever been able to raise his voice in protest or stand up against them, not even Moses. In Numbers 16, Korah arose and asserted that they were all holy people of God, and asked why Moses alone should rule and teach. Since that time, the majority of them have been genuine Korahites; there have been very few true Israelites. For just as Korah persecuted Moses, they have never subsequently left a prophet alive or unpersecuted, much less have they obeyed him.

So it became apparent that they were a defiled bride—yes, an incorrigible whore and an evil slut with whom God ever had to wrangle, scuffle, and fight. If he chastised and struck them with his word through the prophets, they contradicted him, killed his prophets, or, like a mad dog, bit the stick with which they were struck. Thus Psalm 95:10 declares: "For forty years I loathed that generation and said, 'They are a people who err in heart, and they do not regard my ways'." And Moses himself says in Deuteronomy 31:27: "For I know how rebellious and stubborn you are; behold, while I am yet alive with you, today you have been rebellious against the Lord; how much more after my death!" And Isaiah 48:4: "Because I know that you are obstinate, and your neck is an iron sinew and your forehead brass…" And so on; anyone who is interested may read more of this. The Jews are well aware that the prophets upbraided the children of Israel from beginning to end as a disobedient, evil people and as the vilest whore, although they boasted so much of the law of Moses, or circumcision, and of their ancestry.

But it might be objected: Surely, this is said about the wicked Jews, not about the pious ones as they are today. Well and good, for the

Part I

present I will be content if they confess as they must confess, that the wicked Jews cannot be God's people, and that their lineage, circumcision, and law of Moses cannot help them. Why, then, do they all, the most wicked as well as the pious, boast of circumcision, lineage, and law? The worse a Jew is, the more arrogant he is, solely because he is a Jew—that is, a person descended from Abraham's seed, circumcised, and under the law of Moses. David and other pious Jews were not as conceited as the present-day, incorrigible Jews. However wicked they may be, they presume to be the noblest lords over against us Gentiles, just by virtue of their lineage and law. Yet the law rebukes them as the vilest whores and rogues under the sun.

Furthermore, if they are pious Jews and not the whoring people, as the prophets call them, how does it happen that their piety is so concealed that God himself is not aware of it, and they are not aware of it either? They have, as we said, prayed, cried, and suffered almost 1,500 years already, and yet God refuses to listen to them. We know from Scripture that God will hear the prayers or sighing of the righteous, as the Psalter says [Ps 145:19]: "He fulfills the desire of all who fear him, he also hears their cry." And Psalm 34:17: "When the righteous cry for help, the Lord hears." As he promised in Psalm 50:15: "Call upon me in the day of trouble; I will deliver you." The same is found in many more verses of the Scripture. If it were not for these, who would or could pray? In brief, he says in the first commandment that he will be their God. Then, how do you explain that he will not listen to these Jews? They must assuredly be the base, whoring people, that is, no people of God, and their boast of lineage, circumcision, and law must be accounted as filth. If there were a single pious Jew among them who observed these, he would have to be heard; for God cannot let his saints pray in vain, as Scripture demonstrates by many examples. This is conclusive evidence that they cannot be pious Jews, but must be the multitude of the whoring and murderous people.

Such piety is, as already has been said, so concealed among them that they themselves also can know nothing of it. How then shall God know of it? They are full of malice, greed, envy, hatred toward one another, pride, usury, conceit, and curses against us Gentiles. Therefore, a Jew would have to have very sharp eyes to recognize a pious Jew, to say nothing of the fact that they all should be God's people as they claim. They surely hide their piety effectively under their manifest vices; and yet they all, without exception, claim to be Abraham's blood, the people of the circumcision and of Moses, that is, God's nation, compared with whom the Gentiles must surely be sheer stench. Although they know that God cannot tolerate this, nor did he tolerate it among the angels, yet he should and must listen to their lies and blasphemies to the effect that they are his people by virtue of the law he gave them, and because he conversed with their forefathers at Mount Sinai.

Why should one make many words about this? If the boast that God spoke with them and that they possess his word or commandment were sufficient so that God would on this basis regard them as his people, then the devils in hell would be much worthier of being God's people than the Jews, yes, than any people. The devils have God's word and know far better than the Jews that there is a God who created them, whom they are obliged to love with all their heart, to honor, fear, and serve, whose name they dare not misuse, whose word they must hear on the Sabbath and at all times; they know that they are forbidden to murder or to inflict harm on any creature. But what good does it do them to know and to possess God's commandment? Let them boast that this makes them God's own special, dear angels, in comparison with whom other angels are nothing! How much better off they would be if they didn't have God's commandment or if they were ignorant of it. If they didn't have it, they would not be condemned. The very reason for their condemnation is that they possess his commandment and yet don't keep it, but violate it constantly.

In the same manner, murderers and whores, thieves and rogues and all evil men might boast that they are God's holy, peculiar people; for they, too, have his word and know that they must fear and obey him,

Part I

love and serve him, honor his name, refrain from murder, adultery, theft, and every other evil deed. If they didn't have God's holy and true word, they could not sin. But since they do sin and are condemned, it is certain that they do have the holy, true word of God, against which they sin. Let them boast, like the Jews, that God has sanctified them through his law and chosen them above all other men as a peculiar people!

It's the same kind of boasting when the Jews boast in their synagogues, praising and thanking God for sanctifying them through his law and setting them apart as a peculiar people, although they know full well that they are not at all observing this law, that they are full of conceit, envy, usury, greed, and all sorts of malice. The worst offenders are those who pretend to be very devout and holy in their prayers. They are so blind that they not only practice usury—not to mention the other vices—but they teach that it is a right which God conferred on them through Moses.[15] Thereby, as in all the other matters, they slander God most infamously. However, we lack the time to dwell on that now.

But when they declare that even if they are not holy because of the Ten Commandments—since all Gentiles and devils are also duty-bound to keep these, or else are polluted and condemned on account of them—they still have the other laws of Moses, besides the Ten Commandments, which were given exclusively to them and not also to the Gentiles, and by which they are sanctified and singled out from all other nations... O Lord God, what a lame, loose, and vain excuse and pretext this is! If the Ten Commandments are not obeyed, what does the keeping of the other laws amount to, other than mere jugglery and

---

[15] Usury, or lending money at interest, was long a sin in Christian tradition, but permitted to the Jews. As Luther rightly states, the Old Testament prohibits Jews from lending at interest to each other, but permits it for non-Jews. See Ex 23:25: "If you lend money to any of my [Jewish] people with you who is poor, you shall not be to him as a creditor, and you shall not exact interest from him"; and Lev 25:35: "And if your [Jewish] brother becomes poor, and cannot maintain himself with you, you shall maintain him... Take no interest from him or increase... You shall not lend him your money at interest." But for non-Jews, the rule is different: "You shall not lend upon interest to your brother, interest on money... To a foreigner you may lend upon interest, but to your brother you shall not lend upon interest" (Deut 23:19).

hypocrisy, indeed, a veritable mockery that treats God as a fool. It's just as if an evil, devilish fellow among us were to parade about in the garb of a pope, cardinal, bishop, or pastor and observe all the precepts and the ways of these persons, but underneath this spiritual dress would be a genuine devil, a wolf, an enemy of the church, a blasphemer who trampled both the gospel and the Ten Commandments under foot and cursed and damned them. What a fine saint he would be in God's sight!

Or let's suppose that somewhere a pretty girl came along, adorned with a wreath, and observed all the manners, the duties, the deportment and discipline of a chaste virgin, but underneath was a vile, shameful whore, violating the Ten Commandments. What good would her fine obedience in observing outwardly all the duties and customs of a virgin's station do her? It would help her this much—that one would be seven times more hostile to her than to an impudent, public whore. Thus, God constantly chided the children of Israel through the prophets, calling them a vile whore because, under the guise and decor of external laws and sanctity, they practiced all sorts of idolatry and villainy, as especially Hosea laments in chapter 2.

To be sure, it is commendable when a pious virgin or woman is decently and cleanly dressed and adorned, and outwardly conducts herself with modesty. But if she is a whore, her garments, adornments, wreath, and jewels would better befit a sow that wallows in the mire. As Solomon says [Prov 11:22]: "Like a gold ring in a swine's snout is a beautiful woman without discretion." That is to say, she's a whore. Therefore, this boast about the external laws of Moses, apart from obedience to the Ten Commandments, should be silenced; indeed, this boast makes the Jews seven times more unworthy to be God's people than the Gentiles are. The external laws were not given to make a nation the people of God, but to adorn and enhance God's people externally. Just as the Ten Commandments were not given that any might boast of them and haughtily despise all the world because of them, as if they were holy and God's people because of them; rather they were given to be observed, and that obedience to God might be shown in them, as

Part I

Moses and all the prophets most earnestly teach. Not he who *has* them shall glory, as we saw in the instance of the devils and of evil men, but he who *keeps* them. He who has them and fails to keep them must be ashamed and terrified because he will surely be condemned by them.

But this subject is beyond the ken of the blind and hardened Jews. Speaking to them about it is much the same as preaching the gospel to a sow. They cannot know what God's commandment really is, much less do they know how to keep it. After all, they couldn't listen to Moses, nor look into his face; he had to cover it with a veil. This veil is there to the present day, and they still do not behold Moses' face, that is, his doctrine. It's still veiled to them.[16] Thus they couldn't hear God's word on Mount Sinai when he talked to them, but they retreated, saying to Moses: "You speak to us, and we will hear; but let not God speak to us, lest we die" [Ex 20:19]. To know God's commandment and to know how to keep it requires a high prophetic understanding.

Moses was well aware of that when he said in Exodus 34 that God forgives sin and that no one is guiltless before him, which is to say that no one keeps his commandments but he whose sins, God forgives. As David also testifies in Psalm 32:1, "Blessed is he whose transgression is forgiven…to whom the Lord imputes no iniquity." And in the same psalm [v. 6]: "Therefore let everyone who is godly offer prayer to thee for forgiveness," which means that no saint keeps God's commandments. But if the saints fail to keep them, how will the ungodly, the unbelievers, the evil people keep them? Again we read in Psalm 143:2: "O Lord, enter not into judgment with thy servant; for no man living is righteous before thee." That attests clearly enough that even the holy servants of God are not justified before him unless he sets aside his judgment and deals with them in his mercy; that is, they do not keep his commandments, and stand in need of forgiveness of sins.

This calls for a Man who will assist us in this, who bears our sin for us, as Isaiah 53:6 says: "The Lord has laid on him the iniquity of us all." Indeed, that is truly to understand God's law and its observance—when

---

[16] See for example Ex 34:33 or 2 Cor 3:13.

we know, recognize, yes, and feel that we have it, but do not keep it and cannot keep it; that in view of this, we are poor sinners and guilty before God; and that it's only out of pure grace and mercy that we receive forgiveness for such guilt and disobedience through the Man on whom God has laid this sin. Of this we Christians speak and this we teach, and of this the prophets and apostles speak to us and teach us. They are the ones who were and still are our God's bride and pure virgin; and yet they boast of no law or holiness as the Jews do in their synagogues. They rather wail over the law and cry for mercy and forgiveness of sins. The Jews, on the other hand, are as holy as the barefoot friars who possess so much excess holiness that they can use it to help others to get to heaven, and still retain a rich and abundant supply to sell. It's of no use to speak to any of them about these matters, for their blindness and arrogance are as solid as an iron mountain. They are in the right; God is in the wrong. Let them go their way, and let us remain with those who pray the *Miserere*, Psalm 51, that is, with those who know and understand what the law is, and what it means to keep and not to keep it.

Learn from this, dear Christian, what you are doing if you permit the blind Jews to mislead you. Then the saying will truly apply, "When a blind man leads a blind man, both will fall into the pit".[17] You cannot learn anything from them except how to misunderstand the divine commandments, and, despite this, boast haughtily over against the Gentiles—who really are much better before God than they, since they do not have such pride of holiness and yet keep far more of the law than these arrogant saints and damned blasphemers and liars.

Therefore, be on your guard against the Jews, knowing that wherever they have their synagogues, nothing is found but a den of devils in which sheer self-glory, conceit, lies, blasphemy, and defaming of God and men are practiced most maliciously and vehemently, just as the devils themselves do. And where you see or hear a Jew teaching, remember that you are hearing nothing but a venomous basilisk who poisons and kills people merely by fastening his eyes on them. God's

---

[17] A paraphrase of Luke 6:39.

Part I

wrath has consigned them to the presumption that their boasting, their conceit, their slander of God, their cursing of all people are a true and a great service rendered to God—all of which is very fitting and becoming to such noble blood of the fathers and circumcised saints. This they believe, despite the fact that they know they are steeped in manifest vices. And with all this, they claim to be doing right. Be on your guard against them!

ARROGANCE REGARDING THE PROMISED LAND

In the fourth place, they pride themselves tremendously on having received the land of Canaan, the city of Jerusalem, and the temple from God. God has often squashed such boasting and arrogance, especially through the king of Babylon, who led them away into captivity and destroyed everything[18]—just as the king of Assyria earlier had led all of Israel away and had laid everything low.[19] Finally, they were exterminated and devastated by the Romans over 1,400 years ago—so that they might well perceive that God did not regard, nor will regard, their country, city, temple, priesthood, or principality, and view them on account of these as his own peculiar people. Yet their iron neck, as Isaiah calls it [48:4] is not bent, nor is their brass forehead red with shame. They remain stone-blind, obdurate, immovable, ever hoping that God will restore their homeland to them and give everything back to them.[20]

Moses had informed them a great many times, first, that they were not occupying the land because their righteousness exceeded that of other heathen—for they were a stubborn, evil, disobedient people—and second, that they would soon be expelled from the land and perish if they did not keep God's commandments. And when God chose the

---

[18] Circa 600 BC, in which some 20,000 Jews were led away as captives.

[19] Circa 720 BC. The king in question was Sennacherib, whom Luther mentions explicitly in Part II.

[20] Arguably, God did "restore their homeland" in 1948, when the nation of Israel was established.

city of Jerusalem, he added very clearly in the writings of all the prophets that he would utterly destroy this city of Jerusalem, his seat and throne, if they would not keep his commandments. Furthermore, when Solomon had built the temple,[21] had sacrificed and prayed to God, God said to him (1 Kings 9:3), "I have heard your prayer and your supplications... I have consecrated this house," etc.; but then he added shortly thereafter:

> But if you turn aside from following me...and do not keep my commandments...then I will cut off Israel from the land which I have given them; and the house which I have consecrated for my name I will cast out of my sight; and Israel will become a proverb and a byword among all peoples.

With an utter disregard for this, they stood, and still stand, firm as a rock or as an inert stone image, insisting that God gave them country, city, and temple, and that therefore they have to be God's people or church.

They neither hear nor see that God gave them all of this that they might keep his commandments, that is, regard him as their God, and thus be his people and church. They boast of their race and of their descent from the fathers, but they neither see nor pay attention to the fact that he chose their race that they should keep his commandments. They boast of their circumcision; but why they are circumcised—namely, that they should keep God's commandments—counts for naught. They are quick to boast of their law, temple, worship, city, land and government; but why they possess all of this, they disregard.

The devil with all his angels has taken possession of this people, so that they always exalt external things—their gifts, their deeds, their works—before God, which is tantamount to offering God the empty

---

[21] This would be the 'First Temple' of the Jews, traditionally held to be built circa 950 BC.

Part I

shells without the kernels. These they expect God to esteem and by reason of them accept them as his people, and exalt and bless them above all Gentiles. But that he wants his laws observed and wants to be honored by them as God, this they don't want to consider. Thus, the words of Moses are fulfilled when he says [Deut 32:21] that God will not regard them as his people, since they don't regard him as their God. Hosea 2 expresses the same thought.

Indeed, if God had not allowed the city of Jerusalem to be destroyed and had them driven out of their country, but had permitted them to remain there, no one could have convinced them that they are not God's people, since they would still be in possession of temple, city, and country regardless of how base, disobedient, and stubborn they were. [They would not have believed it] even if it had rained nothing but prophets daily and even if a thousand Moseses had stood up and shouted: "You are not God's people, because you are disobedient and rebellious to God." Why, even today they cannot refrain from their nonsensical, insane boasting that they are God's people, although they have been cast out, dispersed, and utterly rejected for almost 1,500 years. By virtue of their own merits, they still hope to return there again. But they have no such promise with which they could console themselves other than what their false imagination smuggles into Scripture.

Our apostle St. Paul was right when he said of them that "they have a zeal for God, but it is not enlightened," etc. [Rom 10:2]. They claim to be God's people by reason of their deeds, works, and external show, and not because of sheer grace and mercy, as all prophets and all true children of God have to be, as was said. Therefore, they are beyond counsel and help. In the same way as our papists, bishops, monks, and priests, together with their following, who insist that they are God's people and church; they believe that God should esteem them because they are baptized, because they have the name, and because they rule the roost. There they stand like a rock. If 100,000 apostles came along and said: "You are not the church because of your behavior or your many doings and divine services, even though these were your best efforts; no, you must despair of all this and adhere simply and solely to the grace and mercy of Christ, etc. If you fail to do this, you are the devil's whore or a school of knaves and not the church," they would wish to murder, burn at the stake, or banish such apostles. As for believing them and abandoning their own devices, of this there is no hope; it will not happen.

The Turks follow the same pattern with their worship, as do all fanatics. Jews, Turks, papists, radicals abound everywhere. All of them claim to be the church and God's people in accord with their conceit and boast, regardless of the one true faith and the obedience to God's commandments through which alone people become and remain God's children. Even if they don't all pursue the same course, but one chooses this way, another that way, resulting in a variety of forms, they nonetheless all have the same intent and ultimate goal, namely, by means of their own deeds they want to manage to become God's people. And thus they boast and brag that they are the ones whom God will esteem. They are the foxes of Samson that are tied together tail to tail, but whose heads turn away in different directions.[22]

But as we noted earlier, that's beyond the comprehension of the Jews, as well as of the Turks and papists. As St. Paul says in 1 Corinthians, "The unspiritual man does not receive the gifts of the Spirit of God, because they are spiritually discerned" [2:14]. Thus the words of Isaiah 6:9 come true: "Hear and hear, but do not understand; see and see, but do not perceive." They don't know what they hear, see, say, or do. And yet they don't concede that they are blind and deaf.

---

[22] See Judges 15:4.

PART II

THE COMING OF THE MESSIAH

That shall be enough about the false boast and pride of the Jews, who would move God with sheer lies to regard them as his people. Now we come to the main subject, their asking God for the Messiah.[23] Here at last they show themselves as true saints and pious children. At this point they certainly do not want to be accounted liars and blasphemers but reliable prophets, asserting that the Messiah has not yet come but will still appear. Who will take them to task here for their error or mistake? Even if all the angels and God himself publicly declared on Mount Sinai or in the temple in Jerusalem that the Messiah had come long ago and that he was no longer to be expected, God himself and all the angels would have to be considered nothing but devils. So convinced are these most holy and truthful prophets that the Messiah has not yet appeared but will still come. Nor will they listen to us. They turned a deaf ear to us in the past and still do so, although many fine scholarly people, including some from their own race,[24] have refuted them so thoroughly that even stone and wood, if endowed with a particle of reason, would have to yield.

Yet they rave consciously against recognized truth. Their accursed rabbis, who indeed know better, wantonly poison the minds of their poor youth and of the common man and divert them from the truth. I believe that if these writings were read by the common man and the youth, they would stone all their rabbis and hate them more violently

---

[23] The bulk of Part II covers Luther's analysis of the coming of the Messiah. His argument turns on four key passages: (1) Genesis 49:10, (2) 2 Samuel 23:5, (3) Haggai 2:6, and (4) Daniel 9:24. Each is addressed in turn in this part of the book.

[24] Including Paul of Burgos.

than they do us Christians. But these villains prevent our sincere views from coming to their attention.

If I hadn't had the experience with my papists, it would have seemed incredible to me that the earth should harbor such base people who knowingly fly in the face of open and manifest truth, that is, of God himself. I never expected to encounter such hardened minds in any human breast, but only in that of the devil. However, I'm no longer amazed by either the Turks' or the Jews' blindness, obduracy, and malice, since I have to witness the same thing in the most holy fathers of the church, in pope, cardinals, and bishops. O you terrible wrath and incomprehensible judgment of the sublime Divine Majesty! How can you be so despised by the children of men that we do not forthwith tremble to death before you? What an unbearable sight you are, also to the hearts and eyes of the holiest men, as we see in Moses and the prophets. Yet these stony hearts and iron souls mock you so defiantly.

However, although we perhaps labor in vain on the Jews—for I said earlier that I don't want to dispute with them—we nonetheless want to discuss their senseless folly among ourselves, for the strengthening of our faith and as a warning to weak Christians against the Jews, and, chiefly, in honor of God, in order to prove that our faith is true and that they are entirely mistaken on the question of the Messiah. We Christians have our New Testament, which furnishes us reliable and adequate testimony concerning the Messiah. That the Jews don't believe it does not concern us; we believe their accursed glosses still less. We let them go their way and wait for their Messiah. Their unbelief doesn't harm us; but as to the help they derive and thus far have derived from it, they may ask of their long-enduring exile. That will, indeed, supply the answer for us.

Let him who will not follow lag behind. They act as though they were of great importance to us. Just to vex us, they corrupt the sayings of Scripture. We do not at all desire or require their conversion for any advantage, usefulness, or help accruing to us. All that we do in this regard is prompted rather by a concern for their welfare. If they don't

Part II

want it, they can disregard it; we are excused and can easily dispense with them, together with all that they are, have, and can do for salvation. We have a better knowledge of Scripture, thanks be to God; of this we are certain, and all the devils shall never deprive us of it, much less the miserable Jews.

Genesis 49

First, we want to submit the verse found in Genesis 49:10: "The scepter shall not depart from Judah, nor the ruler's staff from between his feet, until Shiloh[25] comes, and to him shall be the obedience of the peoples." This saying of the holy patriarch Jacob, spoken at the very end of his life, has been tortured and crucified in many ways down to the present day by the modern, strange Jews, in violation of their own conscience. They realize fully that their twisting and perverting is nothing but wanton mischief. Their glosses remind me very much of an evil, stubborn shrew who clamorously contradicts her husband and insists on having the last word although she knows she is in the wrong. Thus, these blinded people also suppose that it suffices to bark and prattle against the text and its true meaning; they are entirely indifferent to the fact that they are lying impudently. I believe they would be happier if this verse had never been written rather than that they should change their mind. This verse pains them intensely, and they cannot ignore it.

The ancient, true Jews understood this verse correctly, as we Christians do, namely, that the government or scepter should remain with the tribe of Judah until the advent of the Messiah; then "to him shall be the obedience of the peoples," to him they will adhere. That is, the scepter shall then not be confined to the tribe of Judah, but, as the prophets later explain, it shall be extended to all peoples on earth at the time of the Messiah. However, until he appears, the scepter shall remain

---

[25] This is a disputed biblical term. Luther (and most Christians) assume it refers to the coming Messiah, i.e. Jesus. Most Jews, however, consider it a town or village, located near the present-day town of Shilo in the West Bank. In theory, it could be both. Luther discusses it at length below.

in that small nook and corner, Judah. That, I say, is the understanding of the prophets and of the ancient Jews; this they cannot deny. Also their Chaldaean Bible,[26] which they dare oppose as little as the Hebrew Bible itself, shows this clearly.

In translation it reads thus: "The *shultan* shall not be put away from the house of Judah nor the *saphra* from his children's children eternally until the Messiah comes, whose is the kingdom, and the peoples will make themselves obedient to him." This is a true and faithful translation of the Chaldaean text, as no Jew or devil can deny.

For Moses' Hebrew term *shebet* ["scepter"] we use the word *Zepter* in German, whereas the Chaldaean translator chooses the word *shultan*. Let's explain these words. The Hebrew *shebet* is the designation for a *virga* ['rod']; it's really not a rod in the usual sense, for this term suggests to the German the thought of birch switches with which children are punished. Nor is it a staff used by invalids and the aged for walking. But it designates a mace held upright, such as a judge holds in his hand when he acts in his official capacity. As luxury increased in the world, this mace was made of silver or of gold. Now it's called a scepter, that is, a royal rod. *Skeptron* is a Greek word, but it has now been taken up into the German language. In his first book, Homer describes his King Achilles as having a wooden scepter adorned with small silver nails.[27] From this we learn what scepters originally were and how they gradually came to be made entirely of silver and gold. In brief, it is the rod, whether of silver, wood, or gold, carried by a king or his representative. It symbolizes nothing other than dominion or kingdom. No one questions this.

To make it very clear: The Chaldaean translator does not use the word *shebet*, mace or scepter; but he substitutes the person who bears this rod, saying *shultan*, indicating that a prince, lord, or king shall not depart from the house of Judah; there shall be a sultan in the house of

---

[26] That is, the Targumim, which are Aramic versions of passages from the Old Testament.

[27] *Iliad*, Book I, lines 270-290.

PART II

Judah until the Messiah comes. "Sultan" is also a Hebrew term, and a word well known to us Christians, who have waged war for more than 600 years against the sultan of Egypt, and have gained very little to show for it. The Saracens [Muslims] call their king or prince "sultan," that is, lord or ruler or sovereign. From this the Hebrew word *schilt* is derived, which has become a thoroughly German word (*Schild* ["shield"]). It's as though one wished to say that a prince or lord must be his subjects' shield, protection, and defense, if he is to be a true judge, sultan, or lord, etc. Some people even try to trace the German term *Schultheiss* ["village mayor"] back to the word "sultan"; but I won't enter into this.

Saphra is the same as the Hebrew *sopher*—for Chaldee and Hebrew are closely related, indeed they are almost identical, just as Saxons and Swabians both speak German, but still there's a great difference. The word *sopher* we commonly translate into the German by means of *Kanzler* ["chancellor"]. Everyone, including Burgensis, translates the word *saphra* with *scriba* or scribe. These people are called scribes in the Gospel. They are not ordinary scribes who write for wages or without official authority. They are sages, great rulers, doctors and professors, who teach, order, and preserve the law in the state. I suppose that it also encompasses the chancelleries, parliaments, councilors, and all who by wisdom and justice aid in governing. That's what Moses wishes to express with the word *mehoqeq* ["ruler's staff"], which designates one who teaches, composes, and executes commands and decrees. Among the Saracens, for instance, the sultan's scribes or secretaries, his doctors, teachers, and scholars, are those who teach, interpret, and preserve the Koran as the law of the land. In the papacy, the pope's scribes or *saphra* are the canonists or jackasses who teach and preserve his decretals and laws. In the empire, the *doctores legum*, the secular jurists, are the emperor's *saphra* or scribes who teach, administer, and preserve the imperial laws.

Thus Judah, too, had scribes who taught and preserved the law of Moses, which was the law of the land. Therefore we have translated the word *mehoqeq* with "master," that is, doctor, teacher, etc. So this passage, "The *mehoqeq*, i.e., master, will not be taken from between his feet," means that teachers and listeners who sit at their feet will remain in an orderly government. Every country, if it is to endure, must have these two things: power and law. The country, as the saying goes, must have a lord, a head, a ruler. But it must also have a law by which the ruler is guided. These are the mace and the *mehoqeq*, or sultan and *saphra*. Solomon indicates this also, for when he had received the rod, that is, the kingdom, he prayed only for wisdom so that he might rule the people justly (1 Kings 3). Wherever sheer power prevails without the law, where the sultan is guided by his arbitrary will and not by duty, there is no government, but tyranny, akin to that of Nero, Caligula, Dionysius, Henry of Brunswick, and their like. Such does not endure long. On the other hand, where there is law but no power to enforce it, there the wild mob will also do its will and no government can survive. Therefore, both must be present: law and power, sultan and *saphra*, to supplement one another.

Thus, the councilors who gathered in Jerusalem and who were to come from the tribe of Judah were the *saphra*; the Jews called them the Sanhedrin. Herod, a foreigner, an Edomite, did away with this, and he himself became both sultan and *saphra*, mace and *mehoqeq* in the house of Judah, lord and scribe.[28] Then the saying of the patriarch began to be fulfilled, that Judah was no longer to retain the government or the *saphra*. Now it was time for the Messiah to come and to occupy his kingdom and sit on the throne of David forever, as Isaiah 9:6 prophesies. Therefore, let us now study this saying of the patriarch.

"Judah," he declares, "your brothers shall praise you," etc. [Gen 49:8]. This, it seems to me, requires no commentary; it states clearly enough that the tribe of Judah will be honored above all of his brothers

---

[28] Herod (also known as 'Herod the Great' and 'Herod I') ruled Judea from 37 to 4 BC. He was born an Edomite, that is, not a true Jew, but converted to the religion—hence, a "foreigner," as Luther says. Herod was appointed provincial governor of Judea by the Romans, and thus was viewed as puppet ruler and traitor by the local Jews.

Part II

and will enjoy the prerogative. The text continues: "Your hand shall be on the neck of your enemies," etc. This also declares plainly that the famous and prominent tribe of Judah must encounter enemies and opposition, but that all will end successfully and victoriously for it. We continue: "Your father's sons shall bow down before you," etc. Again, it's clear that this doesn't refer to the captivity but to the rule over his brothers, all of which was fulfilled in David. But not only did the tribe of Judah, in David, become lord over his brothers; he also spread his rule beyond, like a lion, forcing other nations into submission; for instance, the Philistines, the Syrians, the Moabites, the Ammonites, the Edomites.

This is what he praises in these beautiful words [Gen 49:9]: "Judah is a lion's whelp [or 'cub']; from the prey, my son, you have gone up. He stooped down, he crouched as a lion, and as a lioness; who dares rouse him up?" This is to say that he was enthroned and established a kingdom that no one could overwhelm, though the adjacent nations frequently and mightily tried to do so.

All right, up to this point the patriarch has established, ordained, and confirmed the kingdom, the sultan, the rod, the *saphra* in the tribe of Judah. There Judah, the sultan, sits enthroned for his rule. What is to happen now? This, he says: He shall remain thus until the Messiah comes; that is, many will oppose him, attempting to overthrow and destroy the kingdom and simply make it disappear from the earth. The histories of the kings and the prophets amply testify that all the Gentile nations ever earnestly strove to do this. And the patriarch himself declares, as we heard before, that Judah must have its foes. Such is the course of events in the world that wherever a kingdom or principality rises to a position of might, envy will not rest until it is destroyed. All of history illustrates this with numerous examples.

However, in this instance the Holy Spirit states: This kingdom in the tribe of Judah is mine, and no one shall take it from me, no matter how angry and mighty he may be, even if the gates of hell should try. The words will still prove true: *Non auferetur*, "It shall not be taken away." You devils and Gentiles may say: *Auferetur*, we shall put an end to it, we shall devour it, we shall silence it, as Psalm 74 bemoans. But it shall remain undevoured, undevastated. "The *shebet* or sultan shall not depart from the house of Judah, nor the *saphra* from his children's children," until the *shiloh* or Messiah comes—no matter how you all rant and rage.

And when he does appear, the kingdom will become far different and still more glorious. Since you would not tolerate the tribe of Judah in a little, narrow corner, I shall change him into a truly strong lion who will become sultan and *saphra* in all the world. I will do this in such a way that he will not draw a sword nor shed a drop of blood, but the nations will voluntarily and gladly submit themselves to him and obey him. Such shall be his kingdom. After all, the kingdom and all things are his.

Approach the text, both Chaldaean and Hebrew, with this understanding and this thought, and I wager that your heart together with the letters will surely tell you: By God! that is the truth, that is the patriarch's meaning. And then consult the histories to ascertain whether this has not happened and come to pass in this way and still continues to do so. Again you will be compelled to say: It is verily so. It is undeniable that the sultan and *saphra* remained with the tribe of Judah until Herod's time, even if it was at times feeble and was not maintained without the opposition of mighty foes. Nevertheless, it was preserved. Under Herod and after Herod, however, it fell into ruin and came to an end. It was so completely destroyed that even Jerusalem, once the throne-seat of the tribe of Judah, and the land of Canaan, were wiped out.[29] Thus the verse was fulfilled which said that the sultan has departed and the Messiah has come.

I don't have the time at present to demonstrate what a rich fountainhead this verse is and how the prophets drew so much information from it

---

[29] Again, in 70 AD.

Part II

concerning the fall of the Jews and the election of the Gentiles, about which the modern Jews and bastards know nothing at all. But we have clearly and forcefully seen from this verse that the Messiah had to come at the time of Herod. The alternative would be to say that God failed to keep his promise and, consequently, lied. No one dare do that, save the accursed devil and his servants, the false bastards and strange Jews. They do this incessantly. In their eyes, God must be a liar. They claim that they are right when they assert that the Messiah has not yet come, despite the fact that God declared in very plain words that the Messiah would come before the scepter had entirely departed from Judah. And this scepter has been lost to Judah for almost 1,500 years now. The clear words of God vouch for this, and so do the visible effect and fulfillment of these same words.

What do you hope to accomplish by engaging an obstinate Jew in a long dispute on this? It's just as though you were to talk to an insane person and prove to him that God created heaven and earth, according to Genesis 1, pointing out heaven and earth to him with your hands, and he would nevertheless prattle that these are not the heaven and earth mentioned in Genesis 1, or that they were not heaven and earth at all, but were called something else, etc. This verse, "The scepter shall not depart from Judah," etc., is as clear and plain as the verse, "God created heaven and earth." And the fact that this scepter has been removed from Judah for almost 1,500 years is as patent and manifest as heaven and earth are, so that one can readily perceive that the Jews are not simply erring and misled but that they are maliciously and willfully denying and blaspheming the recognized truth, in violation of their conscience. No one should consider such a person worthy of wasting a single word on him, even if it dealt with Markolf the mockingbird,[30] much less if it deals with such exalted divine words and works.

But if anyone is tempted to become displeased with me, I will serve his purpose and give him the Jews' glosses on this text. First I will present those who do not dismiss this text but adhere to it, particularly to the

---

[30] That is, a swindler or imposter.

Chaldean version, which no sensible Jew can deny. These twist and turn as follows: To be sure, they say, God's promise is certain; but our sins prevent the fulfillment of the promise. Therefore we still look forward to it until we have atoned, etc. Is this not an empty pretext, even a blasphemous one? As if God's promise rested on our righteousness, or fell with our sins! That's tantamount to saying that God would have to become a liar because of our sin, and conversely, that he would have to become truthful again by reason of our righteousness. How could one speak more shamefully of God than to imply that he's a shaking reed that is easily swayed back and forth either by our falling down or standing up?

If God were not to make a promise or keep a promise until we were rid of sin, he would have been unable to promise or do anything from the very beginning. As David says in Psalm 130:3: "If thou, O Lord, shouldst mark iniquity, Lord, who could stand?" And in Psalm 143:2: "Enter not into judgment with thy servant; for no man living is righteous before thee." And there are many more such verses. The example of the children of Israel in the wilderness can be cited here. God led them into the land of Canaan without any righteousness on their part, in fact, with their great sins and shame, solely on account of his promise. In Deuteronomy 9:5 Moses says:

> Know therefore that the Lord your God is not giving you this good land to possess because of your righteousness; for you are a stubborn and a disobedient people (it seems to me that this may indeed be called sin), but because of the promise which the Lord gave to your fathers, ...

By way of example he often wanted to exterminate them, but Moses interceded for them. So little was God's promise based upon their holiness.

It's true that wherever God promises anything conditionally, or with reservation, saying: "If you will do that, I will do this," then the fulfillment is contingent on our action; for instance, when he declared to Solomon [1 Kings 9], "If you will keep my statutes and my ordinances,

Part II

then this house shall be consecrated to me; if not I shall destroy it." However, the promise of the Messiah is not thus conditional. He doesn't say: "If you will do this or that, then the Messiah will come; if you fail to do it, he will not come." But he promises him unconditionally, saying: "The Messiah will come at the time when the scepter has departed from Judah." Such a promise is based only on divine truth and grace, which ignores and disregards our doings. That renders this subterfuge of the Jews inane, and, moreover, very blasphemous.

The others who depart from this text subject almost every single word of it to severe and violent misinterpretation. They really don't deserve to have their drivel and filth heard; still, in order to expose their disgrace, we must exercise a bit of patience and also listen to their nonsense. Since they depart from the clear meaning of the text, they already stand condemned by their own conscience, which would constrain them to heed the text; but to vex us, they conjure up the Hebrew words before our eyes, as though we were not conversant with the Chaldean text.

Some engage in fantasies here and say that Shiloh refers to the city of that name, where the ark of the covenant was kept (Judges 21),[31] so that the meaning would be that the scepter shall not depart from Judah until Shiloh comes, that is, until Saul is anointed king of Shiloh. That is surely foolish prattle. Prior to King Saul, not only did Judah have no scepter, but neither did all of Israel.[32] How, then, can it have departed when Saul became king? The text declares that Judah had first been lord over his brothers and that he then became a lion, and therefore received the scepter. Likewise, before Saul's time, no judge was lord or prince over the people of Israel, as we gather from Gideon's speech to the people in reply to their wish that he and his descendants rule over them: "I will not rule over you, and my son will not rule over you; the Lord will rule over you" (Judg 8:23). Nor was there a judge from the tribe of

---

[31] See also 1 Sam 4:3.

[32] Saul was the traditional first king of Israel as a unified nation-state, circa 1000 BC. But the historical accuracy of his reign is disputed.

Judah, except perhaps for Othniel [Judg 3:9], Joshua's immediate successor. All the others down to Saul were from the other tribes. And although Othniel is called Caleb's youngest brother, this doesn't prove that he was of the tribe of Judah, since he may have had a different father. And it doesn't make sense that Shiloh should here refer to a city or to Saul's coronation in Shiloh, for Saul was anointed by Samuel in Ramath (1 Sam 10) and confirmed at Gilgal.

In any case, what's the meaning of the Chaldean text that says that the kingdom belongs to Shiloh and that nations shall be subject to it? When was the city of Shiloh or Saul ever accorded such an honor? Israel is one nation, not many, with one body of laws, one divine worship, one name. There are many nations, however, which have different and various laws, names, and gods. Now Jacob declares that not the one nation Israel—which was already his or was under Judah's scepter—but other nations would fall to Shiloh. Therefore this foolish talk reflects nothing other than the great stubbornness of the Jews, who will not submit to this saying of Jacob, although they stand convicted by their own conscience.

Others indulge in the fancy that Shiloh refers to King Jeroboam, who was crowned in Shiloh, and to whom ten tribes of Israel had defected from Rehoboam, the king of Judah (1 Kings 12). Therefore, they say, this is Jacob's meaning: The scepter shall not depart from Judah until Shiloh, that is, Jeroboam, comes. This is just as inane as the other interpretation; for Jeroboam was not crowned in Shiloh but in Shechem (1 Kings 12). Thus the scepter did not depart from Judah, but the kingdom of Judah remained, together with the tribe of Benjamin and many of the children of Israel who dwelt in the cities of these two tribes, as we hear in 1 Kings 12. Moreover, the entire priesthood, worship, temple, and everything remained in Judah. Furthermore, Jeroboam never conquered the kingdom of Judah, nor did other nations fall to him, as they were to fall to Shiloh.

The third group babbles thus: "Shiloh means 'sent,' and this term applies to Nebuchadnezzar of Babylon".[33] So the meaning is that the

---

[33] Nebuchadnezzar II was king of Babylon, circa 605 – 560 BC.

Part II

scepter shall not depart from Judah until Shiloh, that is, the king of Babylon, comes. He was to lead Judah into exile and destroy it. This also doesn't hold water, and even a child learning the alphabet can disprove it. For Shiloh and *shiloch* are two different words. The latter may mean "sent." But that's not the word found here; it is Shiloh, and that, as the Chaldee says, means "Messiah." But the king of Babylon is not the Messiah who is to come from Judah, as the Jews and all the world know very well. Nor did the scepter depart from Judah even though the Jews were led captive into Babylon. That was just a punishment for 70 years. Also during this time, great prophets—Jeremiah, Daniel, Ezekiel—appeared who upheld the scepter and said how long the exile would be. Furthermore, Jehoiachin, the king of Judah, was regarded as a king in Babylon. And many of those who were led away into captivity returned home again during their lifetime (Haggai 2). This cannot be viewed as loss of the scepter, but as a light flogging. Even if they were deprived of their country for a while by way of punishment, God nonetheless pledged his precious word that they could remain assured of their land. But during the past 1,500 years, not even a dog, much less a prophet, has any assurance concerning the land. Therefore the scepter has now definitely departed from Judah. I have written more about this against the Sabbatarians.

The fourth group twists the word *shebet* and interprets it to mean that the rod will not depart from Judah until Shiloh, that is, his son, will come, who will weaken the Gentiles. These regard the rod as the punishment and exile in which they now live. But the Messiah will come and slay all the Gentiles. That is humbug. It ignores the Chaldean text entirely—something they may and dare not do—and is a completely arbitrary interpretation of the word *shebet*. They overlook the preceding words in which Jacob makes Judah a prince and a lion or a king, adding immediately thereafter that the scepter, or *shebet*, shall not depart from Judah. How could such an odd meaning about punishment follow right on the heels of such glorious words about a principality or kingdom? The sins that provoked such a punishment would have to have been proclaimed first. But all that we find mentioned here are praise, honor, and glory to the tribe of Judah.

And even if the word *shebet* does designate a rod for punishment, how would that help them? For the judge's or the king's rod is also a rod of punishment for the evildoers. Indeed, the rod of punishment cannot be any but a judge's or sultan's rod, since the right to administer punishment belongs solely to the authority (Deut 32): *Mihi vindicatam*, "Vengeance is mine." In any event, this meaning remains unshaken—that the scepter or rod of Judah shall remain—even if this rod is one of punishment. But this arbitrary interpretation of the rabbis points to a foreign rod that does not rest in Judah's hand but on Judah's back and is wielded by a foreign hand. Even if this meaning were possible—which it's not—what would we do with the other passage that speaks of the *saphra* or *mehoqeq* at his feet? This would then also have to be a foreign lord's *mehoqeq* and a foreign nation's feet. But since Jacob declares that it is to be Judah and the *mehoqeq* of his feet, the other term, the rod, must also represent the rule of his tribe.

Some twist the word *donec* ("until") and try to make "because" (*quia*) out of it. So they read: "The scepter of Judah will not depart *donec*, that is, because (*quia*) the Messiah will come." He who perpetrated this is a precious master, worthy of being crowned with thistles. He reverses the correct order of things in this manner: The Messiah will come; therefore, the scepter will remain. Jacob, however, first makes Judah a prince and a lion to whom the scepter is assigned prior to the coming of the Messiah; he then, in turn, will give it to the Messiah. Thus Judah retains neither the principality nor the role of lion nor the scepter, which Jacob assigned to him. Furthermore, the fool arbitrarily makes out of the term "until" a new term, "because." This, of course, the language does not permit.

And finally, there is a rabbi who twists the word "come" and claims that it means "to set," just as the Hebrew uses the word "to come" for the setting of the sun. This fellow is given to such nonsense that I'm at a loss to know whether he is trying to walk on his head or on his ears.

Part II

For I fail to understand the purport of his words when he says that the scepter will not depart from Judah until Shiloh (the city) goes down (sets). Then David, the Messiah, will come. Where, to repeat what was said above, was the scepter of Judah prior to Shiloh or Saul? But they who rage against their own conscience and patent truth must necessarily speak such nonsense. In brief, Lyra is right when he says that even if they invent these and many other similar glosses, the Chaldean text topples all of them and convicts them of being willful liars, blasphemer, and perverters of God's word. However, I wanted to present this to us Germans so that we might see what rascals the blind Jews are, and how powerfully the truth of God in our midst stands with us and against them.

And now that some have noticed that such evasions and silly glosses are null and void, they admit that the Messiah came at the time of the destruction of Jerusalem; but, they say, he's in the world secretly, sitting in Rome among the beggars and doing penance for the Jews until the time for his public appearance is at hand. These are not the words of Jews or of men but those of the arrogant, jeering devil, who most bitterly and venomously mocks us Christians and our Christ through the Jews, as if to say: "The Christians glory much in their Christ, but they have to submit to the yoke of the Romans; they must suffer and be beggars in the world, not only in the days of the emperors, but also in those of the pope. After all, they are impotent in my kingdom, the world, and I will surely remain their master." Yes, vile devil, just mock and laugh your fill over this now; you will still tremble enough for it.

Thus the words of Jacob fared very much the same as did these words of Christ in our day: "This is my body which is given for you." The enthusiasts distorted each word singly and collectively, putting the last things first, rather than accept the true meaning of the text, as we have observed. It's clear in this instance too that Christians such as Lyra, Raymund, Burgensis, and others certainly went to great lengths in an effort to convert the Jews. They hounded them from one word to another, just as foxes are hunted down. But after having been hounded a long time, they still persisted in their obstinacy and now set to erring consciously and would not depart from their rabbis. Thus, we must let them go their way and ignore their malicious blasphemy and lying.

I once experienced this myself. Three learned Jews came to me, hoping to discover a new Jew in me because we were beginning to read Hebrew here in Wittenberg, and remarking that matters would soon improve since we Christians were starting to read their books. When I debated with them, they gave me their glosses, as they usually do. But when I forced them back to the text, they soon fled from it, saying that they were obliged to believe their rabbis as we do the pope and the doctors, etc. I took pity on them and gave them a letter of recommendation to the authorities, asking that for Christ's sake they let them freely go their way. But later, I found out that they called Christ a *tola*, that is, a hanged highwayman. Therefore, I don't want to have anything more to do with any Jew. As St. Paul says, they are consigned to wrath; the more one tries to help them, the baser and more stubborn they become. Leave them to their own devices.

We Christians, however, can greatly strengthen our faith with this statement of Jacob, assuring us that Christ is now present and that he has been present for almost 1,500 years—but not, as the devil jeers, as a beggar in Rome; rather, as a ruling Messiah. If this were not so, then God's word and promise would be a lie. If the Jews would only let Holy Scripture be God's word, they would also have to admit that there has been a Messiah since the time of Herod (no matter where), rather than awaiting another. But before doing this, they will rather tear and pervert Scripture until it is no longer Scripture. And this is in fact their situation: They have neither Messiah nor Scripture, just as Isaiah 28 prophesied of them.

2 Samuel 23

But may this suffice on the saying of Jacob. Let's take another saying that the Jews did not and cannot twist and distort in this way. In the last words

Part II

of David, we find him saying (2 Sam 23:2): "The Spirit of the Lord speaks by me, his word is upon my tongue. The God of Israel has spoken, the Rock of Israel…" And a little later [v. 5]: "Does not my house stand so with God?" Or, to translate it literally from the Hebrew: "My house is of course not thus," etc. That is to say: "My house is, after all, not worthy; this is too glorious a thing and it is too much that God does all of this for a poor man like me." [Continuing with v. 5:] "For he has made with me an everlasting covenant, ordered in all things and secure." Note well how David exults with so numerous and seemingly superfluous words that the Spirit of God has spoken through him and that God's word is upon his tongue. Thus he says: "The God of Israel has spoken, the Rock of Israel," etc. It's as if he were to say: "My dear people, give ear. Whoever can hear, let him hear. Here is God, who is speaking and saying, 'Listen'," etc. What is it, then, that you exhort us to listen to? What is God saying through you? What does he wish to say to you? What shall we hear?

This is what you are to hear: that God made an everlasting, firm, and sure covenant with me and my house, a covenant of which my house is not worthy. Indeed, my house is nothing compared to God; and yet he did this. What is this everlasting covenant? Oh, open your ears and listen! My house and God have bound themselves together forever through an oath. This is a covenant, a promise which must exist and endure forever. For it is God's covenant and pledge, which no one shall or can break or hinder. My house shall stand eternally; it is "ordered in all things and secure." The word *aruk* ("ordered") conveys the meaning that it will not disappoint or fail one in the least. Have you heard this? And do you believe that God is truthful? Yes, without doubt. My dear people, do you also believe that he can and will keep his word?

Well and good, if God is truthful and almighty and spoke these words through David—which no Jew dares to deny—then David's house and government (which are the same thing) must have endured since the time he spoke these words, and must still endure and will endure forever—that is, eternally. Otherwise, God would be a liar. In brief, either we must have David's house or heir, who reigns from the time of David to the present and in eternity, or David died as a flagrant liar to his last day, uttering these words (as it seems) as so much idle chitchat: "God speaks, God says, God promises." It's futile to join the Jews in giving God the lie, saying that he did not keep these precious words and promises. We must, I say, have an heir of David from his time onward, in proof of the fact that his house has never stood empty—no matter where this heir may be. His house must have been continuous and must ever remain so. Here we find God's word that this is an everlasting, firm, and sure covenant, without a flaw, but everything in it must be *aruk*, magnificently ordered, as God orders all his work. Psalm 111:3: "Full of honor and majesty in his work."

Now let the Jews produce such an heir of David. They must do so, since we read here that David's house is everlasting, a house that no one will destroy or hinder, but rather as we also read here [2 Sam 23:4], it shall be like the sun shining forth, which no cloud can hinder. If they are unable to present such an heir or house of David, then they stand fully condemned by this verse, and they show that they are surely without God, without David, without Messiah, without everything, that they are lost and eternally condemned. Of course, they cannot deny that the kingdom or house of David endured uninterruptedly until the Babylonian captivity, even throughout the Babylonian captivity, and following this to the days of Herod. It endured, I say, not by its own power and merit but by virtue of this everlasting covenant made with the house of David. Most of their kings and rulers were evil, practicing idolatry, killing the prophets, and living shamefully. For example, Rehoboam, Joram, Joash, Ahaz, Manasseh, etc., surpassed all the Gentiles or the kings of Israel in vileness. Because of them, the house and tribe of David fully deserved to be exterminated. That was what finally happened to the kingdom of Israel. However, the covenant made with David remained in effect. The books of the kings and of the prophets exultantly declare that God preserved a lamp or a light to the house of David that he would not permit to be extinguished. Thus we read in 2 Kings 8:19 and in 2 Chronicles 21:7: "Yet the Lord would not

Part II

destroy the house of David because of the covenant which he had made with David, since he had promised to give a lamp to him and to his sons forever." The same thought is expressed in 2 Samuel 7:12.

By way of contrast, look at the kingdom of Israel, where the rule never remained with the same tribe or family beyond the second generation, with the exception of Jehu who, by reason of a special promise, carried it into the fourth generation of his house.[34] Otherwise it always passed from one tribe to another, and at times scarcely survived for one generation; moreover, it was not long until the kingdom died out completely. But through the wondrous deeds of God, the kingdom of Judah remained within the tribe of Judah and the house of David. It withstood strong opposition on the part of the surrounding Gentiles, from Israel itself, from uprisings within, and from gross idolatries and sins, so that it would not have been surprising if it had perished in the third generation under Rehoboam, or at least under Joram, Ahaz, and Manasseh. But it had a strong Protector who did not let it die or let its light become extinguished. The promise was given that it would remain firm, eternally firm and secure. And so it has remained and must remain down to the present and forever; for God does not and cannot lie.

The Jews drivel that the kingdom perished with the Babylonian captivity. As we said earlier, this is empty talk; for this constituted but a short punishment, definitely confined to a period of 70 years. God had pledged his word for that. Moreover, he preserved them during this time through splendid prophets. Furthermore, King Jehoiachin was exalted above all the kings in Babylon, and Daniel and his companions ruled not only over Judah and Israel but also over the Babylonian Empire.[35] Even if their seat of government was not in Jerusalem for a short span of time, they nonetheless ruled elsewhere much more gloriously than in Jerusalem. Thus we may say that the house of David did not become extinct in Babylon but shone more resplendently than in Jerusalem. They only had to vacate their homeland for a while by way of punish-

---

[34] See 2 Kings 9.
[35] See Dan 2:48.

ment. When a king takes the field of a foreign country, he cannot be regarded as an ex-king because he is not in his homeland, especially if he is attended by great victory and good fortune against many nations. Rather one should say that he's more illustrious abroad than at home.

If God kept his covenant from the time of David to that of Herod, preserving his house from extinction, he must have kept it from that time on to the present, and he will keep it eternally, so that David's house has not died and cannot die eternally. We dare not rebuke God as half truthful and half untruthful, saying that he kept his covenant and preserved David's house faithfully from David's time to that of Herod, but that after the time of Herod he began to lie and to become deceitful, ignoring and altering his covenant. No, for as the house of David remained and shone up to Herod's time, thus it had to remain under Herod and after Herod, shining to eternity.

Now we note how nicely this saying of David harmonizes with that of the patriarch Jacob: "The scepter shall not depart from Judah, nor the *mehoqeq* from his feet until Messiah comes, and to him shall be the obedience of the peoples" [Gen 49:10]. How can it be expressed more clearly or differently that David's house will shine forth until the Messiah comes? Then, through him, the house of David will shine not only over Judah and Israel but also over the Gentiles, or over other and more numerous countries. This indeed does not mean that it will become extinct, but that it will shine farther and more lustrously than before his advent. And thus, as David says, this is an eternal kingdom and an eternal covenant. Therefore it follows most cogently from this that the Messiah came when the scepter departed from Judah—unless we want to revile God by saying that he did not keep his covenant and oath. Even if the stiff-necked, stubborn Jews refuse to accept this, at least our faith has been confirmed and strengthened by it. We don't give a fig for their crazy glosses, which they have spun out of their own heads. We have the clear text.

These last words of David—to revert to them once more—are founded on God's own word, where he says to him, as he here boasts at

Part II

his end: "Would you build me a house to dwell in?" (2 Sam 7:5). You can read what follows there—how God continues to relate that, until now, he has lived in no house, but that he had chosen him [David] to be a prince over his people, to whom he would assign a fixed place and grant him rest, concluding, "I will make you a house".[36] That is to say: Neither you nor anyone else will build me a house to dwell in; I am far, far too great for that, as we read also in Isaiah 66. No, I will build you a house. Thus says the Lord, as Nathan asserts: "The Lord declares to you that the Lord will make you a house" [2 Sam 7:11]. Everyone is familiar with a house built by man—a very perishable structure fashioned of stone and wood. But a house built by God means the establishing of the father of a family who would ever after have heirs and descendants of his blood and lineage. Thus Moses says in Exodus 1:21 that God built houses for the midwives because they did not obey the king's command, but let the infants live and did not kill them. On the other hand, he breaks down and extinguishes the houses of the kings of Israel in the second generation.

Thus David has here a secure house, built by God, which is to have heirs forever. It isn't a plain house; no, he says, "You shall be prince over my people Israel" [2 Sam 7:8]. Therefore it shall be called a princely, a royal house—that is, the house of Prince David or King David, in which your children shall reign forever and be princes such as you are. The books and histories of the kings prove this true, tracing it down to the time of Herod. Until that time, the scepter and *saphra* are in the tribe of Judah.

Now follows the second theme, concerning Shiloh. How long shall my house thus stand and how long shall my descendants rule? He answers thus [2 Sam 7:12-16]:

> When your days are fulfilled and you lie down with your fathers, I will raise up your offspring after you who shall come forth from your body (*utero*—that is, from your flesh and

---
[36] See 2 Sam 7:11.

blood), and I will establish his kingdom. He shall build a house for my name, and I will establish the throne of his kingdom forever. I will be his father, and he shall be my son. When he commits iniquity, I will chastise him with the rod of men (as one whips children), with the stripes of the sons of men; but I will not take my steadfast love from him, as I took it from Saul, whom I put away from before you. And your house and your kingdom shall be made sure forever before me; your throne shall be established forever.

This statement is found almost verbatim also in 1 Chronicles 17:11-14, where you may read it.

Whoever would refer these verses to Solomon would indeed be an arbitrary interpreter. Although Solomon was not yet born at this time, indeed the adultery with his mother Bathsheba had not yet even been committed, he is nonetheless not the seed of David born after David's death, of whom the text says, "When your days are fulfilled and you lie down with your fathers, I will raise up your seed after you." Solomon was born during David's lifetime.[37] It would be foolish, yes, ridiculous, to say that the term "raised up" here means that Solomon should be raised up after David's death to become king or to build the house; for three other chapters (1 Kings 1, 1 Chronicles 28, and 1 Chronicles 29) attest that Solomon was not only instated as king during his father's lifetime, but that he also received command from his father David, as well as the entire plan of the temple, of all the rooms, its detailed equipment, and the organization of the whole kingdom. It's obvious that Solomon didn't build the temple or order the kingdom or the priesthood according to his own plans but according to those of David, who prescribed everything, in fact, already arranged it during his lifetime.

There is also a great discrepancy and a difference in words between 2 Samuel 7 and 1 Chronicles 28 and 29. The former states that God will

---

[37] David (reign 1010 – 970 BC) is considered the 3rd king of Israel. His son, Solomon, reigned as the 4th king from 970 to his death in 932 BC.

Part II

build David an eternal house, the latter that Solomon shall build a house in God's name. The former passage states without any condition or qualification that it shall stand forever and be hindered by no sin. The latter passage conditions its continuance on Solomon's and his descendants' continued piety. Since he didn't remain pious, he not only lost the ten tribes of Israel but was also exterminated in the seventh generation. The former is a *promissio gratiae* ["a promise of grace"], the latter a *promissio legis* ["a promise of law"]. In the former passage David thanks God that his house will stand forever, in the latter he does not thank God that Solomon's temple will stand forever. In other words, the two passages refer to different times and to different things and houses. And although God does call Solomon his son in the latter also and says that he will be his father, this promise is dependent on the condition that Solomon will remain pious. Such a condition is not found in the former passage. It's not at all rare that God calls his saints, as well as the angels, his children. But the son mentioned in 2 Samuel 7:14 is a different and special son who will retain the kingdom unconditionally and be unhindered by sin.

Also the prophets and the psalms quote 2 Samuel 7, which speaks of David's seed after his death, whereas they pay no attention to 1 Chronicles 28 and 29, which speak of Solomon. In Psalm 89:1-4 we read:

> I will sing of thy steadfast love, O Lord, forever; with my mouth I will proclaim thy faithfulness to all generations. For thy steadfast love was established forever, thy faithfulness is firm as the heavens. Thou hast said, "I have made a covenant with my chosen one, I have sworn to David my servant: 'I will establish your descendants forever, and build your throne for all generations'."

These too are clear words. God vows and swears an oath to grant David his grace forever, and to build and preserve his house, seed, and throne eternally.

Later, in verse 19, we have an express reference to the true David. This verse contains the most beautiful prophecies of the Messiah, which cannot apply to Solomon. He was not the sovereign of all kings on earth, nor did his rule extend over land and sea. These facts cannot be glossed over. Furthermore, the kingdom did not remain with Solomon's house. He had no absolute promise with regard to this, but only a promise conditional on his piety. But it was the house of David that had the promise, and he had more sons than Solomon. And as the history books report, the scepter of Judah at times passed from brother to brother, from cousin to cousin, but always remained in the house of David. For instance, Ahaziah left no son, and Ahaz left none, so according to the custom of Holy Scripture the nephews had to be heirs and sons.[38]

Anyone who would venture to contradict such clear and convincing statements of Scripture regarding the eternal house of David, which are borne out by the histories, showing that there were always kings or princes down to the Messiah, must be either the devil himself or whoever is his follower. I can readily believe that the devil, or whoever it may be, would be unwilling to acknowledge a Messiah, but still he would have to acknowledge David's eternal house and throne. He cannot deny the clear words of God in his oath, vowing that his word would not be changed and that he would not lie to David, not even by reason of any sin, as the aforementioned psalm [Ps 89] impressively and clearly states.

Now, such an eternal house of David is nowhere to be found unless we place the scepter before the Messiah and the Messiah after the scepter, and then join the two together: namely, by asserting that the Messiah appeared when the scepter departed and that David's house was thus preserved forever. In that way, God is found truthful and faithful in his word, covenant, and oath. It's obvious that the scepter of Judah completely collapsed at the time of Herod, but much more so when the Romans destroyed Jerusalem and the scepter of Judah. Now, if David's house is eternal and God truthful, then the true King of Judah, the Messiah, must have come at that time. No barking, interpreting, or glossing will change this. The text is too authoritative and too clear. If the Jews refuse to admit it, we don't care.

---

[38] See 2 Kings 1:17, 2 Kings 16:20, and 2 Chron 28:27.

Part II

For us it's enough that, first of all, our Christian faith finds here most substantial proof, and that such verses afford me very great joy and comfort that we have such strong testimony also in the Old Testament. Second, we are certain that even the devil and the Jews themselves cannot refute this in their hearts and that in their own consciences they are convinced. This can surely and certainly be noted by the fact that they twist this saying of Jacob concerning the scepter—as they do all of Scripture—in so many ways, betraying that they are convinced and won over, and yet refuse to admit it. They are like the devil, who knows very well that God's word is the truth and yet with deliberate malice contradicts and blasphemes it. The Jews feel distinctly that these verses are solid rock and their interpretation nothing but straw or spiderweb. But with willful and malicious resolve, they won't admit this; yet they insist on being and on being known as God's people, solely because they are of the blood of the patriarchs. Otherwise they have nothing of which to boast. As to what lineage alone can effect, we have spoken above. It's just as if the devil were to boast that he was of angelic stock, and by reason of this was the only angel and child of God, even though he is really God's foe.

Now that we have considered these verses, let's hear what Jeremiah says. His words sound very strange. We know that he was a prophet long after the kingdom of Israel had been destroyed and exiled, when only the kingdom of Judah still existed, which itself was soon to go into captivity in Babylon, as he foretold to them and even experienced during his lifetime.[39] Yet despite this, he dares to say in chapter 33:17-26,

> "For thus says the Lord: David shall never lack a man to sit on the throne of the house of Israel, and the Levitical priests shall never lack a man in my presence to offer burnt offerings, to burn cereal offerings, and to make sacrifices forever."

---

[39] Jeremiah is a possibly-fictional prophet who is said to have lived roughly from 650 – 580 BC.

On the Jews and Their Lies

The word of the Lord came to Jeremiah: "Thus says the Lord: If you can break my covenant with the day and my covenant with the night, so that day and night will not come at their appointed time, then also my covenant with David my servant may be broken, so that he shall not have a son to reign on his throne, and my covenant with the Levitical priests my ministers…"

The word of the Lord came to Jeremiah: "Have you not observed what these people are saying, 'The Lord has rejected the two families which he chose'? Thus they have despised my people so that they are no longer a nation in their sight. Thus says the Lord: If I have not established my covenant with day and night and the ordinances of heaven and earth, then I will reject the descendants of Jacob and David my servant and will not choose one of his descendants to rule over the seed of Abraham, Isaac, and Jacob. For I will restore their fortunes, and will have mercy upon them."

What can we say to this? Whoever can interpret it, let him do so. Here we read that not only David but also the Levites will endure forever; and the same for Israel, the seed of Abraham, Isaac, and Jacob. It is emphasized that David will have a son who will sit on his throne eternally, just as surely as day and night continue forever. On the other hand, we hear that Israel will be led away into captivity, and also Judah after her, but that Israel will not be brought home again as Judah will be. Tell me, how does all this fit together? God's word cannot lie. Just as God watches over the course of the heavens, so that day and night follow in endless succession, so too David (that is, Abraham, Isaac, and Jacob), must have a son on his throne uninterruptedly. God himself draws this comparison. It's impossible for the Jews to make sense of it; they see with their very eyes that neither Israel nor Judah has had a government for nearly 1,500 years; in fact Israel has not had one for over 2,000 years. Yet God must be truthful, do what we will. The kingdom

Part II

of David must rule over the seed of Jacob, Isaac, and Abraham, as Jeremiah states here, or Jeremiah is not a prophet but a liar.

We shall let the Jews reconcile and interpret this as they will or can. For us this passage leaves no doubt; it affirms that David's house will endure forever, also the Levites, and Abraham's, Isaac's, and Jacob's seed under the son of David, as long as day and night—or as it is otherwise expressed, as long as sun and moon—endure. If this is true, then the Messiah must have come when David's house and rule ceased to exist. Thus David's throne assumed more splendor through the Messiah, as we read in Isaiah 9:6:

> For to us a child is born, to us a son is given; and the government will be upon his shoulder, and his name will be called *Pele, Joets, El, Gibbor, Abi-gad, Sar shalom.*[40] Of the increase of his government and of peace there will be no end, upon the throne of David, and over his kingdom, to establish it, and to uphold it with justice and with righteousness from this time forth and for evermore.

We may revert to this later, but here we shall refrain from discussing how the blind Jews twist these six names of the Messiah. They accept this verse and admit—as they must admit—that it speaks of the Messiah. We quote it because Jeremiah states that David's house will rule forever: first through the scepter up to the time of the Messiah, and after that much more gloriously through the Messiah. So it must be true that David's house has not ceased up to this hour and that it will not cease to eternity. But since the scepter of Judah departed 1,500 years ago, the Messiah must have come that long ago; or, as we have said above, 1,468 years ago. All of this is convincingly established by Jeremiah.

However, some among us may wonder how it's possible that at the time of Jeremiah and then up to the advent of the Messiah, the seed of

---

[40] In English: "Wonderful Counselor, Mighty God, Everlasting Father, Prince of Peace."

Abraham, Isaac, and Jacob existed and remained under the tribe of Judah or the throne of David, even though only Judah remained whereas Israel was exiled. These persons must be informed that the kingdom of Israel was led into captivity and destroyed, that it never returned home and never will return home, but that Israel, or the seed of Israel, always continued to a certain extent under Judah, and that it was exiled with Judah and returned again with her. You may read about this in 1 Samuel, 1 Kings 11 and 12, and 2 Chronicles 30 and 31. Here you will learn that the entire tribe of Benjamin—thus a good part of Israel—remained with Judah, as well as the whole tribe of Levi together with many members of the tribes of Ephraim, Manasseh, Asher, Isachar, and Zebulun who remained in the country after the destruction of the kingdom of Israel, and who held to Hezekiah in Jerusalem and helped to purge the land of Israel of idols. Furthermore, many Israelites dwelt in the cities of Judah.

Since we find so many Israelites living under the rule of the son of David, Jeremiah is not lying when he says that Levites and the seed of Abraham, Isaac, and Jacob will be found under the rule of David's house. All of these, or at least a number of them, were taken to Babylon and returned from it with Judah, as Ezra enumerates and recounts.[41] Undoubtedly many more returned of those who were led away under Sennacherib, since the Assyrian or Median kingdom was brought under the Persian rule through Cyrus, so that Judah and Israel were very likely able to join and return together from Babylon to Jerusalem and the land of Canaan. I know for certain that we find these words in Ezra 2:70: "And all Israel (or all who were there from Israel) lived in their towns." And how could they live there if they had not come back? In the days of Herod and of the Messiah, the land was again full of Israelites; for in the 70 weeks of Daniel, that is, in 490 years, they had assembled again.[42] However, they didn't again establish a kingdom.

---

[41] See Ezra 2:1.

[42] The passage in Daniel is highly disputed, as we will see. In the esoteric language of the Old Testament, a "week" (7 days) stands for 7 years. Thus "70 weeks" represents (70 x 7 =) 490 years.

Part II

Therefore, the present-day Jews are very ignorant teachers and indolent pupils of Scripture when they allege that Israel has not yet returned, as though all of Israel would have to return. Actually not all of Judah returned either, but only a small number, as we gather from Ezra's enumeration. The majority of them remained in Babylon, as did Daniel, Nehemiah, and Mordecai themselves. Similarly, the majority of the Israelites remained in Media, though they perhaps traveled to Jerusalem for the high festivals and then returned to their homes again, as Luke writes in the Acts of the Apostles [2:5]. God never promised that the kingdom or scepter of Israel would be restored like that of Judah. But he did promise this to Judah. The latter had to recover it by virtue of God's promise that he would establish David's house and throne forever and not let it die out. As Jeremiah declares here, God will not tolerate that anyone slander him by saying that he had rejected Judah and Israel entirely, so that they should no longer be his people and that David's throne should come to an end, as if he had forgotten his promise, when he had promised and pledged to David an eternal house. Even though they would now have to sojourn in Babylon for a little while, still, he says, it will remain an eternal house and kingdom.

I'm saying this to honor and to strengthen our faith and to shame the hardened unbelief of the blinded and stubborn Jews, for whom God must ever and eternally be a liar, as though he had let David's house die out and forgotten his covenant and his oath sworn to David. If they would admit that God is truthful, they would have to confess that the Messiah came 1,500 years ago, so that David's house and throne should not be desolate for so long as they suppose, just because Jerusalem has lain in ashes and has been devoid of David's throne and house so long. If God kept his promise from the time of David to the Babylonian captivity and from then to the days of Herod when the scepter departed, he must also have kept it subsequently and forever after, or else David's house is not an eternal but a perishable house, which has ceased together with the scepter at the time of Herod.

But as we have already said, God will not tolerate this. No, David's house will be everlasting, like "day and night and the ordinances of heaven and earth," as Jeremiah puts it [33:25]. However, since the scepter of Judah was lost at the time of Herod, it cannot be eternal unless the son of David, the Messiah, has come, seated himself on David's throne, and become the Lord of the world. If the Jews are correct, then David's house must have been extinct for 1,568 years, contrary to God's promise and oath. This is impossible to believe. Now this is a thorough exposition of the matter, and no Jew can adduce anything to refute it. Outwardly he may pretend that he doesn't believe it, but his heart and his conscience are devoid of anything to contradict it.

And how could God have maintained the honor of his divine truthfulness, having promised David an eternal house and throne, if he then let it stand desolate longer than intact? Let's figure this out. In the opinion of the Jews, the time from David to Herod covers not quite a thousand years. David's house or throne stood for that length of time, inclusive of the 70 years spent in Babylon. (We would add over 100 years to this total.) From Herod's time, or rather let us say—for this is not far from correct—from the destruction of Jerusalem to the year 1542 there are 1,568 years, as stated above. According to this computation, David's house and throne has been empty 400 or 500 years longer than it was occupied. Now inquire of stone and log whether such may be called an eternal house, especially constructed by God and preserved by his sublime faithfulness and truthfulness—a house that stands for 1,000 years and lies in ashes for 1,400 or 1,500 years!

Though the Jews be as hard or harder than a diamond, the lightning and thunder of such clear and manifest truth should smash, or at least soften, them. But as I said before, our faith is cheered thereby, it is strengthened, it is made sure and certain that we do have the true Messiah, who surely came and appeared at the time when Herod took away the scepter of Judah and the *saphra*, so that David's house might be eternal and forever have a son upon his throne, as God said and swore to him and made a covenant with him.

PART II

Some crafty Jew might try to cast up to me my book against the Sabbatarians, in which I demonstrated that the word "eternally," *le-olam*, often means not really an eternity, but merely "a long time." Thus, Moses says in Exodus 21:8 that the master shall take the slave who wants to stay with him and bore through his ear with an awl on the door, "and he shall serve him eternally." Here the word designates a human eternity, that is, a lifetime. But also said in the same treatise that when God uses the word "eternal, it's a truly divine eternity. And he commonly adds another phrase to the effect that it shall not be otherwise, as in Psalm 110:4, "The Lord has sworn and will not change his mind." Similarly, in Psalm 132:11: "The Lord swore to David a sure oath from which he will not turn back," etc. Wherever such a "not" is added, this surely means eternal and not otherwise. Thus, we read in Isaiah 9:7, "Of peace there will be no end." And in Daniel [7:14], "His dominion is an everlasting dominion…and his kingdom one that shall not be destroyed." This is eternal not before men, who do not live eternally, but before God, who lives eternally.

The promise states that David's house and throne shall be eternal before God. He says: "Before me, before me," a son shall forever sit upon your throne. In Psalm 89:35-37 he also adds the little word "not": "Once for all I have sworn by my holiness, I will not lie to David. His line shall endure forever, his throne as long as the sun before me. Like the moon it shall be established forever; it shall stand firm while the skies endure." The last words of David convey the same thought: "He has made with me an everlasting covenant, ordered in all things and secure." These words "ordered and secure" mean the same as firm, sure, eternal, never-failing. The same applies to the saying of Jacob in Genesis 49:10: "The scepter shall not depart." "Not depart" signifies eternally, until the Messiah comes; and that surely means eternally. All the prophets assign to the Messiah an eternal kingdom, a kingdom without end.

But if we assume that this refers to a human or temporal eternity or an indefinite period of time (which is impossible), then the meaning would necessarily be as follows: Your house shall be eternal before me, that is, your house shall stand as long as it stands, or for your lifetime. This would pledge and promise David the equivalent of exactly nothing; for even in the absence of such an oath, David's house would stand "eternally," that is, as long as it stands, or as long as he lives. But let's dismiss such nonsense from our minds, which would occur to none but a blinded rabbi. When Scripture glories in the fact that God didn't want to destroy Judah because of the sins committed under Rehoboam, but that a lamp should remain to David, as God has promised him regarding his house (2 Kings 8:19), it shows that all understood the word "eternal" in its true sense.

Someone might also cite here the instance of the Maccabees.[43] After Antiochus the Noble had ruthlessly ravaged the people and the country, so that the princes of the house of David became extinct, the Maccabees ruled, who were not of the house of David but of the tribe of the priests.[44] This meant that the scepter had departed from Judah and that a son of David did not sit eternally on the throne of David. Thus the eternal house of David could not be really eternal. We reply: The Jews cannot disturb us with this argument, and we need not answer them; none of this is found in Scripture, because Malachi is the last prophet and Nehemiah the last historian, who, as we can gather from his book, lived until the time of Alexander. Therefore both parties must rely, so far as this question is concerned, on Jeremiah's statement that a son of David was to occupy his throne or rule forever. For apart from Scripture, whoever wants to concern himself with this may regard it as an open question whether the Maccabees themselves ruled or whether they served the rulers. As to the reliability of the historians, we shall have some comments later on.

It seems to me, however, that the following incident recorded in Scripture should not be treated lightly.[45] At the time of Queen Athaliah, for fully six years, no son of David occupied his throne; she, Athaliah

---

[43] See 1 Macc 1:10.

[44] The Maccabees were a group of Jewish rebels who ruled Judea from 167 to 63 BC, when Rome took over control.

[45] See 2 Kings 11:1.

Part II

the tyrant, reigned alone. She had had all the male descendants of David slain, with the single exception of Joash, an infant a quarter or a half year old, who had been secretly removed, hidden in the temple, and reared by the excellent Jehosheba, the wife of the high priest Jehoiada, daughter of King Joram and sister of King Ahaziah, whom Jehu slew. Here the eternal covenant of God made with David was in great peril indeed, resting on one young lad in hiding, who was far from occupying the throne of David. At this time, his house resembled a dark lantern in which the light is extinguished, since a foreign queen, a Gentile from Sidon, was sitting and reigning on David's throne. However, she burned her backside thoroughly on that throne!

Still, all of this didn't mean that the scepter had departed or that God's eternal covenant was broken. Even if the light of David was not shining brightly at this time, it was still glimmering in that child Joash, who would again shine brightly in the future and rule. He was already born as a son of David, and these six years were nothing but a *tentatio*, a temptation. God often gives the appearance that he is unmindful of his word and is failing us. This he did with Abraham when he commanded him to burn to ashes his dear son Isaac, in whom, after all, God's promise of the eternal seed was embodied. Likewise when he led the children of Israel from Egypt. In fact, he seemed to be leading them into death, with the sea before them, high cliffs on both sides, and the enemy at their back blocking their way of escape. But matters proceeded according to God's word and promises; the sea had to open, move, and make way for them. If the sea hadn't done this, then the cliffs would have had to split asunder and make a path for them, and they would have squeezed and squashed Pharaoh between them, just as the sea drowned the foe. For all creatures would rather have to perish a thousand thousand times than that God's word should fail and deceive, however strange things may appear. Thus Joash is king through and in God's word, and occupies the throne of David before God, although he still lies in the cradle—yes, even if he lay dead and buried under the ground; in spite of all he would have to rise, like Isaac, from the ashes.

In such a manner we might also account for that story of the Maccabees; but this is unnecessary, for it has an entirely different meaning. The Babylonian captivity might be viewed similarly; however, thanks to splendid prophets and miracles, the situation at that time was much brighter. But Joash posed a terrible temptation for the house of David, against the covenant and the oath of God, although the house and rule of David still flourished; it was only the ruler, or the head, that was suffering and that faltered in God's covenant. But this is the manner of his divine grace, that he sometimes plays and jokes with his own. He hides himself and disguises himself so that he may test us to see whether we will remain firm in faith and love toward him, just as a father sometimes does with his children. Such jesting of our heavenly Father pains us immeasurably, since we don't understand it. However, this is out of place here.

Haggai 2

We have been speaking about a statement of Jeremiah. We will now turn our attention to one of the last prophets.[46] In Haggai 2:6-9 we read:

> For thus says the Lord of hosts: once again, in a little while, I will shake the heavens and the earth and the sea and the dry land; and I will shake all nations, so that the consolation of the Gentiles (*chemdath*) shall come, and I will fill this house with splendor, says the Lord of hosts. The silver is mine, and the gold is mine, says the Lord of hosts. The splendor of this latter house shall be greater than the former, says the Lord of hosts; and in this place I will give prosperity, says the Lord of hosts.

This is another of those passages that pains the Jews intensely. They test it, twist it, interpret and distort almost every word, just as they do the statement of Jacob in Genesis 49. But it doesn't help them. Their conscience pales before this passage; it senses that their glosses are null and

---

[46] Haggai apparently lived sometime around 500 BC.

Part II

void. Lyra does well when he plies them hard with the phrase *adhuc modicum*, "in a little while." They cannot elude him, as we shall see. "In a little while," he says, cannot possibly mean a long period of time. Lyra is surely right here; no one can deny it, not even a Jew, try as hard as he may. In a little while, he says, the Consolation of the Gentiles will come, after this temple is built—that is, he will come when this temple is still standing. And the splendor of this latter temple will be greater than that of the former. And this will happen shortly, i.e., "in a little while."

It's easily understood that if the consolation of the Gentiles, whom the ancients interpret as the Messiah, didn'ot come while that temple was still standing, but is still to come—the Jews have been waiting 1,568 years already since the destruction of that temple, and this cannot be termed "a little while," especially since they cannot foresee the end of this long time—then he will never come, for he neglected to come in this little, short time, and now has entered upon the great, long time, which will never result in anything. The prophet speaks of a short, not a long time.

But they extricate themselves from this difficulty as follows. Since they cannot ignore the words "in a little while," they take up and crucify the expression "consolation of the Gentiles," in Hebrew *chemdath*, just as they did earlier with the words *shebet* and *shiloh* in the saying of Jacob. They insist that this term does not refer to the Messiah, but that it designates the gold and silver of all the Gentiles. Grammatically, the word *chemdath* really means 'desire' or 'pleasure'; thus it would mean that the Gentiles have a desire for or take pleasure and delight in something. So the text must read thus: "In a short time, the desire of all Gentiles will appear." And what does this mean? What do the Gentiles desire? Gold, silver, gems! You may ask why the Jews make this kind of gloss here. I'll tell you. Their breath stinks with lust for the Gentiles' gold and silver; no nation under the sun is greedier than they were, still are, and always will be, as is evident from their accursed usury. So they comfort themselves that when the Messiah comes, he will take the gold and silver of the whole world and divide it among them. Therefore, wherever they can quote Scripture to satisfy their insatiable greed, they do so outrageously. One is led to believe that God and his prophets knew of nothing else to prophesy than of ways and means to satisfy the bottomless greed of the accursed Jews with the Gentiles' gold and silver.

However, the prophet hasn't chosen his words properly to accord with this greedy understanding. He should have said: "In a little while, the desire of *the Jews* shall come." *The Jews* are the ones who desire gold and silver more avidly than any other nation on earth. In view of that, the text should more properly speak of the desire of the Jews than of the Gentiles. Although the Gentiles do desire gold and silver, nevertheless here are the Jews who desire and covet this desire of the Gentiles, who desire that it be brought to them so that they may devour it and leave nothing for the Gentiles. Why? Because they are the noble blood, the circumcised saints who have God's commandments and do not keep them, but are stiff-necked, disobedient, prophet-murderers, arrogant, usurers, and filled with every vice, as the whole of Scripture and their present conduct bear out. Such saints, of course, are properly entitled to the Gentiles' gold and silver. They honestly and honorably deserve it for such behavior—just as the devil deserves paradise and heaven.

Further, how does it happen that such very intelligent teachers and wise, holy prophets don't also apply the word "desire" (*chemdath*) to all the other desires of the Gentiles? The Gentiles desire not only gold and silver but also pretty girls, and the women desire handsome young men. Wherever we find among the Gentiles anything other than Jews (I almost said "misers"), who will not bestow any good on their bodies, they desire also beautiful houses, gardens, cattle, and property, as well as good times, clothes, food, drink, dancing, playing, and all sorts of enjoyment. Why, then, do the Jews not interpret this verse of the prophet to mean that such desires of all the Gentiles also will shortly come to Jerusalem, so that the Jews alone might fill their bellies and feast on the world's joys? Muhammad promises such a mode of life to

PART II

his Saracens. In that respect, he is a genuine Jew, and the Jews are genuine Saracens, according to this interpretation.

The Gentiles have another desire. How could these wise, clever interpreters overlook it? I'm surprised at it. The Gentiles die, and they are afflicted with much sickness, poverty, and all kinds of distress and fear. There isn't one of them who does not most ardently wish that he did not have to die, that he could avoid need, misery, and sickness, or be quickly freed from them and secure against them. This desire is so pronounced that they would gladly surrender all others for its fulfillment, as experience shows daily. Why, then, do the Jews not explain that such desire of all the Gentiles will also come to the temple in Jerusalem in a little while? Shame on you, here, there, or wherever you may be, you damned Jews, that you dare to apply this earnest, glorious, comforting word of God so despicably to your mortal, greedy belly, which is doomed to decay, and that you aren't ashamed to display your greed so openly. You aren't worthy of looking at the cover of the Bible, much less of reading it. You should read only the bible that's found under the sow's tail, and eat and drink the letters that drop from there.[47] That would be a bible for such prophets, who root about like sows and tear apart like pigs the words of the divine Majesty, which should be heard with all honor, awe, and joy.

Furthermore, when the prophet says that "the splendor of this latter house shall be greater than the former," let's listen to the noble and filthy—I meant to say, circumcised—saints and wise prophets who want to make Jews of us Christians. The greater splendor of the latter temple compared to the former consists [they say] in this: that it—that is, the

---

[47] Luther refers here to the *Judensau*, or Jew-pig. It is an anti-Jewish image, dating from the 1200s, in which Jewish scholars or rabbis peer into the anus of a large hog in an attempt to 'read' their Talmud. In his work *Von Schem Hamphoras* (1543), Luther explains it concisely: "Here on our church in Wittenberg a sow is sculpted in stone. Young pigs and Jews lie suckling under her. Behind the sow a rabbi is bent over the sow, lifting up her right leg, holding her tail high and looking intensely under her tail and into her Talmud, as though he were reading something acute or extraordinary, which is certainly where they get their *Shemhamphoras* [unknowable name]." For a good recent discussion of the *Judensau*, see Joyce (2019).

temple of Haggai—stood ten years longer than the temple of Solomon, etc. Alas, if they had only had a good astronomer who could have worked out the time a little more precisely. Perhaps he would have found the difference between the two to be three months, two weeks, five days, seven hours, twelve minutes, and ten half-minutes over and above the ten years. If there were a store anywhere that offered blushes for sale, I might give the Jews a few florins to go and buy a pound of them to smear over their forehead, eyes, and cheeks, if they would refuse to cover their impudent heart and tongue with them. Or do these ignorant, stupid asses suppose that they are talking to sticks and blocks like themselves?

There were many old, gray men and women, very likely also beggars and villains, in Jerusalem when Solomon, a young man of 20 years, became a glorious king.[48] Should these, for that reason, be more glorious than Solomon? Perhaps David's mule, on which Solomon became king, was older than Solomon. Should he by reason of that be greater than Solomon? But thus those will bump their heads, stumble, and fall who incessantly give God the lie and claim that they are in the right. They deserve no better fate than to compose such glosses on the Bible, such foolishness and ignominy. This they indeed do most diligently. Therefore, dear Christian, be on your guard against the Jews, who, as you discover here, are consigned by the wrath of God to the devil, who has not only robbed them of a proper understanding of Scripture, but also of ordinary human reason, shame, and sense, and only works mischief with Holy Scripture through them.

Therefore they cannot be trusted and believed in any other matter either, even though a truthful word may occasionally drop from their lips. For anyone who dares to juggle the awesome word of God so frivolously and shamefully as you see it done here, and as you also noted earlier with regard to the words of Jacob, cannot have a good spirit dwelling in him. Therefore, wherever you see a genuine Jew, you may with a good conscience cross yourself and bluntly say: "There goes a devil incarnate."

---

[48] Again, this would have been around 970 BC.

Part II

These impious scoundrels know very well that their ancient predecessors applied this verse of Haggai to the Messiah, as Lyra, Burgensis, and others testify. And still they wantonly depart from this and compose their own Bible out of their own mad heads, so that they hold their wretched Jews with them in their error, in violation of their conscience and to our vexation. They think that in this way they are hurting us greatly, and that God will reward them wherever for his sake (as they imagine) they have opposed us Gentiles even in open, evident truth. But what happens, as you have seen, is that they disgrace themselves and do not harm us, and further, forfeit God and his Scripture.

Thus the verse reads: "Once again, in a little while, I will shake the heavens and the earth and the sea and the dry land (these are the islands of the sea) and the *chemdath* of all Gentiles shall come"—that is, the Messiah, the Desire of all Gentiles, which we translated into German with the word *Trost* ["consolation"]. The word "desire" does not fully express this thought, since in German it reflects the inward delight and desire of the heart (active). But here the word designates the external thing (passive) that a heart longs for. It would surely not be wrong to translate it with "the joy and delight of all Gentiles." In brief, it's the Messiah who would be the object of displeasure, disgust, and abomination for the unbelieving and hardened Jews, as Isaiah 53 prophesies. The Gentiles, on the other hand, would bid him welcome as their heart's joy, delight, and every wish and desire. He brings them deliverance from sin, death, devil, hell, and every evil, eternally. This is, indeed, the Gentiles' desire, their heart's delight, joy, and comfort.

This agrees with the saying of Jacob in Genesis 49:10, "And to Shiloh (or the Messiah) shall be the obedience of the peoples." That is to say, they will receive him gladly, hear his word and become his people, without coercion, without the sword. It's as if he wished to say: The ignoble, uncircumcised Gentiles will do this, but my noble rascals, my circumcised, lost children won't do it, but will rather rave and rant against it. Isaiah 2:2 and Micah 4:1 also agree with this:

> It shall come to pass in the latter days that the mountain of the house of the Lord shall be established as the highest of the mountains, and shall be raised above the hills; and all the nations shall flow to it (doubtless voluntarily, motivated by desire and joy) and many people shall come, and say: 'Come, let us go up to the mountain of the Lord, to the house of the God of Jacob; that he may teach us his ways and that we may walk in his path.' For out of Zion shall go forth the law, and the word of the Lord from Jerusalem.

Thus the prophets speak throughout of the kingdom of the Messiah established among the Gentiles.

Yes, this is it, this is the bone of contention, which is the source of the trouble, which makes the Jews so angry and foolish and spurs them to arrive at such an accursed meaning, forcing them to pervert all the statements of Scripture so shamefully: namely, they don't want, they cannot endure, that we Gentiles should be their equal before God and that the Messiah should be our comfort and joy as well as theirs. I say, before they would have us Gentiles—whom they incessantly mock, curse, damn, defame, and revile—share the Messiah with them, and be called their co-heirs and brethren, they would crucify ten more Messiahs and kill God himself if this were possible, together with all angels and all creatures, even at the risk of incurring thereby the penalty of a thousand hells instead of one. Such an incomprehensibly stubborn pride dwells in the noble blood of the fathers and circumcised saints. They alone want to have the Messiah and be masters of the world. The accursed Goyim must be servants, give their desire (that is, their gold and silver) to the Jews, and let themselves be slaughtered like wretched cattle.[49] They [the Jews] would rather remain lost consciously and eternally than give up this view.

---

[49] These attitudes are well-documented in the Old Testament. See for example: Gen 27:29: "Let peoples serve you, and nations bow down to you". Deut 15:6: "You shall rule over many nations," and 28:10, "they shall be afraid of you". Isaiah 60:10: "Foreigners shall build up your walls, and their kings shall minister to you…that men may bring you the wealth of nations," and 61:5, "you shall eat the wealth of nations."

Part II

From their youth, they have imbibed such venomous hatred against the Goyim from their parents and their rabbis, and they still continuously drink it. As Psalm 109:18 declares, it has penetrated flesh and blood, marrow and bone, and has become part and parcel of their nature and their life. And as little as they can change flesh and blood, marrow and bone, so little can they change such pride and envy. They must remain thus and perish, unless God performs extraordinarily great miracles. If I wished to vex and anger a Jew severely, I would say: "Listen, Jehudi, do you realize that I am a real brother of all the holy children of Israel and a co-heir in the kingdom of the true Messiah?" Without doubt, I would meet with a nasty rebuff. If he could stare at me with the eyes of a basilisk, he would surely do it. And all the devils could not execute the evil he would wish me, even if God were to give them leave—of that I'm certain. However, I shall refrain from doing this, and I ask also that no one else do so, for Christ's sake. For the Jews' heart and mouth would overflow with a cloudburst of cursing and blaspheming of the name of Jesus Christ and of God the Father. We must conduct ourselves well and not give them cause for this if we can avoid it, just as I must not provoke a madman if I know that he will curse and blaspheme God. Quite apart from this, the Jews hear and see enough in us for which they ever blaspheme and curse the name of Jesus in their hearts; they really are possessed.

As we have already said, they cannot endure to hear or to see that we accursed Goyim should glory in the Messiah as our *chemdath*, and that we are as good as they are or as they think they are. Therefore, dear Christian, be advised and do not doubt that, next to the devil, you have no more bitter, venomous, and vehement foe than a real Jew who earnestly seeks to be a Jew. There may perhaps be some among them who believe what a cow or goose believes, but their lineage and circumcision infect them all. Therefore the history books often accuse them of contaminating wells, of kidnaping and piercing children, as for example at Trent, Weissensee, etc.[50] They, of course, deny this. Whether it's true

---

[50] Simon of Trent (Trento, Italy) was a 3-year-old boy who died in 1475, allegedly at

or not, I do know that they do not lack the complete, full, and ready will to do such things either secretly or openly where possible. This you can assuredly expect from them, and you must govern yourself accordingly.

If they do perform some good deed, you may rest assured that they are not prompted by love, nor is it done with your benefit in mind. Since they are compelled to live among us, they do this for reasons of expediency; but their heart remains and is as I have described it.[51] If you don't want to believe me, read Lyra, Burgensis, and other truthful and honest men. And even if they hadn't recorded it, you would find that Scripture tells of the two seeds, the serpent's and the woman's. It says that these are enemies, and that God and the devil are at variance with each other. Their own writings and prayer books also state this plainly enough.

A person who is unacquainted with the devil might wonder why they are so particularly hostile toward Christians. They have no reason to act this way, since we show them every kindness. They live among us, enjoy our shield and protection, they use our country and our highways, our markets and streets. Meanwhile our princes and rulers sit there and snore with mouths hanging open and permit the Jews to take, steal, and rob from their open moneybags and treasures whatever they want. That is, they let the Jews, by means of their usury, skin and fleece them and their subjects, and make them beggars with their own money. The Jews, who are exiles, should really have nothing, and whatever they have must surely be our property. They don't work, and they don't earn anything from us, nor do we give or present it to them, and yet they are in possession of our money and goods, and are our masters in our own country and in their exile. A thief is condemned to hang for the theft of ten florins, and if he robs anyone on the highway, he forfeits his

---

the hands of Jews. A group of local Jews confessed to the murder, possibly under duress, and 16 were eventually put to death. Conrad of Weissensee (Germany) was a 13-year-old boy likewise allegedly killed by Jews in 1303; eventually over 100 Jews were executed in retaliation. These are only two of many so-called "blood libel" charges against medieval Jews.

[51] This recalls similar present-day charges against wealthy Jewish 'philanthropists.'

Part II

head. But when a Jew steals and robs ten tons of gold through his usury, he is more highly esteemed than God himself.

In proof of this, we cite the bold boast with which they strengthen their faith and give vent to their venomous hatred of us, as they say among themselves: "Be patient and see how God is with us, and does not desert his people even in exile. We do not labor, and yet we enjoy prosperity and leisure. The accursed Goyim have to work for us, but we get their money. This makes us their masters and them our servants. Be patient, dear children of Israel, better times are in store for us, our Messiah will still come if we continue thus and acquire the *chemdath* of all the Gentiles by usury and other methods." Alas, this is what we endure for them. They are under our shield and protection, and yet, as I have said, they curse us. But we shall address this later.

We are now speaking about the fact that they cannot tolerate having us as co-heirs in the kingdom of the Messiah, and that he is our *chemdath*, as the prophets abundantly attest. What does God say about this? He says that he will give the *chemdath* to the Gentiles, and that their obedience shall be pleasing to him, as Jacob affirms in Genesis 49, together with all the prophets. He says that he will oppose the obduracy of the Jews most strenuously, rejecting them and choosing and accepting the Gentiles, even though the latter are not of the noble blood of the fathers or circumcised saints. Thus says Hosea 2:23: "And I will say to Not my people, 'You are my people'; and he shall say, 'Thou are my God'." But to the Jew he says [in Hos 1:9]: "Call his name Not my people (*lo-ammi*), for you are not my people and I am not your God." Moses, too, had sung this long ago in his song [Deut 32:21]: "They have stirred me to jealousy with what is no god; they have provoked me with their vain deeds. So I will stir them to jealousy with those who are no people; I will provoke them with a foolish nation." This verse has been in force now for nearly 1,500 years. We foolish Gentiles, who were not God's people, are now God's people. That drives the Jews to distraction and stupidity, and over this they became Not-God's-people, who were once his people and really should still be.

But let's conclude our discussion of the saying of Haggai. We have convincing proof that the Messiah, the Gentiles' *chemdath*, appeared at the time when this temple was standing. Thus the ancients understood it, and the inane flimsy glosses of the present-day Jews also testify to this, since they don't know how to deny it except by speaking of their own shame. He who gives a hollow, meaningless, and irrelevant answer shows that he is defeated and condemns himself. It would have been better and less shameful if he had kept quiet, rather than giving a pointless answer that disgraces him. Thus Haggai 2:6 says, "Once again, in a little while, I will shake the heavens and the earth and the sea and the dry land; and I will shake all nations, and the desire of all the Gentiles shall come." This is how I, in the simplicity of my mind, understand these words: Since the beginning of the world there has been enmity between the seed of the serpent and that of the woman, and there has always been conflict between them—sometimes more, sometimes less.

Wherever the Seed of the woman is or appears, he causes strife and discord. This he says in the Gospel: "I have not come to bring peace on earth, but a sword and disunity" [Matt 10:34]. He takes the armor from the strong man fully armed who had peace in his palace [Luke 11:22]. The latter cannot tolerate this, and the strife is on; angels contend against the devils in the air, and man against man on earth—all on account of the woman's Seed. To be sure, there is plenty of strife, war, and unrest in the world otherwise too; but since it is not undertaken on account of this Seed, it is an insignificant thing in God's eyes, for in this conflict all the angels are involved.

Since the advent of this Seed, or of the Messiah, was close at hand, Haggai says "in a little." This means that until now the strife has been confined solely to my people Israel, that is, restricted to a small area. The devil was ever intent upon devouring them and he set all the surrounding kings upon them. He was well aware that the promised Seed was in the people of Israel, the Seed that was to despoil him. Therefore he was always eager to harass them. And he instigated one disturbance,

Part II

dissatisfaction, war, and strife after another. Well and good, now it will be but "a little while," and I shall give him strife aplenty. I will initiate a struggle, and a good one at that—not only in a narrow nook and corner among the people of Israel, but as far as heaven and earth extend, on the sea and on dry land, that is, where it is wet and where it is dry, whether on the mainland or on the islands, at the sea or on the waters, wherever human beings dwell. Or as he says, "I will shake all the Gentiles," so that all the angels will contend with all the devils in heaven or in the air, and all men on earth will quarrel over the Seed.

I shall send the *chemdath* to all Gentiles. They will love him and adhere to him, as Genesis 49 says, "The Gentiles will gather about him," and, on the other hand, they will grow hostile to the devil, the old serpent, and defect from him. Then all will take its due course when the god and the prince of the world grows wrathful, raves and rages because he is obliged to yield his kingdom, his house, his equipment, his worship, his power, to the *chemdath* and Shiloh, the woman's Seed. Anyone can read the histories that date back to the time of Christ and learn how first the Jews and Gentiles, then the heretics, finally Muhammad, and at present the pope, have raged and still are raging "against the Lord and his Messiah" (Psalm 2:2), and he will understand the words of Haggai that speak of shaking all the nations, etc. There is not a corner in the world nor a spot in the sea where the gospel has not resounded and brought the *chemdath*, as Psalm 19:3-4 declares: "There is no speech, nor are there words; their voice is not heard; yet their voice goes out through all the earth, and their words to the end of the world." The devil too appeared promptly on the scene with murder by the hands of tyrants, with lies spoken by heretics, with all his devilish wiles and powers, which he still employs to impede and obstruct the course of the gospel. This is the strife in question.

I shall begin the story of this struggle with that great villain, Antiochus the Noble.[52] Approximately 300 years elapsed between the time of Haggai and that of Antiochus. This is the short span of time in

---

[52] This would be Antiochus IV Epiphanes, who ruled from 175 to 164 BC.

which peace prevailed. The kings in Persia were very kind to them, nor did Alexander harm them, and they fared well also under his successors, up to the time of this filthy Antiochus, who ushered in the unrest and the misfortune. Through him, the devil sought to exterminate the woman's Seed. He pillaged the city of Jerusalem, the temple, the country and its inhabitants, he desecrated the temple and raged as his god, the devil, impelled him. Practically all the good fortune of the Jews terminated right here. Down to the present, they have never recovered their former position, and they never will.

This will serve to supply a proper understanding of the Jews' glosses, which say that the "*chemdath* of all the Gentiles," that is, gold and silver, flowed into this temple. If the earlier kings had put anything into it, then this one took it all away again. This turns their glosses upside down to read: Antiochus distributes the *chemdath* of all Jews among the Gentiles. Thus this verse of Haggai cannot be understood of the Gentiles' shirt or coat. Following these 300 years, or this "little while," and from then on, they didn't get much from the Gentiles, but rather were compelled to give them much. Soon after this, the Romans came and made a clean sweep of it, and placed Herod over them as king. What Herod gave them, they soon learned. Therefore, from the time of Antiochus on, they enjoyed but a small measure of peace. Daniel's report also stops with Antiochus, as if to say: Now the end is at hand and all is over, now the Messiah is standing at the door, who will stir up ever more contention.

The detestable Antiochus not only despoiled and desecrated the temple but he also suppressed the *shebet* or sultan, the prince in the house of David, namely, the last prince, John Hyrcanus.[53] None of his descendants again ascended the throne of David or became ruler. Only the *saphra* or *mehoqeq* remained till Herod. From that point on, David's house looked as if its light had been extinguished, and as if there were no *shultan* or scepter in Judah. It had in fact come to an end, although there were about 150 years left until the coming of the Messiah. Such

---

[53] Hyrcanus (164-104 BC) was a Jewish leader and high priest.

Part II

an occurrence is not unusual; anything that is going to break will first crack or burst apart a little. Whatever is going to sink will first submerge or sway a little. The scepter of Judah went through the same process toward the end: it became weak, it groaned and moaned for 150 years until it fell apart entirely at the hands of the Romans and of Herod. During these 150 years, the princes of Judah didn't rule but lived as common citizens, perhaps quite impoverished. For Mary, Christ's mother in Nazareth, states that she is a handmaid of poor and low estate [Luke 1:48].

It's also true, however, that the Maccabees fought victoriously against Antiochus. Daniel 11:34 refers to this as "a little help." Those who in this way ascended the throne of David and assumed the rule were priests from the tribe of Levi and Aaron. One could say with good reason that the royal and the priestly tribes were mixed. In 2 Chronicles 22:11 we read that Jehoshabeath, the daughter of King Jehoram and the sister of King Ahaziah, was the wife of Jehoiada, the high priest. Thus, coming from the royal house of Solomon, she was grafted into the priestly tribe and became one trunk and tree with it. Therefore she was the ancestress of all the descendants of Jehoiada the priest, a true Sarah of the priestly family. Therefore the Maccabees may indeed be called David's blood and children, as viewed from the maternal lineage. Descent from a mother is just as valid as that from a father. This is recognized also in other countries. For instance, our Emperor Charles is king in Spain by virtue of his descent from his mother and not from his father; and his father Philip was duke of Burgundy not because of his father, Maximilian, but because of his mother, Mary.

Thus David calls all the children of Jehoiada and of Jehoshabeath his natural children, his sons and daughters, because Jehoshabeath was descended from his son Solomon. So through the Maccabees, Solomon's family regained rule and scepter through the maternal side, after it had been lost through Ahaziah on the paternal side. It remained in David's family until Herod, who did away with it and abolished both *shultan* and *saphra* or the Sanhedrin. Now finally, there lies the scepter of Judah and the *mehoqeq*, there the house of David is darkened on both the paternal and the maternal sides. Therefore the Messiah must now be at hand, the true Light of David, the true Son, who had sustained his house until that time and who would sustain it and enlighten it from that point on to all eternity. This conforms to God's promise that the scepter of Judah will remain until the Messiah appears and that the house of David will be preserved forever and will never die out. But, as we said, despite all of this, God must be the Jews' liar, who has not yet sent the Messiah as he promised and vowed.

Furthermore, God says through Haggai [2:7]: "I will fill this house with splendor. The silver is mine, and the gold is mine. The splendor of this latter house shall be greater than the former," etc. It's true that this temple displayed great splendor during the 300 years prior to Antiochus, since the Persians and the successors of Alexander, the kings in Syria and King Philadelphus in Egypt, contributed much toward it. But despite all of this, it didn't compare in magnificence with the first temple, the temple of Solomon. The text must refer to a different splendor here, or else Solomon's temple will far surpass it. In the first temple, there was also an abundance of gold and silver, and in addition the ark of the covenant, the mercy-seat, the cherubim, Moses' tablets, Aaron's rod, the bread of heaven in the golden vessel, Aaron's robes, also the Urun and Thuminin and the sacred oil with which the kings and priests were anointed (Burgensis on Daniel 9). When Solomon dedicated this temple, fire fell from heaven and consumed the sacrifice, and the temple was filled with what he called a cloud of divine Majesty. God himself was present in this cloud, as Solomon himself says: "The Lord has said that he would dwell in thick darkness" [2 Chron 6:1]. He had done the same thing in the wilderness as he hovered over Moses' tabernacle.

There was none of this splendor, surpassing gold and silver, in the temple of Haggai. Yet God says that it will show forth greater splendor than the first one. Let the Jews pipe up and say what constituted this greater splendor. They cannot pass over this in silence, for the text and the confession of the ancient Jews, their forefathers, both state that the

Part II

chemdath of the Gentiles, the Messiah, came at the time when the same temple stood and glorified it highly with his presence. We Christians know that our Lord Jesus Christ, the true *chemdath*, was presented in the temple by his mother, and that he himself often taught and did miracles there. This is the true cloud—his tender humanity, in which God manifested his presence and let himself be seen and heard. The blind Jews may deride this, but our faith is strengthened by it, until they can adduce a splendor of the temple excelling this *chemdath* of all the Gentiles. That they will do when they erect the third temple, that is to say, when God is a liar, when the devil is the truth, and when they themselves again take possession of Jerusalem—not before.

Josephus writes that Herod razed the temple of Haggai because it was not sufficiently splendid, and rebuilt it so that it was equal or superior to the temple of Solomon in splendor.[54] I would be glad to believe the history books; however, even if this temple had been constructed of diamonds and rubies, it would still have lacked the items mentioned from that sublime, old holy place—namely, the ark, the mercy-seat, the cherubim, etc. Furthermore, since Herod had not been commissioned by God to build it but did so as an impious enemy of God and of his people, motivated by vanity and pride, in his own honor, his whole structure and work was not as good as the most puny little stone that Zerubbabel placed into the temple by command of God. Herod certainly didn't merit much grace for tearing down and desecrating the temple that had been commanded, built, and consecrated by the word of God, and then presuming to erect a much more glorious one without God's word and command. God permitted this out of consideration for the place that he had selected for the temple, and so that the destruction of the temple might have the negative significance that the people of Israel should henceforth be without temple, word of God, and all, that it instead would be given wholly to the splendor of the world, under the guise of the service to God.

---

[54] Josephus (37-100 AD) was a Jewish writer under Roman rule. His book *Antiquities of the Jews* documents much of Jewish history. Luther refers to Book 15, chapter 13 of that work.

On the Jews and Their Lies

This temple was not only less splendid than Solomon's, but it was also violated in many ways more terribly than Solomon's temple, and was often completely desecrated. This happened first, against the will of the Jews, when Antiochus robbed it of all its contents, placed an idol on the altar, sacrificed pork, and made a regular pig-sty and an idolatrous desolation of the temple, instituting a horrible slaughter in Jerusalem, as though he were the devil himself—as we read in 1 Maccabees 1 and as Daniel 11 had predicted. No lesser outrage was committed by the Romans, and especially by that filthy Emperor Caligula, who also placed his mark of abomination in the temple. Daniel 9 and 12 speak of this. Such ignominy and disgrace were not experienced by Solomon's temple at the hands of Gentiles and foreigners. This makes it difficult to see how Haggai's words were fulfilled, "I will fill this temple with glory which will exceed the glory of that temple." One might rather say that it was filled with dishonor exceeding the dishonor of that temple, that is, if one thinks of external and outward honor. Consequently, if Haggai's words are to be accounted true, he must be referring to a different kind of splendor.

Second, the Jews themselves also desecrated this temple more viciously than the other one ever was desecrated: namely, with spiritual idolatries. Lyra writes, and others too, in many passages, that the Jews, after their return from the Babylonian captivity, did not commit idolatry or sin by killing prophets as gravely as before. Thereby he wants to prove that their present exile must be due to a more heinous sin than idolatry, the murder of the prophets, etc.—namely, the crucifixion of the Messiah. This argument is good, valid, and cogent. That they no longer killed the prophets is not to be attributed to a lack of evil intentions, but to the fact that they no longer had any prophets who reproved their idolatry, greed, and other vices. That's why they could no longer kill prophets. To be sure, the last prophet, Malachi, who began to rebuke the priests, barely escaped—if indeed he did escape.

But they did practice idolatry more outrageously at the time of this temple than at the time of the other—not the coarse, palpable, stupid

Part II

variety, but the subtle, spiritual kind. Zechariah portrays this under the image of a flying scroll and of an ephah going forth (5:2, 8). And Zechariah 11:12 and 12:10 foretell the infamy of their selling God for 30 pieces of silver and their piercing him through. More on that elsewhere; is it not shame enough that the priests at the same time perverted God's Ten Commandments so flagrantly? Tell me, what idolatry compares with the abomination of changing the word of God into lies? To do that is truly to set up idols, i.e., false gods, under the cloak of God's name; and that's forbidden in the second commandment, which reads: "You shall not take the name of the Lord your God in vain."

Their Talmud and their rabbis record that it's no sin for a Jew to kill a Gentile, but it is only a sin for him to kill a brother Israelite. Nor is it a sin for a Jew to break his oath to a Gentile. Likewise, they say that it's rendering God a service to steal or rob from a Goy, as they in fact do through their usury. Since they believe that they are the noble blood and the circumcised saints and we the accursed Goyim, they cannot treat us too harshly or commit sin against us, for they are the lords of the world and we are their servants, yes, their cattle.

In brief, our evangelists also tell us what their rabbis taught. In Matthew 15:4 we read that they abrogated the fourth commandment, which enjoins honor of father and mother; and in Matthew 23, that they were given to much shameful doctrine, not to mention what Christ says in Matthew 5 about how they preached and interpreted the Ten Commandments so deviously, how they installed money-changers, traders, and all sorts of usurers in the temple, prompting our Lord to say that they had made the house of God into a den of robbers.[55] Now figure out for yourself what a great honor that is and how the temple is filled with such glory that God must call his own house a den of robbers because so many souls had been murdered through their greedy, false doctrine, that is, through double idolatry. The Jews still persist in such doctrine to the present day. They imitate their fathers and pervert God's word. They are steeped in greed, in usury, they steal and murder where they can, and ever teach their children to do likewise.

---

[55] See Matt 21:13 and Luke 19:48.

Even this isn't the greatest shame of this temple. The real abomination of all abominations, the shame of all shames, is this: that at the time of this temple, there were several chief priests and an entire sect which were Sadducean, that is, Epicurean, who did not believe in the existence of any angel, devil, heaven, hell, or life after this life. And such fellows were expected to enter the temple, vested with the priestly office and in priestly garments, and sacrifice, pray, and offer burnt offerings for the people, preach to them, and rule them! Tell me, how much worse could Antiochus have been, with his idol and his sacrifice of pork, than were these Sadducean pigs and sows? In view of this, what remains of Haggai's statement that this temple's glory was greater than that of Solomon's temple? Before God and reason, a real pig-sty might be called a royal hall when compared with this temple, because of such great, horrible, and monstrous sows.

How much more honorably do the pagan philosophers, as well as the poets, write and teach not only about God's rule and about the life to come but also about temporal virtues. They teach that man by nature is obliged to serve his fellow man, to keep faith also with his enemies, and to be loyal and helpful especially in time of need. Thus Cicero and his kind teach.[56] Indeed, I believe that three of Aesop's fables, half of Cato, and several comedies of Terence contain more wisdom and more instruction about good works than can be found in the books of all the Talmudists and rabbis, and more than may ever occur to the hearts of all the Jews.

Someone may think that I'm saying too much. I'm not saying too much, but too little; for I see their writings. They curse us Goyim. In their synagogues and in their prayers, they wish us every misfortune.[57]

---

[56] Marcus Tullius Cicero (106-43 BC) was a renowned Roman philosopher and legislator.

[57] In confirmation of this very point, Burnett (2018: 184) makes this revealing remark: "Since Jews were a tiny religious minority in Europe living in a sea of Christians, they necessarily developed their own subversive counter-history of Christianity, ridiculing its tenets and practicing covertly anti-Christian rituals in order to maintain their own identity." Yuval (2006: 119-134) offers further substantial confirmation. The anti-Christian *rehitim* (prayers) "include sharp condemnations of and curses against

PART II

They rob us of our money and goods through their usury, and they play on us every wicked trick they can. And the worst of it is that they still claim to have done right and well, that is, to have done God a service. And they teach the doing of such things. No pagan ever acted thus; in fact, no one acts thus except the devil himself, or whomever he possesses, as he has possessed the Jews.

Burgensis, who was one of their very learned rabbis, and who through the grace of God became a Christian—a very rare happening—is much agitated by the fact that they curse us Christians so vilely in their synagogues (as Lyra also writes), and he deduces from this that they cannot be God's people. If they were, they would emulate the example of the Jews in the Babylonian captivity. To them Jeremiah wrote, "Seek the welfare of the city where I have sent you into exile, and pray to the Lord on its behalf, for in its welfare you will find your welfare" [29:7]. But our bastards and pseudo-Jews think they must curse us, hate us, and inflict every possible harm upon us, although they have no cause for it. Therefore they surely are no longer God's people. But we shall say more about this later.

To return to the subject of Haggai's temple, it's certain that no house was ever disgraced more than this holy house of God was by such vile sows as the Sadducees and Pharisees. Yet Christ calls it God's house,

---

Gentiles, and a plea to God to bring destruction on them. .... These are texts that demonstrate the abyss of hostility and hatred felt by medieval Jews toward Christians. And we have here not only hatred, but an appeal to God to kill indiscriminately and ruthlessly, alongside vivid descriptions of the anticipated horrors to be brought down upon the Gentiles. ... A detailed description of the ritual curses in the Haggadah [Passover recitations] was written by the apostate Antonius Margaritha..." Luther mentions Margaritha below, at the beginning of Part III, in just such a context. Schramm (2012: 7) further acknowledges that "since at least the 12th century, there had indeed developed in European Jewish circles a strident anti-Christian literature, which satirized Christian beliefs, attacked Christian exegesis, and longed for the destruction of the enemies of the Jewish people"—a polemic that had "filtered down to Luther." And Alex Bein simply states that "With regard to Luther's accusation [of Jewish hatred toward Christians]...that accusation is in principle true." It seems that, once again, Luther was well-justified in his beliefs.

because the four pillars are his.[58] Therefore, to offset this disgrace, a greater and different splendor must have inhered in it than that of silver and gold. If not, Haggai will fare ill with his prophecy that the splendor of this temple will surpass that of Solomon's temple. Amid such colossal shame, no splendor can be found here other than that of the *chemdath*, who will appear in a short time and surpass such shame with his splendor. The Jews can produce no other splendor; their mouth is stopped.

I must break off here and leave the last part of Haggai to others, the section in which he prophesies that the Lord, as he says, "Will give peace in this place" [Hag 2:9]. Can it be possible that this applies to the time from Antiochus up to the present, during which the Jews have experienced every misfortune and are still in exile? There shall be peace in this place, says the Lord. The place is still there; the temple and peace have vanished. No doubt the Jews will be able to interpret this. The history books inform me that there was but little peace prior to Antiochus for about 300 years, and subsequent to that time none at all down to the present hour, except for the peace that reigned at the time of the Maccabees. As I have already said, I shall leave this to others.

DANIEL 9

Finally we must lend an ear to the great prophet Daniel. A special angel with a proper name—Gabriel—talks with him. The like of this is not found elsewhere in the Old Testament. The fact that the angel is mentioned by name marks it as something extraordinary. This is what he tells Daniel [9:24]:

> Seventy weeks of years are decreed concerning your people and your holy city, to finish the transgression, to put an end to sin, and to atone for iniquity, to bring in everlasting righteousness, to seal both vision and prophet, and to anoint a most holy place.

---

[58] The source of Luther's claim here is unknown.

Part II

We cannot now discuss this rich text, which actually is one of the foremost in all of Scripture. And, as is only natural, everyone has reflected on it; it not only fixes the time of Christ's advent but also foretells what he will do—namely, take away sin, bring righteousness, and do this by means of his death. It establishes Christ as the Priest who bears the sin of the whole world. This, I say, we must now set aside and deal only with the question of the time, as we determined to do—whether such a Messiah or Priest has already come or is still to come. [This we do] for the strengthening of our faith, against all devils and men.

In the first place, there is complete agreement on this: that the 70 "weeks" are not weeks of *days* but of *years*; that one week comprises seven years, which produces a sum total of 490 years. That's the first point. Second, it's also agreed that these 70 weeks had ended when Jerusalem was destroyed by the Romans.[59] There is no difference of opinion on these two points, although many are in the dark when it comes to the matter of knowing the precise time of which these 70 weeks began and when they terminated. It isn't necessary for us to settle this question here, since it is generally assumed that they were fulfilled about the time of the destruction of Jerusalem. This will suffice us for the present.

If this is true—as it must be true, since after the destruction of Jerusalem, none of the 70 weeks was left—then the Messiah must have come before the destruction of Jerusalem, while something of those 70 weeks still remained: namely, the last week, as the text later [in Dan 9:25, as explained below] clearly and convincingly attests. After the seven and 62 weeks (that is, after 69 weeks), namely, in the last or 70th week, Christ will be killed—in such a way, however, that he will become alive again. For the angel says that "he shall make a strong covenant with many in the last week" [Dan 9:27]. This he cannot do while dead; he must be alive. "To make a covenant" can have no other meaning than to fulfill God's promise given to the fathers, namely, to disseminate the blessing promised in Abraham's seed to all the Gentiles. As the angel states earlier [v. 24], the visions and prophecies shall be sealed or ful-

---

[59] That is, in 70 AD.

filled. This requires a live Messiah, who, however, has previously been killed. But the Jews will have none of this. Therefore, we shall let it rest at that and hold to our opinion that the Messiah must have appeared during these 70 weeks; this the Jews cannot refute.

In their books as well as in certain histories, we learn that not just a few Jews but all of Jewry at that time assumed that the Messiah must have come or must be present at that very moment. This is what we want to hear! When Herod was forcibly made king of Judah and Israel by the Romans, the Jews surely realized that the scepter would thus depart from them. They resisted this move vigorously, and in the 30 years of their resistance, many thousand Jews were slain, and much blood was shed, until they finally surrendered in exhaustion. In the meantime, the Jews looked about for the Messiah. Thus, a hue and cry arose that the Messiah had been born—as, in truth, he had been. For our Lord Christ was born in the 30th year of Herod's reign.[60] But Herod forcibly suppressed this report, slaying all the young children in the region of Bethlehem, so that our Lord had to be taken for refuge to Egypt.[61] Herod even killed his own son because he was born of a Jewish mother. He was worried that, through this son, the scepter might revert to the Jews and that he might gain the Jews' loyalty, since, as Philo records, the rumor of the birth of Christ had been spread abroad.[62]

As our evangelists relate, more than 30 years later, John the Baptist comes out of the wilderness and proclaims that the Lord had not only been born but also was already among them and would reign shortly after him. Suddenly thereafter, Christ himself appears, preaches, and performs great miracles, so that the Jews hoped that now, after the loss of the scepter, Shiloh had come. But the chief priests, the rulers, and their followers took offense at the person, since he didn't appear as a mighty king but wandered about as a poor beggar. They had made up

---

[60] That is, in 3 BC.

[61] Cited only in Matt 2:13-20. Often referred to as the "flight into Egypt," this incident has no other documentation in the New Testament.

[62] Luther is mistaken here, since Philo never wrote anything about Jesus or the Christians. The work to which he refers was a later work, forged under Philo's name.

Part II

their mind that the Messiah would unite the Jews and not only wrest the scepter from the foreign king but also subdue the Romans and all the world under himself with the sword, installing them as mighty princes over all the Gentiles. When they were disappointed in these expectations, the noble blood and circumcised saints were vexed, as people who had the promise of the kingdom and could not attain it through this beggar. Therefore they despised him and did not accept him.

But when they disdained John and his [Christ's] message and miracles, reviling them as the deeds of Beelzebub, he spoiled and ruined matters entirely. He rebuked and chided them severely—something he should not, of course, have done—for being greedy, evil, and disobedient children, false teachers, seducers of the people, etc.; in brief, a brood of serpents and children of the devil. On the other hand, he was friendly to sinners and tax collectors, to Gentiles and to Romans, giving the impression that he was the foe of the people of Israel and the friend of Gentiles and villains. Now the fat was really in the fire; they grew wrathful, bitter, and hateful, and ranted against him; finally they contrived the plot to kill him. And that's what they did; they crucified him as ignominiously as possible. They gave free rein to their anger, so that even the Gentile Pilate[63] noticed this and testified that they were condemning and killing him out of hatred and envy, innocently and without cause.

When they had executed this false Messiah—which is the conception they wanted to convey of him—they still didn't abandon the delusion that the Messiah had to be at hand or nearby. They constantly murmured against the Romans because of the scepter. Soon, too, the rumor circulated that Jesus, whom they had killed, had again arisen and that he was now really being proclaimed openly and freely as the Messiah. The people in the city of Jerusalem were adhering to him, as well as the Gentiles in Antioch and everywhere in the country. Now they really had their hands full. They had to oppose this dead Messiah and his followers, lest he be accepted as resurrected and as the Messiah. They also

---

[63] Pontius Pilate was the Roman governor of Judea at the time.

had to oppose the Romans, lest their hoped-for Messiah be forever bereft of the scepter. At one place a slaughter of the Christians was initiated, at another an uprising against the Romans. To these tactics they devoted themselves for approximately 40 years, until the Romans finally were constrained to lay waste country and city. This delusion regarding their false Christ and their persecution of the true Christ cost them 1,100,000 men, as Josephus reports,[64] together with the most horrible devastation of country and city, as well as the forfeiture of scepter, temple, priesthood, and all that they possessed.

This deep and cruel humiliation, which is terrible to read and to hear about, surely should have made them pliable and humble. Alas, they became seven times more stubborn, viler, and prouder than before. This was due in part to the fact that, in their dispersion, they had to witness how the Christians daily grew and increased with their Messiah. The saying of Moses found in Deuteronomy 32:21 was now completely fulfilled in them: "They have stirred me to jealousy with what is no god; so I will stir them to jealousy with those who are no people." Likewise, as Hosea says: "I will say to Not my people, 'You are my people,' but you are not my people and I am not your God" (2:23, 1:9). They stubbornly insisted on having their own Messiah in whom the Gentiles should not claim a share, and they persisted in trying to exterminate this Messiah in whom both Jews and Gentiles gloried. Everywhere throughout the Roman Empire they intervened, and wherever they could ferret out a Christian in any corner, they dragged him out before the judges and accused him—they themselves could not pass sentence on him, since they had neither legal authority nor power—until they had him killed.[65] Thus they shed very much Christian blood and made innumerable martyrs, also outside the Roman Empire, in Persia and wherever they could.

---

[64] In his book *The Jewish War* (Book 7, ch. 17).

[65] This is a remarkable statement about Jewish influence with local authorities of the time—namely, that they had the power to have most anyone killed upon command. Such power has echoed down through the centuries, to the present day, with the evident power of the global Jewish Lobby to influence governments and legislators.

Part II

Still they clung to the delusion that the Messiah must have appeared, since the 70 weeks of Daniel had expired and the temple of Haggai had been destroyed. However, they disliked the person of Jesus of Nazareth, and therefore they went ahead and elevated one of their own number to be the Messiah. This came about as follows: They had a rabbi, or Talmudist, named Akiba, a very learned man, esteemed by them more highly than all other rabbis, a venerable, honorable, gray-haired man. He taught the verses of Haggai and of Daniel, also of Jacob in Genesis 49, with ardor, saying that there had to be a Messiah among the people of God since the time fixed by Scripture was at hand. Then he chose one, surnamed Kokhba,[66] which means "a star." According to Burgensis, his right name was Heutoliba. He's well known in all the history books, where he is called Ben Koziba or Bar Koziban. This man had to be their Messiah; and he gladly complied. All the people and the rabbis rallied about him and armed themselves thoroughly with the intention of doing away with both Christians and Romans. Now they had the Messiah fashioned to their liking and their mind, who was proclaimed by the aforementioned passages of Scripture.

This unrest began approximately 30 years after the destruction of Jerusalem, under the reign of the emperor Trajan.[67] Rabbi Akiba was Kokhba's prophet and spirit who inflamed and incited him and vehemently urged him on, applying all the verses of Scripture that deal with the Messiah to him before all the people and proclaiming: "You are the Messiah!" He applied to him especially the saying of Balaam recorded in Numbers 24:17-19, by reason of his surname Kokhba ("star"). In that passage Balaam says, in a vision:

---

[66] Simon bar Kokhba (d. 135 AD) was the leader of the third Jewish revolt against Rome.

[67] Luther's history here is incorrect. Bar Kokhba's revolt began in 132 AD, under the reign of Hadrian, and it was some 60 years after the destruction of Jerusalem. Luther is likely confusing the third revolt with the second, which occurred in 115 AD, under Trajan.

A star shall come forth out of Jacob, and a scepter shall rise out of Israel; it shall crush the forehead of Moab, and break down all the sons of Sheth. Edom shall be dispossessed, Seir also, his enemies, shall be dispossessed, while Israel does valiantly. By Jacob shall dominion be exercised, and the survivors of cities be destroyed!

That was a proper sermon for thoroughly misleading such a foolish, angry, restive mob—which is exactly what happened. To insure the success of this venture and guard against its going awry, that exalted and precious Rabbi Akiba, the old fool and simpleton, made himself Kokhba's guardsman or armor-bearer, his *armiger*, as the history books have it; if I'm not translating the term correctly, let some one else improve on it. The person is meant who is positioned beside the king or prince, and whose chief duty it is to defend him on the battlefield or in combat, either on horse or on foot. To be sure, something more is implied here, since he is also a prophet—a Münzer (to use contemporary terms). So this is where the scepter of Judah and the Messiah now resided; they are sure of it. They carried on like this for some 30 years. Kokhba always had himself addressed as King Messiah, and butchered throngs of Christians who refused to deny our Messiah Jesus Christ. His captains also harassed the Romans where they could. Especially in Egypt, they at one time defeated the Roman captain during the reign of Trajan. Now their heart, brain, and belly began to swell with conceit. God, they inferred, had to be for them and with them. They occupied a town near Jerusalem, called Bittir; in the Bible it's known as Beth-horon.[68]

At this point they were convinced that their Messiah, King Kokhba, was the lord of the world and had vanquished the Christians and the Romans and had carried the day. But Emperor Hadrian sent his army against them, laid siege to Bittir, conquered it, and slew Messiah and prophet, star and darkness, lord and armor-bearer. Their own

---

[68] See Joshua 10:10.

Part II

books lament that there were twice 80,000 men at Bittir who blew the trumpets, who were captains over vast hosts of men, and that 4,000,000 men were slain, not including those slain at Alexandria. The latter are said to have numbered 1,200,000. However, it seems to me that they are exaggerating enormously. I interpret this to mean that the two times 80,000 trumpeters represent that many valiant and able-bodied men equipped for battle, each of whom would have been able to lead large bodies of soldiers in battle. Otherwise this sounds too devilishly mendacious.

After this formidable defeat, they themselves called Kokhba, their lost Messiah, "Kozba," which rhymes with it and has a similar ring. Thus write their Talmudists: You must not read "Kokhba," but "Kozba." Therefore all history books now refer to him as Koziban. "Kozba" means "false." His attempt had miscarried, and he had proved a false and not a true Messiah. Just as we Germans might say by way of rhyme: You are not a *Deutscher* but a *Täuscher* ["not a German but a deceiver"]; not a *Welscher* but a *Fälscher* ["not a foreigner of Romance origin but a falsifier"]. Of a usurer I may say: You are not a *Bürger*, but a *Würger* ["not a citizen but a slayer"]. Such rhyming is customary in all languages. Our Eusebius reports this story in his *Ecclesiastical History*, Book 4, chapter 6. Here he uses the name Barcochabas, saying that this was an extremely cruel battle in which the Jews "were driven so far from their country that their impious eyes were no longer able to see their fatherland even if they ascended the highest mountains."

Such horrible stories are sufficient witness that all of Jewry understood that this had to be the time of the Messiah, since the 70 weeks had elapsed, Haggai's temple had been destroyed, and the scepter had been wrested from Judah, as the statements of Jacob in Genesis 49, of Haggai 2, and of Daniel 9 clearly indicated and announced. God be praised that we Christians are certain and confident of our belief that the true Messiah, Jesus Christ, did come at that time. To prove this, we have not only his miraculous deeds, which the Jews themselves cannot deny, but also the gruesome downfall and misfortune, because of the name of the Messiah, of his enemies who wanted to exterminate him together with all his adherents. How could they otherwise have brought such misery upon their heads if they hadn't been convinced that the time of the Messiah was at hand? And I think this does surely constitute coming to grief and running their heads—now for the second time—against "the stone of offence and the rock of stumbling," to quote Isaiah 8:14. So many hundreds of thousands attempted to devour Jesus of Nazareth, but over this they themselves "stumbled and fell and were broken, snared, and taken," as Isaiah says [8:15].

Since two such terrible and awesome attempts had most miserably failed, the first at Jerusalem under Vespasian, the other at Bittir under Hadrian, they surely should have come to their senses, have become pliable and humble, and concluded: God help us! How does this happen? The time of the Messiah's advent has, in accord with the prophets' words and promises, come and gone, and we are beaten so terribly and cruelly over it! What if our ideas regarding the Messiah—that he should be a secular Kokhba—have deceived us, and he came in a different manner and form? Is it possible that the Messiah is Jesus of Nazareth, to whom so many Jews and Gentiles adhere, who daily perform so many wondrous signs? Alas, they became seven times more stubborn and baser than before. Their conception of a worldly Messiah must be right and cannot fail; there must be a mistake about the designated time. The prophets must be lying and fail rather than they. They will have nothing of this Jesus, even if they must pervert all of Scripture, have no god, and never get a Messiah. That's the way they want it.

Since they were beaten into defenseless impotence by the Romans, from that time on they have turned against Scripture, and have boldly tried to take it from us and to pervert it with strange and different interpretations. They have digressed from the understanding of all their forefathers and prophets, and furthermore from their own reason. Because of this, they have lost so many hundreds of thousands of men, land, and city,

Part II

and have fallen prey to every misery. They have done nothing these 1,400 years but take any verse which we Christians apply to our Messiah and violate it, tear it to bits, crucify it, and twist it in order to give it a different nose and mask. They deal with it as their fathers dealt with our Lord Christ on Good Friday, making God appear as the liar but themselves as the truthful ones, as you heard before. They assign practically ten different interpretations to Jacob's saying in Genesis 49. Likewise they know how to twist the nose of Haggai's statement. Here you have two good illustrations that show you how masterfully the Jews exegete the Scriptures, in such a way that they don't arrive at any definite meaning.

They have also distorted in this way the passage from Daniel. I cannot enumerate all their shameful glosses, but shall submit just one—the one that Lyra and Burgensis consider to be the most famous and widespread among the Jews, from which they dare not depart on pain of losing their souls. It reads as follows. Gabriel says to Daniel: "Seventy weeks of years are decreed concerning your people and your holy city, to finish the transgression, to put an end to sin, and to atone for iniquity, to bring in everlasting righteousness, to seal both vision and prophet, and to anoint a most holy place..." [Dan 9:24]. This is the text. Now their beautiful commentary follows:

"It will still be 70 weeks before Jerusalem will be destroyed and the Jews are led into exile by the Romans. This will happen so that they may be induced by this exile to depart from their sins, that they may be punished for them, pay for them, render satisfaction, atone for them, and thus become pious eternally and merit the fulfillment of the messianic promises, the reconstruction of the holy temple," etc.

Here you perceive, in the first place, that the Jews' immeasurable holiness presumes that God will fulfill his promise regarding the Messiah not because of his sheer grace and mercy but because of their merit and repentance and their extraordinary piety. And how could or should God, that poor fellow, do otherwise? When he promised the Messiah to Jacob, David, and Haggai out of sheer grace, he neither thought nor knew that such great saints—whose merits would exact the Messiah from his—

would appear after 70 weeks and after the destruction of Jerusalem, that he would have to grant the Messiah not out of grace but would be obliged to send him by reason of their great purity and holiness, when, where, and in the way that they desired. Such is the imposing story of the Jews, who repented after the 70 weeks and became so pious.

You can easily infer that they didn't repent, nor were they pious before and during the 70 weeks. As a result, the priests in Jerusalem all starved to death because there was no penance, no sin or guilt offerings—which the priests needed for sustenance. All this was postponed and saved for the penance and holiness, which were to begin after the 70 weeks. Where there is no repentance, or anything to repent for, there is no sin. But where then, we wonder, did the sin come from for which they have to repent after the 70 weeks, since they had atoned daily through so many sacrifices of the priests, ordained by Moses for this purpose, for all previous sin? Why do they have to begin to do penance now after the 70 weeks, when temple, office, sacrifice for sins no longer exist?

But the following even surpasses this. Gabriel says, according to their gloss, that the Jews will repent and become pious after the 70 weeks, so that the Messiah will come on account of their merit. Well and good, here we have it! If Gabriel is speaking the truth and not lying, then the Jews have now repented, they have become pious, they have merited the Messiah ever since the passing of those 70 weeks. He says that all of this will be done by the Jews subsequent to the 70 weeks. What follows now? They confess, indeed they wail, that the Messiah has not come since the end of those 70 weeks, that he has not come to date, approximately 1,468 years later; nor do they know when he will come. So they will also have to confess that they have not done penance for any sin nor become pious during these 1,468 years following the 70 weeks, nor merited the Messiah. It follows that the angel Gabriel must be lying when he promises in God's behalf that the Jews will repent, be pious, and merit the Messiah after the 70 weeks.

In Leviticus 26:40 and in Deuteronomy 4:29 and 30:1, Moses, too, proves very clearly that they have never sincerely done penance for sin

Part II

since the 70 weeks. In many beautiful words he promises that God will return them to their fatherland, even if they are dispersed to the end of the heavens, etc., if they turn to God with all their heart and confess their sin. Moses utters these words as the spokesman of God, whom one must not accuse of lying. Since the Jews have not been returned to their country to date, it is proved that they have never repented for sin with all their heart since the 70 weeks. So it must be falsehood when they incorrectly interpret Gabriel as speaking about their repentance.

We also know that God is so gracious by nature that he forgives man his sin in every hour in which man sincerely repents and is sorry for it, as David says in Psalm 32:5: "I said, I will confess my transgressions to the Lord: then thou didst forgive the guilt of my sin." We also read that when the prophet Nathan rebuked David for his sin and the latter thereupon declared, "I have sinned against the Lord," he was immediately absolved by Nathan, who replied, "The Lord has put away your sin" [2 Sam 12:13]. Even if God in many instances does not remove the punishment as promptly as he did with David, he nonetheless assures man of the remission of his sin. And if neither prophet nor priest were available, an angel would have to appear instead and announce, "Your sins are forgiven you," so that a sinner in his sorrow and punishment might not lose heart and despair. We observe also how, during the Babylonian captivity, God graciously and paternally consoles the people who confess their sins, enabling them to bear the punishment. Nor can the punishment endure forever; it must have its definite time, measure, and end wherever genuine contrition and repentance are found.

But there is no remission of sin for these Jews, no prophet to console them with the assurance of such forgiveness, no definite time limit for their punishment, but only interminable wrath and disfavor, devoid of any mercy. So it's not only an unmitigated lie but also an impossibility to understand Gabriel's promises in terms of their repentance, much less of their merit and righteousness.

But why should we waste so many words and so much time! The land of Canaan was hardly as big as a beggar's alms or as a crust of bread in comparison with the empire of the whole world. Yet they didn't merit even this land through their repentance, or righteousness. Thus Moses declares in Deuteronomy 9:4 that they were not granted the possession of the land because of their righteousness, but it was given to them, a stiff-necked and disobedient people, that is, very sinful and unworthy people, solely by reason of God's gracious promise—although Hosea [11:1] and Balaam (Numbers 24:5) praise them for being at their peak of piety at that time. They still had Moses, Aaron, the divine worship, prophets, God himself with his miracles, bread from heaven, water from the rock, clouds by day, pillars of fire by night, indestructible shoes and garments, etc. And these dreary dregs, this stinking scum, this dried-up froth, this moldy leaven and boggy morass of Jewry should merit, on the strength of their repentance and righteousness, the empires of the whole world—that is, the Messiah and the fulfillment of the prophecies—though they possess none of the aforementioned items and are nothing but rotten, stinking, rejected dregs of their fathers' lineage!

In brief, Moses and all true Israelites understood these verses regarding the Messiah [as signifying that all this would be given them] out of sheer grace and mercy and not because of penitence and merit. This we gathered from the cited verses of Jacob, David, and Haggai. Likewise Daniel does not ask, desire, or think that such a glorious promise of the 70 weeks should be revealed to him, but it is granted him out of grace, far, far beyond his asking.

From this you can learn what fine repentance the Jews practiced, and still practice, after those 70 weeks. They began it with lies and blasphemies, in which they continued and still persist. Whoever wishes may imitate the Jews' example of repentance and say: "God and his angels are liars, they speak about things that are not." Then you will merit grace as they merit the Messiah.

If they weren't so stone-blind, their own vile external life would indeed convince them of the true nature of their penitence. It abounds with witchcraft, conjuring signs, figures, and the tetragrammaton of the name, that is, with idolatry, envy, and conceit. Moreover, they are nothing but thieves and robbers who daily eat no morsel and wear no

Part II

thread of clothing which they have not stolen and pilfered from us by means of their accursed usury. Thus they live from day to day, together with wife and child, by theft and robbery, as arch-thieves and robbers, in the most impenitent security. A usurer is an arch-thief and a robber who should rightly be hanged on the gallows seven times higher than other thieves. Indeed, God should prophesy about such beautiful penitence and merit from heaven through his holy angel and become a flagrant, blasphemous liar for the sake of the noble blood and circumcised saints who boast of being hallowed by God's commandments, although they trample all of them under foot and keep not one of them.

The passage in Daniel continues:

> Know therefore and understand that from the time when the order goes forth to restore and build Jerusalem to the coming of the Messiah, the prince, there shall be seven weeks and sixty-two weeks. It shall be built again with streets and walls, but in a troubled time. And after the sixty-two weeks, the Messiah shall be killed, and shall have nothing [Dan 9:25].

Oh, how ridiculous it seems to these circumcised saints that we accursed Goyim have interpreted and understand this saying thus, especially since we didn't consult their rabbis, Talmudists, and Kokhbaites, whom they regard as more authoritative than all of Scripture. They do a far better job of it. This is what they say: "Know therefore and understand from the going forth of the word to restore and rebuild Jerusalem"—this means, Ponder and understand it well that the word has gone forth that Jerusalem is to be restored. That's one point. Further, "To the coming of the Messiah, the prince"—this means, until the time of King Cyrus[69]—"there shall be seven weeks." That's another point. Further, "For sixty-two weeks it shall be built again with walls and streets, but in a troubled time." That's another point. "And after

---
[69] Cyrus the Great, king of Persia (600-530 BC).

sixty-two weeks the Messiah (that means King Agrippa[70]) will be killed and will not be"—this means, will be no king, etc.

It is indeed tiresome to discuss such confused lies and such tomfoolery. But I have to give our people occasion for pondering the devilish wantonness that the rabbis perpetrate with this splendid saying. So here you see how they separate the text where it should be read connectedly, and join it where it should be separated. This is the way in which it should be connected:

"Know therefore and understand that from the going forth of the word about how Jerusalem is to be restored and rebuilt to the coming of the Messiah, there shall be seven weeks and 62 weeks." These words, I say, are to be joined together to form one complete text. Then follows: "It shall be built again with walls and streets, but in a troubled time." This sentence, separate though it is, they connect with the foregoing words about the 62 weeks, so as to convey the meaning that the building of the walls and the streets will occupy 62 weeks.

That is truly a knavish trick. It reminds me of the rascal of whom I once heard as a young monk. He hacked the Lord's Prayer to pieces and rearranged it to read thus: 'Our Father, hallowed be in heaven; thy name come; thy kingdom be done; thy will as in heaven, so also on earth.' Or as that ignorant priest read the lesson in the Vigils from 1 Corinthians 15: *Ubi est mors stimulus, tuus stimulus autem mortis, peccatum est virtus vero*, etc.

That's the way the Jews tear apart the text wherever they can, solely for the purpose of spoiling the words of Scripture for us Christians, although it serves no purpose for them either. It teaches them nothing, it doesn't comfort them, it gives them nothing; it results in nothing but meaningless words. It's the same as if the angel had said nothing at all. But they would rather surrender such comforting, joyous words and suffer the loss than to have them benefit us. Similarly, Bodenstein maliciously tore the words of the sacrament apart lest they prove useful to us. However, this won't help the rabbis, those night herons and screech

---

[70] Herod Agrippa I (11 BC – 44 AD) ruled Judea for the last three years of his life. He was the grandson of Herod I, discussed at the beginning of Part II.

Part II

owls. With the help of God, we will bring their howling and lying to light. Let's take up the several parts in order.

First I want to ask the Hebraists whether the word *intellige* ["know"] is construed with the word *de* ["from"] in any other place in Scripture. I haven't found any, and this seems to me quite arbitrary. If it is to mean *de* as in the phrase *de subjecta materia*, the Hebrew uses the preposition *al*, just as the Latins use the word *super* ("*Multa super Priamo*," etc.). I know very well, however, that the Jews cannot prove that such a construction obtains here. The biblical examples agree that it stands as an absolute, independently. But to ascribe something to God maliciously of which one is uncertain, and which one cannot prove, is tantamount to tempting him and giving him the lie.

Now let's see how they tear the text apart. "Know therefore and understand, from the going forth of the word, that Jerusalem will again be built." This, they claim, does not speak of the beginning of the 70 weeks but of the word that has gone forth. Then follows: "To the coming of the Messiah, the prince, there shall be seven weeks." Now, it's in agreement with the customary usage of all languages that the word *donec*, "until" [or "to"], presupposes a beginning. However, the Jews assign it none; they refuse to have the text read "from the beginning of the word to the coming of Messiah." I must draw an analogy.

If someone on St. Gall Square here in Wittenberg were to tell you: "You have heard a sermon based on God's word, declaring that the church is holy. Ponder this and mark it well." All right, you look at him expectantly to hear what else he has to say; he does have more to say. Then he abruptly blurts out: "There are still seven weeks till Michaelmas." Or, "It is a distance of three miles to Halle." Here you would look at him and say, What sense is there in that? Are you crazy? Are the seven weeks to begin now on the marketplace? Or are the three miles to begin in Wittenberg? "No," he would reply, "you must understand this to mean from the Day of St. Lawrence to Michaelmas, and from Bitterfeld to Halle." At this point you would be tempted to rejoin: "Go plant a kiss of peace on a sow's rump! Where did you learn to jabber so foolishly? And what do the seven weeks have to do with your statement that I should note well the sermon that I heard at Wittenberg?"

The rabbis treat the angel Gabriel's words in the same way. They make his speech read thus: "There are seven weeks until the Messiah." Suppose now Daniel replies, "My dear Gabriel, what do you mean? Are the seven weeks to begin now that you are speaking with me?" "No," he says, "you must understand this to mean that they begin with the destruction of Jerusalem." Thank you, indeed, you noble, circumcised rabbis, for teaching the angel Gabriel to speak, as though he were unable to tell of the beginning of the seven weeks, which is all-important, as well as of the middle and the end of them. No, Daniel must assume it. This is just nonsense. Shame on you, you vile rabbis, to attribute this foolish talk of yours to the angel of God! With this you disgrace yourselves and convict yourselves of being malicious liars and blasphemers of God's words. But this is just the grammatical side of the matter. Now let's study the theological aspect.

These holy, circumcised ravens say that the 70 weeks begin with the first destruction of Jerusalem and end with its second destruction. What better method could they have pursued for arriving at this conclusion than to close their eyes and ears, ignore Scripture and the history books, and let their imagination run freely, saying: "This is the way it seems right to us, and we insist upon it. Therefore it follows that God and his angel must agree with us. How could we be wrong? We are the ravens who are able to teach God and the angels."

Oh, what a base, vexatious, blasphemous people, that can merit the Messiah with such penitence! But let's listen to their wisdom. The 70 weeks begin with the destruction of Jerusalem by the king of Babylon; from that event until the coming of the Messiah, the prince (that is, King Cyrus), are seven weeks. Now tell me: Where is this written? Nowhere. Who has said it? Markolf the mockingbird. Who else might say or write it?

Part II

In the beginning of this ninth chapter stands Daniel's clear and plain statement that the revelation regarding the 70 weeks had come to him in the first year of the reign of Darius the Mede, who had conquered the Babylonian kingdom, which event had been preceded by the first destruction of Jerusalem 70 years earlier. Daniel clearly states that 70 years of the devastation had been fulfilled, in accordance with Jeremiah 29:10. This we also read in 2 Chronicles, the last chapter [36:22]. And yet these two clear passages of Scripture, Daniel 9 and 2 Chronicles 36, must be accounted as lies by the rabbis. They insist that they are right and that the 70 weeks must have begun 70 years before they were revealed to Daniel. Isn't that great? Now go and believe the rabbis, those ignorant, untutored asses, who look neither at the Scriptures nor at the history books and who spew forth from their vicious mouth whatever they choose against God and angels.

Ten Lies of the Jews

They herewith stand openly convicted of their lies and their erring arbitrariness. Since the 70 weeks that were revealed in the first year of the reign of Darius the Mede cannot begin 70 years previously with the destruction of Jerusalem, all their lies founded on this are simultaneously refuted, and this verse of Daniel regarding the 70 weeks must remain for us undefiled and unadulterated—no thanks to them. Eternal disgrace will be their reward for this impertinent and patent lie.[71] With this lie, another one also collapses; namely, their claim that the words about the Messiah, the prince, refer to King Cyrus, who supposedly appeared seven weeks after the destruction, although in fact he came ten weeks (that is, 70 years) after the destruction. This is recorded in 2 Chronicles 36, Daniel 9, and Ezra 1.

Even if we would assume—which is impossible—that the 70 weeks began with the destruction of Jerusalem, we could still not justify this stupid lie. And with this the third lie collapses: They say that Cyrus came 52 years after the destruction—the equivalent of seven weeks and

---

[71] This is the first of 10 lies that Luther covers in the following paragraphs.

three years, or seven and a half weeks. Thus they tear three years, or half a week, from the 62 weeks and add them to the first seven weeks. It's as though the angel were such a consummate fool or child that he could not count up to seven, and says seven when he should say seven and a half. Why do they do this? So that we might perceive how they indulge in lies for the purpose of tearing apart and turning upside down God's word for us. Therefore they insist that Cyrus came seven and a half weeks (which they call seven weeks) after the destruction, whereas (as was said) he really came ten weeks, i.e., 70 years, later.

Nor does the angel tolerate that these weeks be mangled and mutilated, subtracting three years from one and leaving it only four years, and adding to the one that has seven years three more, making it ten years or one and a half weeks. He says that the 70 weeks are to be taken exactly; they are counted and reckoned precisely.

Much less does he tolerate the fourth lie—that Cyrus is here called the Messiah—even if the other lies were to be upheld, to the effect that Cyrus had appeared after seven weeks, that is, after 49 years. Here we find the unmistakable and simple words of the angel: "Seventy weeks of years are decreed concerning your people and your holy city" [Dan 9:24]. He means to say: "In other chapters I spoke of strange people and kings; but in this verse concerning the 70 weeks I am speaking of your people, of your city, and of your Messiah. And whoever refers this to a different people and to different kings is a wanton, incorrigible liar."

The fourth lie is followed by the fifth, in which they divorce the seven weeks from the 62. But these belong together, and there's no reason to separate them, especially since the lie regarding King Cyrus miscarried. It was for this reason that they severed the seven from the 62 weeks so that they could give him seven, that is, seven and a half. In biblical Hebrew it's customary to count the years thus: first to give the one, then the other number of years, but with both placed together. We find many illustrations for this in Genesis 5 and 11, where reference is made to the deceased fathers. For instance: "When Seth had lived five years and a hundred years, he became the father of Enosh. Seth lived

Part II

after the birth of Enosh seven years and eight hundred years" [Gen 5:6]. Similarly Genesis 11:17: "Eber lived after the birth of Peleg thirty years and four hundred years." And Genesis 25:7: "Abraham lived one hundred years, 70 years, and five years." From these illustrations one can easily see how arbitrary it is to separate the seven years from the 62 years in this verse.

The Latin and German languages prevent such a disruption nicely, since they don't repeat the little word "year" so often, but read the number connectedly, saying: "Abraham lived one hundred seventy-five years." In that way, these words also are to be taken: "From the going forth of the word to the coming of the Messiah, the prince, there are seven weeks and 62 weeks." These two numbers belong together and compose one number, to the coming of the Messiah. The angel has a reason for designating the entire sum of years as seven weeks and 62 weeks. He might have spoken of nine weeks and 60 weeks, or found many different ways to name such a sum, such as five weeks and 64 weeks, or six weeks and 63 weeks, etc. He must have the seven weeks for the construction of the walls and streets of Jerusalem; and he must have the 62, up to the last week, which is all-important, for in it the Messiah will die, fulfill the covenant, etc.

Then comes the sixth lie, which says that the walls and streets of Jerusalem were rebuilt for 62 weeks (minus three years). That would be up to the last week, after which—as they lie for the seventh time—Jerusalem was again destroyed. With the last week, the 70 weeks are ended. According to this, Jerusalem had not stood again for longer than one week, which means seven years. Go ahead, Jew, lie boldly and unashamedly! Nehemiah stands against you with his book and testifies that he built the walls, set the gates, and arranged the city, and that he himself gloriously consecrated it. Thus the temple was already completed in the sixth year of the reign of Darius (Ezra 6:16). Alexander the Great found the city of Jerusalem already long completed. After him, that villain Antiochus found the city even further restored and the temple full of wealth, and he plundered them horribly.

The eighth rude lie follows when they interpret the words of the angel, "And after 62 weeks the Messiah will be killed, and shall have nothing," as if the Messiah refers to King Agrippa, who was killed and had nothing after his death; no king succeeded him. Why would it not be just as true to say that Emperor Nero was the Messiah? He was killed at that time and left no heirs. I believe that they would designate Markolf or Thersites[72] as the Messiah rather than accept the true Messiah. How can God, who loves the truth and who is the truth himself, tolerate such shameful, open lies if these are intolerable even to a person who is given to lies or is untruthful or is at least not so strict a lover of the truth? And this eighth lie is a multiple one—in the first place, because they assign different meanings to the word "Messiah" within such a brief passage: there he has to be Cyrus after the seven weeks, here Agrippa after the 62 weeks. Just as though the angel were a fool who would point to a different Messiah with every other word!

As we heard earlier, the angel is not referring to a foreign people and city, but says, "I am speaking of your people and of your city." Therefore we must conceive of the Messiah in this verse not as two different beings, but as one—namely, the Messiah of this people and of this city, the Shiloh of Judah who came after the scepter departed from Judah, the Son of David, the *chemdath* of Haggai. This verse indeed refers to him, excluding all others. Agrippa was not king in Jerusalem, much less the Messiah, before the last week—that is, after seven and 62 weeks. The Romans had graciously granted him a little country beyond the Jordan. The Roman procurators such as Felix, Festus, Albinus, etc., ruled the land of Judea. Nor was Agrippa killed after the 62 weeks. In brief, all that they say is a lie.

Since they now confess, and have to confess, that a Messiah was killed after the 62 weeks, that is, in the first year of the last week, and since this cannot have been Agrippa—as they would like to have it, in confirmation of their lie—nor anyone else, I'm curious to learn where

---

[72] Tersites was a foul and obnoxious warrior in Homer's *Iliad* (2.245-320), "the ugliest man who ever came to Troy." 'Markolf' again refers to a generic swindler or imposter.

Part II

they might find one. It must be someone who lived before the expiration of the 70 weeks and who was killed after 62 weeks. Furthermore, as Gabriel says, he must have come from among their people, undoubtedly from the royal tribe of Judah. It's certain that since Herod's time, they had had no king who was a member of their people or race. But, on the other hand, it's just as certain that Gabriel must be believed, with his statement regarding a Messiah of their nation. How is this difficulty to be solved?

And there's more. They themselves confess that they had no Messiah, that is, no anointed king ("Messiah" means "the anointed one"), between the first and the last destruction of Jerusalem, for the sacred anointing oil, of which Moses writes in Exodus 30:22, with which kings and priests were anointed, no longer existed after the first destruction. Consequently, Zedekiah was the last anointed king; his descendants were princes, not kings, down to the time of Herod, when the scepter departed and Shiloh, the true Messiah, was to appear.

We want to purge out their lies completely. With reference to Daniel's saying, "And he shall make a strong covenant with many for one week" [Dan 9:27], that is, the last week, they perpetrate the ninth lie, saying that the Romans agreed to a peace or a truce for this last week (or seven years) with the Jews; but since the Jews grew rebellious, the Romans returned in three years and destroyed Jerusalem. Now, how does this bear out Gabriel, who says that the peace or truce—as they interpret the word "covenant"—is to last seven years? If it did not endure longer than three years, then Gabriel, who speaks of seven years or the last week, must be lying. Thus the mendacious hearts of these incorrigible liars falsely impugn the truthfulness of the angel Gabriel. Alas, what truce? What peace? Read Josephus and the history books and you will learn that the Romans slew many thousands of Jews a long time before, and that there was no peace up to the time when they were constrained to destroy Jerusalem and the country.

The tenth and final lie concerns the assertion that the destruction of Jerusalem will last until the end of the strife. They interpret this as meaning:

until the strife of their Messiah, who will kill Gog and Magog and conquer the whole world.[73] This is a vicious, miserable lie that's dead before it's born. Let those who maintain that the Messiah appeared before the expiration of the 70 weeks be informed that such a lie was discredited as long as 1,500 years ago. Thus the Jews don't retain a single word of Gabriel's statement intact; they pervert all his words into lies, with the exception of the angel's prophecy regarding the destruction of Jerusalem. But no one need thank them for believing that and admitting the truth of it now. While they still inhabited Jerusalem, they believed this prophecy still less than they believe now in our Messiah, although it was foretold plainly enough, here in Daniel 9 as well as in Zechariah 14. If they were still dwelling in Jerusalem today, they would invent 100,000 lies before they would believe it, just as their ancestors did prior to the first destruction. The latter were not persuaded by any prophet that the holy city of God would be laid waste. They harried them, they raved like mad dogs until they stood face to face with the fulfillment of the prophecy. This has always been a stiff-necked, unbelieving, proud, base, incorrigible people, and so it ever remains.

From all of this, we gather that Daniel with his 70 weeks takes our position against the Jews' lies and folly, a position as reliable and firm as an iron wall and an immovable rock, affirming that the true Messiah must have come before the termination of the 70 weeks; that he was killed and made alive again; that he fulfilled God's covenant (why should Daniel here be speaking of the Gentiles' covenant, which, moreover, did not even exist at the time?) in the last week; that he thereby took leave of the city and the people at the end of the 70 weeks; that the city was razed by the Romans shortly after; that the people were destroyed, with their government and all they had—all of this in accordance with the angel's words: "Seventy weeks of years are decreed or reckoned concerning your people and your holy city" [Dan 9:24]. But enough!

No doubt it's necessary for the Jews to lie and to misinterpret in order to maintain their error in light of such a clear and powerful text. Their pre-

---

[73] Gog and Magog are obscure terms that refer, variously, to individual people, to groups of people, or to lands. They are cited in Genesis 10:2 (Magog only), Ezekiel 38-39, and Revelation 20:8.

Part II

vious lies broke down under their own weight. But even if they were to lie for 100,000 years and call all the devils in to aid them, they would still come to naught. It's impossible to name a Messiah at the time of the 70 weeks, as Gabriel's revelation would necessitate, other than our Lord Jesus Christ. We are certain, sure, and cheerful about this, as we snap our fingers at all the gates of hell and defy them, together with all the gates of the world and everything that wants to be or might be exalted, smart, and wise against us. I, a plain insignificant saint in Christ, venture to oppose all of them singlehandedly and to defend this viewpoint easily, comfortably, and gladly. However, it's impossible to convert the devil and his own, nor are we commanded to attempt this. It suffices to uncover their lies and to reveal the truth. Whoever is not motivated to believe the truth for the sake of his own soul will surely not believe it for my sake.

We will limit ourselves for the time being to these four texts—those of Jacob, David, Haggai, and Daniel—wherein we see what a fine job the Jews have done these 1,500 years with Scripture, and what a fine job they still do. Their treatment of these texts parallels their treatment of all others, especially those that are in favor of us and our Messiah. These, of course, must be accounted as lies, whereas they themselves cannot err or be mistaken. However, the Jews have not acquired a perfect mastery of the art of lying; they lie so clumsily and ineptly that anyone who is just a little observant can easily detect it.

But for we Christians, they stand as a terrifying example of God's wrath. As St. Paul declares in Romans 11, we must fear God and honor his word as long as the time of grace remains, so that we don't meet with a similar or worse fate. We have seen this happen in the case of the papacy and of Muhammad. The example of the Jews demonstrates clearly how easily the devil can mislead people, after they once have digressed from the proper understanding of Scripture, into such blindness and darkness that it can be readily grasped and perceived simply by natural reason, yes, even by irrational beasts. And yet they who daily teach and hear God's word don't recognize this darkness but regard it as the true light. O Lord God, have mercy on us!

On the Jews and Their Lies

If I had to refute all the other articles of the Jewish faith, I would be obliged to write against them as much and for as long a time as they have used for inventing their lies—that is, longer than 2,000 years. I stated earlier that they corrupt their circumcision with human ordinances and ruin their heritage with their arrogance. In the same manner, they also desecrate their Sabbath and all their festivals. In brief, all their life and all their deeds, whether they eat, drink, sleep, wake, stand, walk, dress, undress, fast, bathe, pray, or praise, are so sullied with rabbinical, foul ordinances and unbelief, that Moses can no longer be recognized among them. This corresponds to the situation of the papacy in our day, in which Christ and his word can hardly be recognized because of the great vermin of human ordinances. However, let this suffice for the time being on their lies against doctrine or faith.

PART III

SLANDER AGAINST THE LORD

To conclude the above, we want to examine their lies against persons, which, after all, don't make the doctrine either worse or better, whether the persons are pious or base. Specifically, we want to look at their lies about the person of our Lord, as well as those about his dear mother and about ourselves and all Christians. These lies are such as the devil resorts to when he cannot assail the doctrine. Then he turns against the person—lying, maligning, cursing, and ranting against him.[74] That's what the papists' Beelzebub did to me.[75] When he was unable to refute my gospel, he wrote that I was possessed of the devil, that I was a changeling, that my dear mother was a whore and a bathhouse attendant. Of course, no sooner had he written this than my gospel was destroyed, and the papists carried the day!

Similarly, John the Baptist and Christ himself were charged with having a devil[76] and were called Samaritans—and shortly thereafter John's and Christ's doctrine was shown to be false, and that of the Pharisees true. The same thing happened to all the prophets. Recently also, when the stealthy, murdering arsonist of Wolfenbüttel[77]—who, next to the archbishop of Mainz, is the holy Roman Church's one relic and jewel—shamefully slandered and defamed the persons of the elector of Saxony and the landgrave of Hesse, both were instantly doomed; but he, the holy man, king over all kings, was crowned with a diadem and gold so heavy that he couldn't bear it and had to flee.

---

[74] This is the classic *ad hominem* logical fallacy.

[75] Probably Johann Eck (1486-1543).

[76] See Matt 11:18 and John 8:20.

[77] Henry V, Duke of Brunswick-Luneberg (1489-1568).

On the Jews and Their Lies

Therefore, whenever you wish to win in an evil cause, do as they do and as the glib babblers do in court when the silver- or gold-fever seizes them: Scold and lie boldly about the person, and your cause will win out. It's like the mother who instructed her child: "Dear son, if you cannot win otherwise, start a brawl." These are lies in which the liar doesn't fabricate or err in the chief question at issue—as happens also in religious disputes—but nevertheless is well aware that he's lying and wants to lie against the person. He doesn't dream of proving his point, either by appearances or by truth, and is unable to do so.

That's how the Jews, too, are acting in this instance. They blatantly inveigh and lie against and curse the person, against their own conscience. In that way, they have long since won their case, so that God had to listen to them. Already for 1,500 years, they have been sitting in Jerusalem, in a golden city, as we can clearly see. They are the lords of the world, and all the Gentiles flock to them with their *chemdath*, their coats, pants, and shoes, and permit themselves to be slain by the noble princes and lords of Israel, giving them land and people and all that they have, while the Jews curse, spit on, and malign the Goyim.

And you can well imagine that if they would not lie so outrageously, curse, defame, blaspheme, and revile the persons, God would not have heard them, and their cause would have been lost long ago; they would not be lords in Jerusalem today but live dispersed over the world, without seeing Jerusalem, and making their living among the accursed Goyim by means of lying, cheating, stealing, robbing, usury, and all sorts of other vices. So effective is it, to curse the person if the cause in question is evil and therefore doomed! Consequently, if you have a poor cause to defend, don't overlook this example of the Jews. They are the noble princes of Israel who are capable of everything. When their cause is lost, they still can curse the Goyim thoroughly.

In the first place, they defame our Lord Jesus Christ, calling him a sorcerer and tool of the devil. This they do because they cannot deny his miracles. Thus, they imitate their forefathers, who said, "He casts out demons by Beelzebub, the prince of demons" [Luke 11:15]. They

Part III

invent many lies about the name of God, the tetragrammaton, saying that our Lord was able to define this name—which they call *Schem Hamphoras*[78]—and whoever is able to do that, they say, is also able to perform all sorts of miracles. However, they cannot cite a single instance of any men who worked a miracle worth a gnat by means of this *Schem Hamphoras*. It's evident that as consummate liars, they fabricate this about our Lord. If such a rule of *Schem Hamphoras* were true, someone else would have employed it before or afterward. Otherwise, how could one know that such power inhered in the *Schem Hamphoras*? But this is too big a subject; after this booklet is finished, I plan to issue a special essay and relate what Porchetus writes on this subject. It serves them right that, rejecting the truth of God, they have to believe instead such abominable, stupid, inane lies, and that instead of the beautiful face of the divine word, they have to look into the devil's black, dark, lying behind, and worship his stench.

In addition, they rob Jesus of the significance of his name, which in Hebrew means "savior" or "helper." The name Helfrich or Hilfrich was common among the old Saxons; this is the equivalent of the name Jesus. Today we might use the name Hulfrich—that is, one who can and will help. But the Jews, in their malice, call him Jesu, which in Hebrew is neither a name nor a word but three letters, like ciphers or numeral letters. It's as if, for example, I were to take the three numeral letters C, L, and U as ciphers and form the word CLU. That is 155. In this manner, they use the name Jesu, signifying 316. This number then is to denote another word, in which *Hebel Vorik*[79] is found. For further information on their devilish practices with such numbers and words, you may read Anthony Margaritha.[80]

---

[78] 'Unknowable name'.

[79] A phrase from Isaiah 30:7, meaning "utterly worthless." (Sometimes written '*hebel wariq*'.)

[80] Margaritha (ca. 1500 – 1570) was a scholarly Jew who converted to Christianity in 1522. He subsequently published a book, *The Whole Jewish Faith* (1530), that exposed the many sordid practices of Jews in their synagogues.

On the Jews and Their Lies

When a Christian hears them utter the word "Jesu," as will happen occasionally when they are obliged to speak to us, he assumes that they are using the name Jesus. But in reality they have the numeral letters Jesu in mind, that is, the numeral 316 in the blasphemous word *Vorik*. And when they utter the word "Jesu" in their prayer, they spit on the ground three times in honor of our Lord and of all Christians, moved by their great love and devotion. But when they are conversing with one another, they say, *Deleatur nomen eius*, which means in plain words, "May God exterminate his name," or "May all the devils take him."

They treat us Christians similarly in receiving us when we go to them. They pervert the words *Seid Gott willkommen* ["Be welcome to God"] and say, *Sched wil kem!* which means: "Come, devil," or "There comes a devil." Since we aren't conversant with the Hebrew, they can vent their wrath on us secretly. While we suppose that they are speaking kindly to us, they are calling down hellfire and every misfortune on our heads. Such splendid guests we poor, pious Christians are, harboring in our country in the persons of the Jews—we who mean well with them, who would gladly serve their physical and spiritual welfare, and who suffer so many coarse wrongs from them.

Then they also call Jesus a whore's son, saying that his mother Mary was a whore, who conceived him in adultery with a blacksmith. I have to speak in this coarse manner, although I do so with great reluctance, to combat the vile devil. Now, they know very well that these lies are inspired by sheer hatred and spite, solely for the purpose of bitterly poisoning the minds of their poor youth and the simple Jews against the person of our Lord, lest they adhere to his doctrine, which they cannot refute. Still they claim to be the holy people to whom God must grant the Messiah by reason of their righteousness! In the eighth commandment, God forbade us to speak falsehoods against our neighbor, to lie, to deceive, to revile, to defile. This prohibition also includes one's enemies. When Zedekiah did not keep faith with the king of Babylon, he was severely rebuked for his lie by Jeremiah and Ezekiel and was also led into wretched captivity because of it.

PART III

However, our noble princes of the world and circumcised saints, against this commandment of God, invented this beautiful doctrine: namely, that they may freely lie, blaspheme, curse, defame, murder, rob, and commit every vice, however, whenever, and on whom they wish. Let God keep his own commandment: the noble blood and circumcised people will violate it as they desire and please. Despite this, they insist that they are doing right and good and meriting the Messiah and heaven thereby. They challenge God and all the angels to refute this, not to speak of the devil and the accursed Goyim who find fault with it; here is the noble blood which cannot sin and which is not subject to God's commands.

What harm has the poor maiden Mary done to them? How can they prove that she was a whore? She did no more than bear a son, whose name is Jesus. Is it such a great crime for a young wife to bear a child? Or are all who bear children to be accounted whores? What, then, is to be said about their own wives and about themselves? Are they, too, all whores and children of whores? You accursed Goyim, that's a different story! Don't you know that the Jews are Abraham's noble blood, circumcised, and kings in heaven and on earth? Whatever they say is right. If there were a virgin among the accursed Goyim as pure and holy as the angel Gabriel, and the least of these noble princes were to say that she is an arch-whore and viler than the devil, it would necessarily have to be so. The fact that a noble mouth of the lineage of Abraham said this would be sufficient proof. Who dares contradict him? Conversely, any arch-whore of the noble blood of the Jews, though she were as ugly as the devil himself, would still be purer than any angel if the noble lords were pleased to say this. The noble, circumcised lords have the authority to lie, to defame, revile, blaspheme, and curse the accursed Goyim as they wish. On the other hand, they are privileged to bless, honor, praise, and exalt themselves, even if God disagrees with them. Do you suppose that a Jew is such a bad fellow? God in heaven and all the angels have to laugh and dance when they hear a Jew pass wind, so that you accursed Goyim may know what excellent fellows the Jews are. How could they be so bold as to call Mary a whore, with whom they can find no fault, if they were not vested with the power to trample God and his commandment under foot?

Well and good, you and I, as accursed Goyim, wish to submit a simple illustration by means of which we, as benighted heathen, might comprehend this lofty wisdom of the noble, holy Jews a little. Let's suppose that I had a cousin or another close blood relative of whom I knew no evil, and in whom I had never detected any evil; and other people, against whom I bore a grudge, praised and extolled her, regarded her as an excellent, pious, virtuous, laudable woman, and said: This dunce is not worthy of having such a fine, honorable woman as his cousin; a she-dog or a she-wolf would be more fit for him. Then I, upon hearing such eulogies of my cousin spoken, would begin to say, against my own conscience: They are all lying, she is an arch-whore. And now I would, though lacking any proof, demand that everyone believe me, despite the fact that I was well aware of my cousin's innocence, while I, a consummate liar, was cursing all who refused to believe my lie—which I knew in my heart to be just that.

Tell me, how would you regard me? Would you not feel impelled to say that I was not a human being but a monster, a repulsive fiend, unworthy of gazing at sun, leaves, grass, or any creature? Indeed, you would consider me to be possessed by devils. I should rather treat my cousin's disgrace, if I knew of any, as though it were my own, and cover it up if it threatened to become public, just as all other people do. But although no one, including myself, knows anything but honorable things about her, I dare to step to the fore and defame my cousin as a scoundrel, with false slander, oblivious to the fact that this shame reflects on me.

«««—»»»

That's the type of human beings—if I should or could call them that—that these noble, circumcised saints are. We Goyim, with whom they are

Part III

hostile and angry, confess that Mary is not ours but rather the Jews' cousin and blood relative, descended from Abraham.[81] When we praise and laud her highly, they proceed to defame her viciously. If there were a genuine drop of Israelite blood in such miserable Jews, do you not suppose that they would say: "'What are we to do? Can she help it that her son provoked our ire? Why should we slander her? After all, she is our flesh and blood. It has undoubtedly happened before that a bad son issued from a pious mother." No, such human and responsible thoughts won't occur to these holy people; they must entertain nothing but devilish, base, lying thoughts, so that they may in that way do penance and merit the Messiah soon—as they have, of course, merited him now for 1,500 years.

They further lie and slander him and his mother by saying that she conceived him at an unnatural time. About this they are most malicious and malignant and malevolent. In Leviticus 20:18 Moses declares that a man must not approach a woman, nor a woman a man, during the female's menstrual uncleanness. This is forbidden on pain of loss of life and limb; whatever is conceived at such a time results in imperfect and infirm fruit, that is, in insane children, mental deficients, demon's offspring, changelings, and the like—people who have unbalanced minds all their lives. In this way the Jews would defame us Christians, by saying that we honor as the Messiah a person who was mentally deficient from birth, or some sort of demon. These most intelligent, circumcised, highly enlightened saints regard us as such stupid and accursed Goyim. Truly, these are the devil's own thoughts and words!

Do you ask what prompts them to write this, or what is the cause of it? You stupid, accursed Goy, why should you ask that? Does it not satisfy you to know that this is said by the noble, circumcised saints? Are you so slow to learn that such a holy people is exempt from all the decrees of God and cannot sin? They may lie, blaspheme, defame, and

---

[81] It's clear that Mary was Jewish. She was "born under the law [of Judaism]" (Gal 4:4), and was a relative of Elizabeth of the tribe of Levi (Luke 1:5). She and Joseph attended Passover every year (Luke 2:41), and both of them "performed everything according to the [Jewish] law" (Luke 2:39).

murder whom they will, even God himself and all his prophets. All of this must be accounted as nothing but a fine service rendered to God. Did I not tell you earlier that a Jew is such a noble, precious jewel that God and all the angels dance when he farts? And if he were to go on to do something coarser than that, they would nevertheless expect it to be regarded as a golden Talmud. Whatever issues from such a holy man, from above or from below, must surely be considered by the accursed Goyim to be pure holiness.

If a Jew were not so precious and noble, how would it be possible for him to despise all Christians with their Messiah and his mother so thoroughly, to vilify them with such malicious and poisonous lies? If these fine, pure, smart saints would only concede us the qualities of geese or ducks, since they refuse to let us pass for human beings! The stupidity that they ascribe to us I could not assign to any sow, which, as we know, covers itself with mire from head to foot and doesn't eat anything much cleaner. Alas, it cannot be anything but the terrible wrath of God that permits anyone to sink into such abysmal, devilish, hellish, insane baseness, envy, and arrogance. If I were to avenge myself on the devil himself, I would be unable to wish him such evil and misfortune as God's wrath inflicts on the Jews, compelling them to lie and to blaspheme so monstrously, in violation of their own conscience. Anyway, they have their reward for constantly giving God the lie.

In his Bible, Sebastian Münster relates that a malicious rabbi does not call the dear mother of Christ *Maria* but *haria*—i.e., *sterquilinium*, a dung heap. And who knows what other villainy they may indulge in among themselves, unknown to us? One can readily perceive how the devil constrains them to the basest lies and blasphemies he can contrive. Thus they also begrudge the dear mother Mary, the daughter of David, her right name, although she has done them no harm. If they do that, why should they not also begrudge her, her life, her goods, and her honor? And if they wish and inflict all kinds of disgrace and evil on their own flesh and blood, which is innocent and about which they know nothing evil, what, do you suppose, might they wish us accursed Goyim?

Part III

Yet they presume to step before God with such a heart and mouth; they utter, worship, and invoke his holy name, entreating him to return them to Jerusalem, to send them the Messiah, to kill all the Gentiles, and to present them with all the goods of the world. The only reason that God doesn't visit them with thunder and lightning, that he doesn't deluge them suddenly with fire as he did Sodom and Gomorrah, is this: This punishment would not be commensurate with such malice. Therefore, he strikes them with spiritual thunder and lightning, as Moses writes in Deuteronomy 28:28 among other places: "The Lord will smite you with madness and blindness and confusion of mind." Those are, indeed, the true strokes of lightning and thunder: madness, blindness, confusion of mind.

Although these terrible, slanderous, blasphemous lies are directed particularly against the person of our Lord and his dear mother, they are also intended for our own persons. They want to offer us the greatest affront and insult for honoring a Messiah whom they curse and malign so terribly that they don't consider him worthy of being named by them or any human being, much less of being revered. Thus we must pay for believing in him, for praising, honoring, and serving him.

I would like to ask, however: What harm has the poor man Jesus done to these holy people? If he was a false teacher, as they allege, he was punished for it; for this he received his due, for this he suffered with a shameful death on the cross, for this he paid and rendered satisfaction. No accursed heathen in all the world will persecute and malign forever and ever a poor dead man who suffered his punishment for his misdeeds. How, then, does it happen that these most holy, blessed Jews outdo the accursed heathen? To begin with, they declare that Jerusalem was not destroyed nor were they led into captivity for their sin of crucifying Jesus. They claim to have done the right thing when they meted out justice to the seducer and thus merited their Messiah. Is it the fault of the dead man, who has now met his judgment, that we Goyim are so stupid and foolish as to honor him as our Messiah? Why do they not settle the issue with us, convince us of our folly and demonstrate their

On the Jews and Their Lies

lofty, heavenly wisdom? We have never fled from them; we are still standing our ground and defying their holy wisdom. Let's see what they are able to do. It is most unseemly for such great saints to crawl into a corner and to curse and scold in hiding.

Now as I began to ask earlier: What harm has the poor Jesus done to the most holy children of Israel that they cannot stop cursing him after his death, with which he paid his debt? Is it perhaps that he aspires to be the Messiah, which they cannot tolerate? Oh no, for he is dead. They themselves crucified him, and a dead person cannot be the Messiah. Perhaps he's an obstacle to their return into their homeland? No, that's not the reason either; how can a dead man prevent that? What, then, is the reason? I'll tell you. As I said before, it is the lightning and thunder of Moses to which I referred before: "The Lord will smite you with madness and blindness and confusion of mind." It is the eternal fire of which the prophets speak: "My wrath will go forth like fire and burn with none to quench it" [Jer 4:4]. John the Baptist proclaimed the same message to them after Herod had removed their scepter, saying [Luke 3:17]: "His winnowing fork is in his hand, and he will clear his threshing-floor and gather his wheat into his granary, but his chaff he will burn with unquenchable fire." Indeed, such fire of divine wrath we behold descending on the Jews. We see it burning, ablaze and aflame, a fire more horrible than that of Sodom and Gomorrah.

«««—»»»

Now such devilish lies and blasphemy are aimed at the person of Christ and of his dear mother; but our person and that of all Christians are also involved. They are also thinking of us. Because Christ and Mary are dead and because we Christians are such vile people to honor these despicable, dead persons, they also assign us our special share of slander. In the first place, they lament before God that we are holding them captive in exile, and they implore him ardently to deliver his holy people and

Part III

dear children from our power and the imprisonment in which we hold them. They dub us Edom and Haman, with which names they would insult us grievously before God, and hurt us deeply. However, it would carry us too far afield to enlarge on this. They know very well that they are lying here. If it were possible, I would not be ashamed to claim Edom as my forefather. He was the natural son of the saintly Rebekah, the grandson of the dear Sarah; Abraham was his grandfather and Isaac his real father. Moses himself commands them to regard Edom as their brother (Deut 23:7). They indeed obey Moses as true Jews!

Further, they presume to instruct God and prescribe the manner in which he is to redeem them. For the Jews, these very learned saints look upon God as a poor cobbler equipped with only a left last for making shoes. This is to say that he is to kill and exterminate all of us Goyim through their Messiah, so that they can lay their hands on the land, the goods, and the government of the whole world. And now a storm breaks over us with curses, defamation, and derision that cannot be expressed with words. They wish that sword and war, distress and every misfortune may overtake us accursed Goyim. They vent their curses on us openly every Saturday in their synagogues and daily in their homes. They teach, urge, and train their children from infancy to remain the bitter, virulent, and wrathful enemies of the Christians.

This gives you a clear picture of their conception of the fifth commandment and their observation of it. They have been bloodthirsty bloodhounds and murderers of all Christendom for more than 1,400 years in their intentions and would undoubtedly prefer to be such with their deeds. Thus they have been accused of poisoning water and wells, of kidnaping children, of piercing them through with an awl, of hacking them in pieces, and in that way secretly cooling their wrath with the blood of Christians, for all of which they have often been condemned to death by fire. And still God refused to lend an ear to the holy penitence of such great saints and dearest children. The unjust God lets such holy people curse—I wanted to say "pray"—so vehemently in vain against our Messiah and all Christians. He doesn't care to see or have anything to do either with them or with their pious conduct, which is so thickly, thickly, heavily, heavily coated with the blood of the Messiah and his Christians. These Jews are much holier than were those in the Babylonian captivity, who did not curse, who did not secretly shed the blood of children, nor poison the water, but who rather, as Jeremiah had instructed them [Jer 29:7], prayed for their captors, the Babylonians. The reason is that they weren't as holy as the present-day Jews, nor did they have such smart rabbis as the present-day Jews have; for Jeremiah, Daniel, and Ezekiel were big fools to teach this. They would, I suppose, be torn to shreds by the teeth of today's Jews.

Now behold what a fine, thick, fat lie they pronounce when they say that *they* are held captive by *us*. Jerusalem was destroyed over 1,400 years ago, and at that time, we Christians were harassed and persecuted by the Jews throughout the world for about 300 years, as we said earlier. We might well complain that during that time they held us Christians captive and killed us, which is the plain truth. Furthermore, we don't know to the present day which devil brought them into our country. We surely did not bring them from Jerusalem.

In addition, no one is holding them here now. The country and the roads are open for them to proceed to their land whenever they wish. If they did so, we would be glad to present gifts to them on the occasion; it would be good riddance. They are a heavy burden, a plague, a pestilence, a sheer misfortune for our country. Proof for this is found in the fact that they have often been expelled forcibly from a country, far from being held captive in it. Thus they were banished from France[82] (which they call *Tsorfath*, from Obadiah [20][83]), which was an especially fine nest. Very recently they were banished by our dear Emperor Charles from Spain,[84] the very best nest of all (which they called *Sefarad*, also on the basis of Obadiah[85]). This year they were expelled from the entire

---

[82] By King Charles VI in 1394.

[83] Most translations use the name 'Zarephath,' which is generally understood to refer to the city of Sarepta, in present-day Lebanon. Needless to say, this is a long way from France.

[84] In 1492.

Part III

Bohemian crownland, where they had one of the best nests, in Prague.[86] Likewise, during my lifetime they have been driven from Regensburg, Magdeburg, and other places.[87]

If you cannot tolerate a person in a country or home, does that constitute holding him in captivity? In fact, they hold us Christians captive in our own country. They let us work with the sweat of our brow to earn money and property, while they sit behind the stove, idle away the time, fart, and roast pears. They stuff themselves, guzzle, and live in luxury and ease from our hard-earned goods. With their accursed usury, they hold us and our property captive. Moreover, they mock and deride us because we work and let them play the role of lazy squires at our expense and in our land. Thus they are our masters and we are their servants, with our property, our sweat, and our labor. And by way of reward and thanks, they curse our Lord and us! Should the devil not laugh and dance if he can enjoy such a fine paradise at the expense of us Christians? He devours what is ours through his saints, the Jews, and repays us by insulting us, in addition to mocking and cursing both God and man.

They couldn't have enjoyed such good times in Jerusalem under David and Solomon with their own possessions as they now do with ours, which they daily steal and rob. And yet they wail that *we* have taken *them* captive. Indeed, we have captured them and hold them in captivity, just as I hold captive my gallstone, my bloody tumor, and all the other ailments and misfortunes that I have to nurse and take care of with money and goods and all that I have. Alas, I wish that they were in Jerusalem with the Jews and whomever else they would like to have there.

---

[85] Spanish Jews referred to the entire Iberian Peninsula (i.e. Spain and Portugal) as 'Sefarad' or 'Sepharad.' To this day, Jews whose ancestry is based there are called Sephardic Jews.

[86] In 1543.

[87] Jews were expelled from Regensburg in 1519, and from Magdeburg in 1492. Jewish expulsions also occurred in England (1290), Hungary (1360), Switzerland (1392), Austria (1421), Lithuania (1495), Portugal (1497), and the cities of Nuremburg (1499) and Naples (1510).

On the Jews and Their Lies

Since it has now been established that we do not hold them captive, how does it happen that we deserve the enmity of such noble and great saints? We don't call their women whores, as they do Mary, Jesus' mother. We don't call them children of whores, as they do our Lord Jesus. We don't say that they were conceived at the time of cleansing and were thus born as idiots, as they say of our Lord. We don't say that their women are *haria*, as they do with regard to our dear Mary. We don't curse them but wish them well, physically and spiritually. We lodge them, we let them eat and drink with us. We don't kidnap their children and pierce them through; we don't poison their wells; we don't thirst for their blood. How, then, do we incur such terrible anger, envy, and hatred on the part of such great and holy children of God?

There's no other explanation for this than the one cited earlier from Moses—namely, that God has struck them with "madness and blindness and confusion of mind." So we are even at fault in not avenging all this innocent blood of our Lord and of the Christians which they shed for 300 years after the destruction of Jerusalem, and the blood of the children they have shed since then—which still shines forth from their eyes and their skin. We are at fault in not slaying them.

Rather we allow them to live freely in our midst, despite all their murdering, cursing, blaspheming, lying, and defaming; we protect and shield their synagogues, houses, life, and property. In this way we make them lazy and secure and encourage them to fleece us boldly of our money and goods, as well as to mock and deride us, with a view to finally overcoming us, killing us all for such a great sin, and robbing us of all our property—as they daily pray and hope. Now tell me whether they don't have every reason to be the enemies of us accursed Goyim, to curse us and to strive for our final, complete, and eternal ruin!

PART IV

A PLAN OF ACTION

From all of this, we Christians see—for the Jews cannot see it—what terrible wrath of God these people have incurred and still incur without ceasing, what a fire is gleaming and glowing there, and what they achieve who curse and detest Christ and his Christians. O dear Christians, let's take this horrible example to heart, as St. Paul says in Romans 11, and fear God lest we also finally fall victim to such wrath, and even worse! Rather, as we said also earlier, let's honor his divine word and not neglect the time of grace, as Muhammad and the pope have already neglected it, becoming not much better than the Jews.

What shall we Christians do with this rejected and condemned people, the Jews? Since they live among us, we dare not tolerate their conduct, now that we are aware of their lying and reviling and blaspheming. If we do, we become sharers in their lies, cursing, and blasphemy. Thus, we cannot extinguish the unquenchable fire of divine wrath, of which the prophets speak, nor can we convert the Jews. With prayer and the fear of God, we must practice a sharp mercy[88] to see whether we might save at least a few from the glowing flames. We dare not avenge ourselves. Vengeance a thousand times worse than we could wish them already has them by the throat. I shall give you my sincere advice:

First, to set fire to their synagogues or schools, and to bury and cover with dirt whatever won't burn, so that no man will ever again see a stone or cinder of them. This is to be done in honor of our Lord and of Christendom, so that God might see that we are Christians, and don't

---

[88] In original, *"scharfe Barmherzigkeit."*

condone or knowingly tolerate such public lying, cursing, and blaspheming of his Son and of his Christians. Whatever we tolerated in the past unknowingly—and I myself was unaware of it—will be pardoned by God. But if we, now that we are informed, were to protect and shield such a house for the Jews, existing right before our very nose, in which they lie about, blaspheme, curse, vilify, and defame Christ and us (as was heard above), it would be the same as if *we* were doing all this and even worse ourselves, as we very well know.

In Deuteronomy 13:12 Moses writes that any city that is given to idolatry shall be totally destroyed by fire, and nothing of it shall be preserved. If he were alive today, he would be the first to set fire to the synagogues and houses of the Jews. In Deuteronomy 4:2 and 12:32 he commanded very explicitly that nothing is to be added to or subtracted from his law. And Samuel says in 1 Samuel 15:23 that disobedience to God is idolatry. Now, the Jews' doctrine at present is nothing but the additions of the rabbis and the idolatry of disobedience, so that Moses has become entirely unknown among them (as we said before), just as the Bible became unknown under the papacy in our day. So also, for Moses' sake, their schools cannot be tolerated; they defame him just as much as they do us. It's not necessary that they have their own free churches for such idolatry.

Second, I advise that their houses also be razed and destroyed. They pursue in them the same aims as in their synagogues. Instead they might be lodged under a roof or in a barn, like the gypsies. This will bring home to them the fact that they are not masters in our country, as they boast, but that they are living in exile and in captivity, as they incessantly wail and lament about us before God.

Third, I advise that all their prayer books and Talmudic writings, in which such idolatry, lies, cursing, and blasphemy are taught, be taken from them.

Fourth, I advise that their rabbis be forbidden to teach henceforth, on pain of loss of life and limb. They have justly forfeited the right to such an office by holding the poor Jews captive with the saying of

Part IV

Moses (Deuteronomy 17:10) in which he commands them to obey their teachers on penalty of death, although Moses clearly adds: "what they teach you in accord with the law of the Lord." Those villains ignore that. They wantonly employ the poor people's obedience contrary to the law of the Lord and infuse them with this poison, cursing, and blasphemy. In the same way, the pope also held us captive with the declaration in Matthew 18:18, "You are Peter," etc., inducing us to believe all the lies and deceptions that issued from his devilish mind. He didn't teach in accord with the word of God, and therefore he forfeited the right to teach.

Fifth, I advise that safe-conduct on the highways be abolished completely for the Jews. They have no business in the countryside, since they are not lords, officials, tradesmen, or the like. Let them stay at home. I have heard it said that a rich Jew is now traveling across the country with 12 horses—his ambition is to become a Kokhba—devouring princes, lords, lands, and people with his usury, so that the great lords view it with jealous eyes.[89] If you great lords and princes won't forbid such usurers the highway legally, someday a troop may gather against them, having learned from this booklet the true nature of the Jews and how one should deal with them and not protect their activities.[90] You, too, must not and cannot protect them unless you wish to become participants in all their abominations in the sight of God. Consider carefully what good could come from this, and prevent it.

Sixth, I advise that usury be prohibited to them, and that all cash and treasure of silver and gold be taken from them and put aside for safekeeping. The reason for such a measure is that, as said above, they have no other means of earning a livelihood than usury, and by it they have stolen and robbed from us all they possess. Such money should now be used in no other way than the following: Whenever a Jew is sincerely

---

[89] Likely Michael of Derenburg (circa 1490 – 1549), the best-known Jewish banker of the day.

[90] Luther apparently is (rightly) concerned that authorities lack the will to enact such measures, and thus he seems to endorse the idea of vigilante justice—of the people taking action into their own hands.

converted, he should be handed 100, 200, or 300 florins, as personal circumstances may suggest. With this he could set himself up in some occupation for the support of his poor wife and children, and the maintenance of the old or feeble. Such evil gains are cursed if they aren't put to use with God's blessing in a good and worthy cause.

But when they boast that Moses allowed or commanded them to exact usury from strangers, citing Deuteronomy 23:20—apart from this, they cannot adduce as much as a letter in their support—we must tell them that there are two classes of Jews or Israelites. The first comprises those whom Moses, in compliance with God's command, led from Egypt into the land of Canaan. To them he issued his law, which they were to keep in that country and not beyond it, and then only until the advent of the Messiah. The other Jews are those of the emperor and not of Moses. These date back to the time of Pilate, the procurator of the land of Judah. When the latter asked them before the judgment seat, "Then what shall I do with Jesus who is called Christ?" they all said, "Crucify him, crucify him!" He said to them, "Shall I crucify your King?" They shouted in reply, "We have no king but Caesar!" [Matt 27:22; John 19:15]. God had not commanded of them such submission to the emperor; they gave it voluntarily.

But when the emperor *demanded* the obedience due him, they resisted and rebelled against him. Now they no longer wanted to be his subjects. Then he came and visited his subjects, gathered them in Jerusalem, and then scattered them throughout his entire empire, so that they were forced to obey him. From these, the present remnant of Jews descended, of whom Moses knows nothing, nor they of him; they don't deserve a single passage or verse of Moses. If they wish to apply Moses' law again, they must first return to the land of Canaan, become Moses' Jews, and keep his laws. There they may practice usury as much as strangers will endure from them. But since they are dwelling in and disobeying Moses in foreign countries under the emperor, they are bound to keep the emperor's laws and refrain from the practice of usury until they become obedient to Moses. Moses' law has never passed a

Part IV

single step beyond the land of Canaan or beyond the people of Israel. Moses wasn't sent to the Egyptians, the Babylonians, or any other nation with his law, but only to the people whom he led from Egypt into the land of Canaan, as he himself testifies frequently in Deuteronomy. They were expected to keep his commandments in the land that they would conquer beyond the Jordan.

Moreover, since priesthood, worship, government—with which the greater part, indeed, almost all, of those laws of Moses deal—have been at an end for over 1,400 years already, it's certain that Moses' law also came to an end and lost its authority. Therefore the imperial laws must be applied to these imperial Jews. Their wish to be Mosaic Jews must not be indulged. In fact, no Jew has been that for over 1,400 years.

Seventh, I recommend putting a flail, an axe, a hoe, a spade, a distaff, or a spindle into the hands of young, strong Jews and Jewesses and letting them earn their bread with the sweat of their brow, as was imposed on the children of Adam (Gen 3:19). It isn't fitting that they should let us accursed Goyim toil in the sweat of our faces while they, the holy people, idle away their time behind the stove, feasting and farting, and on top of all, boasting blasphemously of their lordship over the Christians by means of our sweat. No, one should toss out these lazy rogues by the seat of their pants.

But if we're afraid that they might harm us or our wives, children, servants, cattle, etc., if they had to serve and work for us—it's reasonable to assume that such noble lords of the world and venomous, bitter worms are not accustomed to working and would be very reluctant to humble themselves so deeply before the accursed Goyim—then let's emulate the common sense of other nations such as France, Spain, Bohemia, etc., compute with them how much their usury has extorted from us, seize and divide this among ourselves, but then eject them forever from the country. For, as we have heard, God's anger with them is so intense that gentle mercy will only tend to make them worse and worse, while sharp mercy will reform them but little. Therefore, in any case, away with them!

On the Jews and Their Lies

«‹‹—›››

I hear it said that the Jews donate large sums of money and thus prove beneficial to governments. Yes, but where does this money come from? Not from their own possessions but from that of the lords and subjects whom they plunder and rob by means of usury. Thus the lords are taking from their subjects what they receive from the Jews, i.e., the subjects are obliged to pay additional taxes and let themselves be ground into the dust for the Jews, so that they may remain in the country, lie boldly and freely, blaspheme, curse, and steal. Shouldn't the impious Jews laugh up their sleeves because we let them make such fools of us and because we spend our money to enable them to remain in the country and to practice every malice? Over and above that, we let them get rich on our sweat and blood, while we remain poor and they suck the marrow from our bones. If it's right for a servant to give his master, or for a guest to give his host, ten florins annually and, in return, to steal 1,000 florins from him, then the servant or the guest will very quickly and easily get rich, and the master or the host will soon become a beggar.

And even if the Jews could give the government such sums of money from their own property, which isn't possible, and thereby buy protection from us, and also the privilege to publicly and freely slander, blaspheme, vilify, and curse our Lord Jesus Christ so shamefully in their synagogues, and in addition to wish us every misfortune, namely, that we might all be stabbed to death and perish with our Haman, emperor, princes, lords, wife, and children—even this would really be selling Christ our Lord, the whole of Christendom together with the whole empire, and ourselves, with wife and children, cheaply and shamefully. What a great saint the traitor Judas would be in comparison with us! Indeed, if each Jew, as many as there are of them, could give 100,000 florins annually, we should nevertheless not give them the right to so freely malign, curse, defame, impoverish by usury a single

Part IV

Christian. That would still be far too cheap a price. How much more intolerable is it that we permit the Jews to purchase with our money such license to slander and curse the whole Christ and all of us and, furthermore, reward them for this with riches and make them our lords, while they ridicule us and gloat in their malice. That would prove a delightful spectacle for the devil and his angels, over which they could secretly grin like a sow grins at her litter, but which would indeed merit God's great wrath.

In brief, dear princes and lords, those of you who have Jews under your rule—if my counsel displeases you, find better advice, so that you and we all can be rid of the unbearable, devilish burden of the Jews, lest we become guilty sharers before God in the lies, the blasphemy, the defamation, and the curses that the mad Jews indulge in so freely and wantonly against the person of our Lord Jesus Christ, his dear mother, all Christians, all authority, and ourselves. Don't grant them protection, safe-conduct, or communion with us. Don't aid and abet them in acquiring your money or your subjects' money and property by means of usury. We have enough sin of our own without this, dating back to the papacy, and we add to it daily with our ingratitude and our contempt of God's word and all his grace; so it isn't necessary to burden ourselves also with these alien, shameful vices of the Jews and, over and above it all, to pay them for it with money and property. Consider that we are now daily struggling with the Turks, which surely calls for a lessening of our sins and a reformation of our life. With this faithful counsel and warning, I wish to cleanse and exonerate my conscience.

«««—»»»

And you, my dear gentlemen and friends who are pastors and preachers, I wish to faithfully remind you of your official duty, so that you too may warn your parishioners concerning their eternal harm, as you know how to do—namely, that they be on their guard against the Jews and avoid them so far as possible. They shouldn't curse them or harm their persons, however. The Jews have cursed and harmed themselves more than enough by cursing the Man Jesus of Nazareth, Mary's son, which they unfortunately have been doing for over 1,400 years. Let the government deal with them in this respect, as I have suggested. But whether the government acts or not, let everyone at least be guided by his own conscience, and form for himself a definition or image of a Jew.

When you lay eyes on or think of a Jew, you must say to yourself: Alas, that mouth which I there behold has cursed and execrated and maligned every Saturday my dear Lord Jesus Christ, who has redeemed me with his precious blood; in addition, it prayed and pleaded before God that I, my wife and children, and all Christians might be stabbed to death and perish miserably. And he himself would gladly do this if he were able, in order to appropriate our goods. Perhaps he has spat on the ground many times this very day over the name of Jesus, as is their custom, so that the spittle still clings to his mouth and beard, if he had a chance to spit. If I were to eat, drink, or talk with such a devilish mouth, I would eat or drink myself full of devils by the dish or cupful, just as I surely make myself a cohort of all the devils that dwell in the Jews and that deride the precious blood of Christ. May God preserve me from this!

We cannot help it that they don't share our belief. It's impossible to force anyone to believe. However, we must avoid confirming them in their wanton lying, slandering, cursing, and defaming. Nor dare we make ourselves partners in their devilish ranting and raving by shielding and protecting them, by giving them food, drink, and shelter, or by other neighborly acts, especially since they boast so proudly and despicably when we do help and serve them that God has ordained them as lords and us as servants. For instance, when a Christian kindles their fire for them on a Sabbath, or cooks for them in an inn whatever they want, they curse and defame and revile us for it, supposing this to be something praiseworthy, and yet they live on our wealth, which they have stolen from us. Such a desperate, thoroughly evil, poisonous, and devilish lot are these Jews, who for these 1,400 years have been and still are our plague, our pestilence, and our misfortune.

Part IV

Especially you pastors who have Jews living in your midst, persist in reminding your lords and rulers to be mindful of their office and of their obligation before God to force the Jews to work, to forbid usury, and to check their blasphemy and cursing. If they punish thievery, robbery, murder, blasphemy, and other vices among us Christians, why should the devilish Jews be scot-free to commit their crimes among us and against us? We suffer more from them than the Italians do from the Spaniards,[91] who plunder the host's kitchen, cellar, chest, and purse, and, in addition, curse him and threaten him with death. Thus the Jews, our guests, also treat us; for we are their hosts. They rob and fleece us and hang about our necks, these lazy weaklings and indolent bellies; they swill and feast, enjoy good times in our homes, and by way of reward they curse our Lord Christ, our churches, our princes, and all of us, threatening us and unceasingly wishing us death and every evil.

Just ponder this: How does it happen that we poor Christians nourish and enrich such an idle and lazy people, such a useless, evil, pernicious people, such blasphemous enemies of God, receiving nothing in return but their curses and defamation and every misfortune they may inflict on us or wish us? Indeed, we are as blind and unfeeling clods in this respect as are the Jews in their unbelief, to suffer such great tyranny from these vicious weaklings, and not perceive and sense that they are our lords, yes, our mad tyrants, and that we are their captives and subjects. Meanwhile they wail that they are *our* captives, and at the same time mock us—as though we had to take this from them!

But if the authorities are reluctant to use force and restrain the Jews' devilish wantonness, the latter should, as we said, be expelled from the country. They should be told to return to their land and their possessions in Jerusalem, where they may lie, curse, blaspheme, defame, murder, steal, rob, practice usury, mock, and indulge in all those infamous abominations that they practice among us, and leave us our govern-

---

[91] A reference to Charles I of Spain's invasion of Italy in 1527, which left a train of destruction in its wake.

ment, our country, our life, and our property, much more leave our Lord the Messiah, our faith, and our church undefiled and uncontaminated with their devilish tyranny and malice. Any privileges that they may plead won't help them; no one can grant privileges for practicing such abominations. These cancel and abrogate all privileges.

If you pastors and preachers have followed my example and have faithfully issued such warnings, but neither prince nor subject will do anything about it, let's follow the advice of Christ (Matthew 10:14) and shake the dust from our shoes, and say, "We are innocent of your blood." I observe and have often experienced how indulgent the perverted world is when it should be strict, and, conversely, how harsh it is when it should be merciful. Such was the case with King Ahab, as we find recorded in 1 Kings 20. That's the way the prince of this world reigns. I suppose that the princes will now wish to show mercy to the Jews, the bloodthirsty foes of our Christian and human name, in order to earn heaven thereby. But that the Jews enmesh us, harass us, torment and distress us poor Christians in every way with the above-mentioned devilish and detestable deeds; this they want us to tolerate, and this is a good Christian deed—especially if there is any money involved, which they have filched and stolen from us.

What are we poor preachers to do meanwhile? In the first place, we will believe that our Lord Jesus Christ is truthful when he declares of the Jews who did not accept but crucified him, "You are a brood of vipers and children of the devil" [Matt 12:34]. This is a judgment in which his forerunner John the Baptist concurred, although these people were his kin. Now our authorities and all such merciful saints as wish the Jews well will at least have to let us believe our Lord Jesus Christ, who, I'm sure, has a more intimate knowledge of all hearts than do those compassionate saints. He knows that these Jews are a brood of vipers and children of the devil, that is, people who will accord us the same benefits as does their father, the devil—and by now we Christians should have learned from Scripture as well as experience just how much he wishes us well.

Part IV

I have read and heard many stories about the Jews that agree with this judgment of Christ, namely, how they have poisoned wells, made assassinations, kidnaped children, as related before. I have heard that one Jew sent another Jew—and this by means of a Christian—a pot of blood, together with a barrel of wine, in which when drunk empty, a dead Jew was found. There are many other similar stories. For their kidnaping of children, they have often been burned at the stake or banished (as we already heard). I'm well aware that they deny all of this. However, it all coincides with the judgment of Christ, which declares that they are venomous, bitter, vindictive, tricky serpents, assassins, and children of the devil, who sting and work harm stealthily wherever they cannot do it openly. For this reason, I would like to see them where there are no Christians. The Turks and other heathen don't tolerate what we Christians endure from these venomous serpents and young devils. Nor do the Jews treat any others as they do us Christians. That's what I had in mind when I said earlier that, next to the devil, a Christian has no more bitter and galling foe than a Jew. There is no other to whom we accord as many benefactions and from whom we suffer as much as we do from these base children of the devil, this brood of vipers.

Now, let me commend these Jews sincerely to whoever feels the desire to shelter and feed them, to honor them, to be fleeced, robbed, plundered, defamed, vilified, and cursed by them, and to suffer every evil at their hands—these venomous serpents and devil's children, who are the most vehement enemies of Christ our Lord and of us all. And if that's not enough, let him stuff them into his mouth, or crawl into their behind and worship this holy object. Then let him boast of his mercy, then let him boast that he has strengthened the devil and his brood for further blaspheming our dear Lord and the precious blood with which we Christians are redeemed. Then he will be a perfect Christian, filled with works of mercy—for which Christ will reward him on the day of judgment, together with the Jews—in the eternal fire of hell!

That's speaking coarsely about the coarse cursing of the Jews. Others write much about this, and the Jews know very well that it is cursing, since they curse and blaspheme consciously. Let's also speak more subtly and, as Christians, more spiritually about this. Thus our Lord Jesus Christ says in Matthew 10:40, "He who receives me receives him who sent me." And in Luke 10:16, "He who rejects you rejects me. And he who rejects me rejects him who sent me." And in John 15:23, "He who hates me hates my father also." In John 5:23, "That all may honor the Son, even as they honor the Father. He who does not honor the Son does not honor the Father who sent him," etc.

These are, God be praised, clear and plain words, declaring that all that is done to the honor or to the dishonor of the Son is surely also done to the honor or to the dishonor of God the Father himself. We Christians cannot have or countenance any doubt of this. Whoever denies, defames, and curses Jesus of Nazareth, the Virgin Mary's Son, also denies, defames, and curses God the Father himself, who created heaven and earth. But that's what the Jews do, etc.

And if you say that the Jews don't believe or know this, since they don't accept the New Testament, I reply that the Jews may know or believe this or that; we Christians, however, know that they publicly blaspheme and curse God the Father when they blaspheme and curse this Jesus. Tell me, what are we going to answer God if he takes us to account now or on the day of judgment, saying: "Listen, you are a Christian. You are aware of the fact that the Jews openly blasphemed and cursed my Son and Me, you gave them opportunity for it, you protected and shielded them so that they could engage in this without hindrance or punishment in your country, city, and house." Tell me: What will we answer to this?

Of course, we accord anyone the right not to believe *omissive et privatim* ["by neglect and privately"]; this we leave to everyone's conscience. But to parade such unbelief so freely in churches and before our very noses, eyes, and ears, to boast of it, to sing it, teach it, and defend it, to revile and curse the true faith, and in this way lure others to them and hinder our people—that's a far, far different story. And this isn't changed by the fact that the Jews don't believe the New Testament,

Part IV

that they are unacquainted with it, and that they pay it no heed. The fact remains that we *are* acquainted with it and that we cannot acquiesce in having the Jews revile and curse it in our hearing. To witness this and keep silent is tantamount to doing it ourselves. Thus, the accursed Jews encumber us with their diabolical, blasphemous, and horrible sins in our own country.

It won't do for them to say at this point: "We Jews care nothing about the New Testament or about the belief of the Christians." Let them express such sentiments in their own country or secretly. In our country and within our earshot, they must suppress these words, or we will have to resort to other measures. These incorrigible rascals know very well that the New Testament deals with our Lord Jesus Christ, God's Son, while they claim to be unacquainted with its contents. My friend, it's not a question of what you know or what you wish to know, but of what you ought to know, what you are obliged to know. As it happens, not only the Jew but all the world is obliged to know that the New Testament is God the Father's book about his Son Jesus Christ. Whoever does not accept and honor that book does not accept and honor God the Father himself. We read, "He who rejects me rejects my Father." And if the Jews don't want to know this, then, as I said, we Christians do know it.

Thus if we ourselves don't wish to stand condemned by their sins, we cannot tolerate that the Jews publicly blaspheme and revile God the Father before our very ears by blaspheming and reviling Jesus our Lord, for as he says, "He who hates me hates my Father also." Similarly we cannot tolerate their stating openly and within our ear-shot that they have no regard for the New Testament but look upon it as a pack of lies. This is tantamount to saying that they care nothing for God the Father and regard him as a liar, for this is God the Father's book, it is the word about his Son Jesus Christ. It will not avail them but rather prejudice their case if they plead ignorance or rejection of the book. It is incumbent on all to know God's book. He didn't reveal it to have it ignored or rejected; he wants it to be known, and he excuses no one from this.

On the Jews and Their Lies

It's as if a king were to instate his only son in his place and command the country to regard him as its sovereign—although he would also be entitled to this by right of natural inheritance—and the country as a whole readily accepted him. A few, however, band together in opposition, alleging that they know nothing about this, despite the fact that the king had in confirmation of his will issued seal and letters and other testimony. They still insist that they don't want to know this or respect it. The king would be obliged to take these people by the nape of the neck and throw them into a dungeon and entrust them to Master Hans,[92] who would teach them to say, "We are willing to acknowledge it." The alternative would be to keep them incarcerated forever, lest they contaminate others with their refractory attitude, who do want to learn it.

This is what God, too, has done. He instated his Son Jesus Christ in Jerusalem in his place and commanded that he be paid homage, according to Psalm 2:11-12: "Kiss the Son, lest he be angry, and you perish in the way".[93] Some of the Jews would not hear of this. God bore witness by the various tongues of the apostles and by all sorts of miraculous signs, and cited the statements of the prophets in testimony. However, they did then what they still do now; they were obstinate, and absolutely refused to listen. Then came Master Hans—the Romans—who destroyed Jerusalem, took the villains by the nape of the neck and cast them into the dungeon of exile, which they still inhabit and in which they will remain forever, or until they say, "We are willing to acknowledge it."

God surely didn't do this secretly or in some nook or corner, so that the Jews would have an excuse for disregarding the New Testament without sin. As we noted above, he gave them a reliable sign through the patriarch Jacob, namely, that they could confidently expect the Messiah when the scepter had departed from Judah. Or, when the 70

---

[92] That is, the torturer or executioner.

[93] This is a paraphrase and slight misreading. The actual passage reads: "Serve the Lord with fear, with trembling kiss his feet, lest he be angry, and you perish in the way."

Part IV

weeks of Daniel had expired; or, a short time after the construction of Haggai's temple but before its destruction. He also informed them through Isaiah that when they would hear a voice in the wilderness (as happened when the scepter had departed)—that is, when they heard the voice of a preacher and prophet proclaiming, "Repent, the Lord is at hand, and is himself coming"—then they should be certain that the Messiah had come [Isa 40:3].

Shortly thereafter, the Messiah himself appeared on the scene, taught, baptized, and performed innumerable great miracles, not secretly but throughout the entire country, prompting many to exclaim, "This is the Messiah" [John 7:41]. Also [John 7:31]: "When the Messiah appears, will he do more signs than this man has done?" And they themselves said, "What are we to do? For this man performs many signs. If we let him go on thus, everyone will believe in him" [John 11:47]. When he was on the cross, they said, "He saved others; he cannot save himself" [Matt 27:42]. Should God concede that these circumcised saints are ignorant of all this, when they already stand convicted by the four statements cited (Jacob's, Haggai's, Daniel's, and David's), all of which show that the Messiah must have come at that time? Several of their rabbis also declared that he was in the world and was begging in Rome, etc.

Furthermore, he saw to it that they were warned not to be offended at his person, for in Zechariah 9:9 he announced that he would come to Jerusalem "riding on an ass," wretched and poor, but as a propitious King who would teach peace, who would "cut off" the chariots, steeds, and bows—that is, not rule in a worldly manner, as the mad Kokhbaites, these bloodthirsty Jews, rave—and that this poor yet peaceful, propitious King's dominion should extend to the ends of the world. That is, indeed, a very clear statement, setting forth that the Messiah should reign in all the world without a sword, with pure peace, as a King bringing salvation. I'm extremely surprised that the devil can be so powerful as to delude a person, to say nothing of an entire nation that boasts of being God's people, into believing something at variance with this clear text.

He faithfully forewarned them, furthermore, not to be offended when they see that such a great miracle-worker and poor King, who had ridden in on an ass, would let himself be killed and crucified. He had had it proclaimed in advance (Daniel 9:26 and Isaiah 53:2 and 52:14) that "his Servant, who will startle the kings, will be smitten and afflicted"; but all of this will occur because "God laid on him the sins of us all and wounded him for our transgressions, but he was to make himself an offering for sin, intercede for the transgressors, and by his knowledge make many to be accounted righteous." Such the text clearly states.

But the sun has never seen or heard anything more disgraceful than the abuse of this passage by these blasphemous Jews. They apply it to themselves in their exile. At the present, we lack the time to deal with this. Alas, should they be the ones who were smitten because of our sin, who bore our transgressions, who made us righteous, and who intercede for us, etc.? There was never a viler people than they, who with their lying, blaspheming, cursing, maligning, their idolatry, their robbery, usury, and all vices accuse us Christians and all mankind more before God and the world than any others. By no means do they pray for us sinners, as the text says; they curse us most vehemently, as we proved earlier from Lyra and Burgensis. Their great slothfulness and malice prompt these blasphemous scoundrels to mock Scripture, God, and all the world with their impudent glosses. This they do in accord with their merit and true worth.

After the crucifixion of the King, God first presented the proper signs that this Jesus was the Messiah. Poor, timid, unlearned, unconsecrated fishermen, who didn't even have a perfect mastery of their own language, stepped forth and preached in the tongues of the whole world.[94] All the world, heaven and earth, is still filled with wonder at this. They interpreted the writings of the prophets with power and correct understanding; in addition, they performed such signs and won-

---

[94] According to Luke in Acts (2:3-4). This, of course, is not an unbiased description, and we have no outside confirmation of uneducated disciples teaching Christian ideas.

Part IV

ders, that their message was accepted throughout the world by Jews and Gentiles. Innumerable people, both young and old, accepted it with such sincerity that they willingly suffered gruesome martyrdom because of it. This message has now endured these 1,500 years down to our day, and it will endure to the end of time.

If such signs didn't move the Jews of that time, what can we expect of these degenerate Jews who haughtily disdain to know anything about this story? Indeed, God, who revealed these things so gloriously to all the world, will see to it that they hear us Christians preach and see us keep this message, which we did not invent but heard from Jerusalem 1,500 years ago. No enemies, no heathen, and especially no Jews have been able to suppress it, no matter how strongly they opposed it. It would be impossible for such a thing to maintain itself if it were not of God.

The Jews themselves in their 1,400-year-exile must confess that this message has been preached in all the world before their very ears, that it was assailed by much heresy and yet survived. Therefore God cannot be accused of having done all this secretly or in hiding, or of never having brought it to the attention of the Jews or of any other people. They have all persecuted it vehemently and vigorously these 1,500 years. And yet the blasphemous Jews oppose it so impudently and sneeringly, as though it had just recently been invented by a drunkard who deserves no credence. They feel free to revile and damn it with impunity, and we Christians have to offer them room and place, house and home in the bargain, we have to protect and defend them all so that they can confidently and freely revile and condemn such a word of God. And by way of reward, we let them take our money and property through their usury.

No, you vile father of such blasphemous Jews, you hellish devil, these are the facts: God has preached long enough to your children, the Jews, publicly and with miraculous signs throughout the world. He has done so for almost 1,500 years now, and still preaches. They were and still are obliged to obey him; but they were hardened and ever resisted, blasphemed, and cursed. Therefore we Christians, in turn, are obliged not to tolerate their wanton and conscious blasphemy. As we heard above, "He who hates the Son also hates the Father" [John 15:23]. If we permit them to do this where we are sovereign, and protect them to enable them to do so, then we are eternally damned together with them because of their sins and blasphemies, even if we in our persons are as holy as the prophets, apostles, or angels. *Quia faciens et consentiens pari poena* ["Doing and consenting deserve equal punishment"]. Whether doer, adviser, accomplice, consenter, or concealer—one is as pious as the other. It doesn't help us (and the Jews still less) that the Jews refuse to acknowledge this. As has already been said, we Christians know it, and the Jews ought to know it, having heard it together with us for almost 1,500 years, having beheld all sorts of miracles and having heard how this doctrine has survived, by nothing but divine strength, against all devils and the whole world.

This is certain, borne out by such an enduring and impressive testimony in all the world, that "He who does not honor the Son does not honor the Father," and that he who does not have the Son cannot have the Father. The Jews ever blaspheme and curse God the Father, the Creator of us all, just by blaspheming and cursing his Son, Jesus of Nazareth, Mary's Son, whom God has proclaimed as his Son for 1,500 years in all the world by preaching and miraculous signs against the might and the trickery of all devils and men; and he will proclaim him as such until the end of the world. They dub him *Hebel Vorik*, that is, not merely a liar and deceiver, but lying and deception itself, viler even than the devil. We Christians must not tolerate that they practice this in their public synagogues, in their books, and in their behavior, openly under our noses, and within our hearing, in our own country, houses, and regimes. If we do, we together with the Jews and on their account will lose God the Father and his dear Son, who purchased us at such cost with his holy blood, and we will be eternally lost, which God forbid!

Part IV

Accordingly, it must and dare not be considered a trifling matter but a most serious one to seek counsel against this and to save our souls from the Jews, that is, from the devil and from eternal death. My advice, as I said earlier,[95] is:

First, that their synagogues be burned down, and that all who are able, toss in sulfur and pitch; it would be good if someone could also throw in some hellfire. That would demonstrate to God our serious resolve and be evidence to all the world that it was in ignorance that we tolerated such houses, in which the Jews have reviled God, our dear Creator and Father, and his Son most shamefully up till now, but that we have now given them their due reward.

Second, that all their books—their prayer books, their Talmudic writings, also the entire Bible—be taken from them, not leaving them one leaf, and that these be preserved for those who may be converted. They use all of these books to blaspheme the Son of God, that is, God the Father himself, Creator of heaven and earth, as was said above; and they will never use them differently.

Third, that they be forbidden on pain of death to praise God, to give thanks, to pray, and to teach publicly among us and in our country. They may do this in their own country or wherever they can, without our being obliged to hear it or know it. The reason for this prohibition is that their praise, thanks, prayer, and doctrine are sheer blasphemy, cursing, and idolatry, because their heart and mouth call God the Father *Hebel Vorik* as they call his Son, our Lord Jesus, this. As they name and honor the Son, thus they also name and honor the Father. It doesn't help them to use many fine words and to make much ado about the name of God. We read, "You shall not take the name of the Lord your God in vain" [Ex 20:7]. It was of no avail that their ancestors at the time of the kings of Israel bore God's name, yet called him Baal.

Fourth, that they be forbidden to utter the name of God within our hearing. We cannot with a good conscience listen to this or tolerate it, because their blasphemous and accursed mouth and heart call God's Son

---

[95] A partial repeat of his earlier list.

Hebel Vorik, and thus also call his Father that. He cannot and will not interpret this otherwise, just as we Christians too cannot interpret it otherwise—we who believe that however the Son is named and honored, thus also the Father is named and honored. Therefore, we mustn't consider the mouth of the Jews as worthy of uttering the name of God within our hearing. He who hears this name from a Jew must inform the authorities, or else throw pig dung at him when he sees him, and chase him away. And may no one be merciful and kind in this regard—for God's honor and the salvation of us all, including that of the Jews, are at stake!

And if they, or someone else in their behalf, were to suggest that they don't intend any such great evil, or that they aren't aware that with such blaspheming and cursing they are blaspheming and cursing God the Father—alleging that though they blaspheme Jesus and we Christians, they nonetheless praise and honor God most highly and beautifully—we answer as we have done before: that if the Jews don't want to admit this or try to put a better face on it, we Christians at least are bound to admit it. The Jews' ignorance is not to be excused, since God has had this proclaimed for almost 1,500 years. They are obliged to know it, and God demands this knowledge of them. If anyone who hears God's words for 1,500 years still constantly remarks, "I don't want to acknowledge this," his ignorance will provide a very poor excuse. He thereby really incurs a sevenfold guilt.

To be sure, they didn't know at that time that it was God's word; but now they have been informed of it these 1,500 years. They have witnessed great signs. Yet they have raged against this, and because of it, lived in such exile for 1,500 years. All right, let them even now hear and believe it, and all will be simple. If they refuse, it's certain that they will never acknowledge it but are bent on cursing it forever, as their forebears have done for these 1,500 years. So we Christians, who do acknowledge it, cannot tolerate or take upon our conscience their willful, everlasting ignorance and blasphemy in our midst. Let them wander back to their country, be ignorant and blaspheme there as long as they can, and not burden us with their wicked sins.

Part IV

<<<—>>>

But what will happen even if we do burn down the Jews' synagogues and forbid them publicly to praise God, to pray, to teach, to utter God's name? They will still keep doing it in secret. If we know that they are doing this in secret, it's the same as if they were doing it publicly. Our knowledge of their secret doings and our toleration of them implies that they are not secret after all, and thus our conscience is encumbered with it before God. So let's beware. In my opinion, the problem must be resolved thus:

If we wish to wash our hands of the Jews' blasphemy and not share in their guilt, we have to part company with them. They must be driven from our country. Let them think of their fatherland; then they need no longer wail and lie before God against us that we are holding them captive, nor need we then any longer complain that they are burdening us with their blasphemy and their usury. This is the most natural and the best course of action, which will safeguard the interest of both parties.

But since they are loath to quit the country, they will boldly deny everything and will also offer the government money enough for permission to remain here. Woe to those who accept such money, and accursed be that money, which they have stolen from us so damnably through usury. They deny just as brazenly as they lie. And wherever they can secretly curse, poison, or harm us Christians, they do so without any qualms of conscience. If they are caught in the act or charged with something, they are bold enough to deny it impudently, even to the point of death, since they don't regard us worthy of being told the truth. In fact, these holy children of God consider any harm they can wish or inflict on us as a great service to God. Indeed, if they had the power to do to us what we are able to do to them, not one of us would live for an hour. But since they lack the power to do this publicly, they remain our daily murderers and bloodthirsty foes in their hearts. Their prayers and curses furnish evidence of that, as do the many stories that relate their torturing of children and all sorts of crimes for which they have often been burned at the stake or banished.

Therefore, I firmly believe that they say and practice far worse things secretly than the histories and others record about them, meanwhile relying on their denials and on their money. But even if they could deny all else, they cannot deny that they curse us Christians openly—not because of our evil life, but because we regard Jesus as the Messiah, and because they view themselves as our captives, although they know very well that the latter is a lie, and that they are really the ones who hold us captive in our own country by means of their usury, and that everyone would gladly be rid of them. Because they curse us, they also curse our Lord; and if they curse our Lord, they also curse God the Father, the Creator of heaven and earth. Thus, their lying cannot avail them. Their cursing alone convicts them, so that we are indeed compelled to believe all the evil things written about them. Undoubtedly, they do more and viler things than those which we know and discover. For Christ doesn't lie or deceive us when he adjudges them to be serpents and children of the devil—that is, his and all his followers' murderers and enemies—wherever they find it possible.

«««—»»»

If I had power over the Jews, as our princes and cities have, I would deal severely with their lying mouth. They have one lie with which they work great harm among their children and their common folk, and with which they slander our faith so shamefully: namely, they accuse us and slander us among their people, declaring that we Christians worship more than one God.[96] Here they vaunt and pride themselves without measure. They beguile their people with the claim that they are the only people, in contrast to all the Gentiles, who worship no more than one God. Oh, how cocksure they are about this!

---

[96] That is, that Christians accept the Trinity: that God, Jesus, and the Holy Spirit are three persons unified in one being. Oddly, this notion has virtually no biblical justification.

Part IV

Even though they are aware that they are doing us an injustice and are lying on this point as malicious and wicked scoundrels, even though they have heard for 1,500 years, and still hear, that all of us Christians disavow this, they still stuff their ears shut like serpents and deliberately refuse to hear us, but rather insist that their venomous lies about us must be accepted by their people as the truth. This they do, even though they read in our writings that we agree with Moses' words in Deuteronomy 6:4: "Hear, O Israel, the Lord our God is one God," and that we confess, publicly and privately, with our hearts, tongues, and writings, our life and our death, that there is but one God, of whom Moses writes here and whom the Jews themselves call upon. I say, even if they know this and have heard and read it about us for almost 1,500 years, it's of no avail; their lies must still stand, and we Christians have to tolerate their slander that we worship many gods.

Consequently, if I had power over them, I would assemble their scholars and their leaders and order them, on pain of losing their tongues down to the root, to convince us Christians within eight days of the truth of their assertions and to prove this blasphemous lie against us, to the effect that we worship more than the one true God. If they succeeded, we would all on the self-same day become Jews and be circumcised. If they failed, they should stand ready to receive the punishment they deserve for such shameful, malicious, pernicious, and venomous lies. For, thanks be to God, we are after all not such ducks, clods, or stones as these most intelligent rabbis, these senseless fools, think us, that we don't know that one God and many gods cannot truly be believed in simultaneously.

Neither Jew nor devil will in any way be able to prove that our belief that the one eternal Godhead is composed of three persons implies that we believe in more than one God. If the Jews maintain that they cannot understand how three persons can be one God, why then must their blasphemous, accursed, lying mouth deny, condemn, and curse what it does not understand? Such a mouth should be punished for two reasons; in the first place, because it confesses that it does not understand this; in the second place, because it nevertheless blasphemes something which it does not understand. Why do they not first ask? Indeed, why have they heard it for 1,500 years and yet refused to learn or understand it? Therefore such lack of understanding cannot help or excuse them, nor us Christians if we tolerate this any longer from them. As already said, we must force them to prove their lies about us or suffer the consequences. He who slanders and maligns us as being idolatrous in this respect, slanders and maligns Christ—that is, God himself—as an idol. It is from him that we learned and received this as his eternal word and truth, confirmed mightily by signs, and confessed and taught now for nearly 1,500 years.

No person has yet been born, or will ever be born, who can grasp or comprehend how foliage can sprout from wood or a tree, or how grass can grow forth from stone or earth, or how any creature can be begotten. Yet these filthy, blind, hardened liars presume to fathom and to know what's happening outside and beyond the creature in God's hidden, incomprehensible, inscrutable, and eternal essence. Though we ourselves can grasp only with difficulty and with weak faith what has been revealed to us about this in veiled words, they give vent to such terrible blasphemy over it as to call our faith idolatrous, which is to reproach and defame God himself as an idol. We are convinced of our faith and doctrine; and they, too, ought to understand it, having heard for 1,500 years that it is by God and from God through Jesus Christ.

If these vulgar people had expressed themselves more mildly and said, "The Christians worship one God and not many gods, and we are lying and doing the Christians an injustice when we allege that they are worshiping more than one God, though they do believe that there are three persons in the Godhead; we cannot understand this but are willing to let the Christians follow their convictions," etc.—that would have been sensible. But now they proceed, impelled by the devil, to fall into this like filthy pigs fall into the trough, defaming and reviling that which they refuse to acknowledge and to understand. Without further ado they declare: We Jews don't understand this and don't want to understand it; therefore it follows that it's wrong and idolatrous.

Part IV

These are the people to whom God has never been God but a liar in the person of all the prophets and apostles, no matter how much God had these preach to them. The result is that they cannot be God's people, no matter how much they teach, clamor, and pray. They don't hear God; so he, in turn, doesn't hear them, as Psalm 18:28 says: "With the crooked thou dost show thyself perverse." The wrath of God has overtaken them.

I am loath to think of this, and it hasn't been a pleasant task for me to write this book, being obliged to resort now to anger, now to satire, in order to avert my eyes from the terrible picture that they present. It has pained me to mention their horrible blasphemy concerning our Lord and his dear mother, which we Christians are grieved to hear. I can well understand what St. Paul means in Romans 9:2 when he says that he is saddened as he considers them. I think that every Christian experiences this when he reflects seriously, not on the temporal misfortunes and exile that the Jews bemoan, but on the fact that they are condemned to blaspheme, curse, and vilify God himself and all that is God's, for their eternal damnation, and that they refuse to hear and acknowledge this but regard all of their doings as zeal for God. O God, heavenly Father, relent and let your wrath over them be sufficient and come to an end, for the sake of your dear Son! Amen.

PART V

CONCLUSION

I wish and I ask that our rulers who have Jewish subjects exercise a sharp mercy toward these wretched people, as suggested above, to see whether this might not help (though it is doubtful). They must act like a good physician who, when gangrene has set in, proceeds without mercy to cut, saw, and burn flesh, veins, bone, and marrow. Such a procedure must also be followed in this instance. Burn down their synagogues, forbid all that I enumerated earlier, force them to work, and deal harshly with them, as Moses did in the wilderness, slaying 3,000 lest the whole people perish.[97] They surely don't know what they are doing; moreover, as people possessed, they don't wish to know it, hear it, or learn it. Therefore, it would be wrong to be merciful and confirm them in their conduct. If this doesn't help, we must drive them out like mad dogs, so that we don't become partakers of their abominable blasphemy and all their other vices and thus merit God's wrath and be damned with them. I have done my duty. Now let everyone see to his. I am exonerated.

Finally, I wish to say this for myself: If God were to give me no other Messiah than such as the Jews wish and hope for, I would much, much rather be a pig than a human being. I will cite you a good reason for this. The Jews ask no more of their Messiah than that he be a Kokhba and worldly king, who will slay us Christians and share out the world among the Jews and make them lords, and who finally will die like other kings, and his children after him. Thus declares a rabbi: You must not suppose that it will be different at the time of the Messiah than it has been since the creation of the world, etc.; that is, there will be

---

[97] See Ex 32:28.

days and nights, years and months, summer and winter, seedtime and harvest, begetting and dying, eating and drinking, sleeping, growing, digesting, eliminating—all will take its course as it does now, only the Jews will be the masters and will possess all the world's gold, goods, joys, and delights, while we Christians will be their servants. This coincides entirely with the thoughts and teachings of Muhammad. He kills us Christians as the Jews would like to do, occupies the land, and takes over our property, our joys and pleasures. If he were a Jew and not an Ishmaelite, the Jews would have accepted him as the Messiah long ago, or they would have made him the Kokhba.

Even if I had all of that, or if I could become the ruler of Turkey or the Messiah for whom the Jews hope, I would still prefer being a pig. For what would all of this benefit me if I could not be secure in its possession for a single hour? Death, that horrible burden and plague of all mankind, would still threaten me. I would not be safe from him; I would have to fear him every moment. I would still have to quake and tremble before hell and the wrath of God. And I would know no end of all this but would have to expect it forever. The tyrant Dionysius illustrated this well when he placed a person who praised his good fortune at the head of a richly laden table. Over his head, he suspended an unsheathed sword attached to a silk thread, and below him he put a red-hot fire, saying: Eat and be merry, etc. That's the sort of joy such a Messiah would dispense. And I know that anyone who has ever tasted of death's terror or burden would rather be a sow than bear this forever and ever.

A sow lies down on her featherbed, on the street, or on a dung-heap; she rests securely, snores gently, sleeps sweetly, fears neither king nor Lord, neither death nor hell, neither the devil nor God's wrath, and lives entirely without care so long as she has her bran. And if the emperor of Turkey were to draw near with all his might and his wrath, she in her pride would not move a bristle for his sake. If someone were to rouse her, she, I suppose, would grunt and say, if she could talk: "You fool, why are you raving? You are not one-tenth as well off as I am. Not for an hour do you live as securely, as peacefully and tranquilly as I do con-

Part V

stantly, nor would you even if you were ten times as great or rich." In brief, no thought of death occurs to her, for her life is secure and serene.

And if the butcher performs his job with her, she probably imagines that a stone or piece of wood is pinching her. She never thinks of death, and in a moment she is dead. Neither before, during, nor in death did she feel death. She feels nothing but life, nothing but everlasting life! No king, not even the Jews' Messiah, will be able to emulate her, nor will any person, however great, rich, holy, or mighty he might be. She never ate of the apple that taught us wretched men in Paradise the difference between good and evil.

What good would the Jews' Messiah do me if he were unable to help a poor man like me, in face of this great and horrible lack and grief, and make my life one-tenth as pleasant as that of a pig? I would say: Dear Lord God, keep your Messiah, or give him to whoever will have him. Instead, make me a pig. It's better to be a live pig than a man who is eternally dying. Yea, as Christ says: "It would have been better for that man if he had not been born" [Matt 28:24].

However, if I had a Messiah who could remedy this grief, so that I would no longer have to fear death but would be always and eternally sure of life, and able to play a trick on the devil and death, and no longer have to tremble before the wrath of God, then my heart would leap for joy and be intoxicated with sheer delight; then would a fire of love for God be enkindled, and my praise and thanks would never cease. Even if he would not, in addition, give me gold, silver, and other riches, all the world would nonetheless be a genuine paradise for me, though I lived in a dungeon.

That's the kind of Messiah we Christians have, and we thank God, the Father of all mercy, with the full, overflowing joy of our hearts, gladly and readily forgetting all the sorrow and harm that we compensated for, and all has been restored to us through this Messiah. Filled with such joy, the apostles sang and rejoiced in dungeons and amid all misfortunes, as did even young girls, such as Agatha, Lucia, etc. The wretched Jews, on the other hand, who rejected this Messiah, have languished and perished since that time in anguish of heart, in trouble, trembling, wrath, impatience, malice, blasphemy, and cursing, as we read in Isaiah 65:14: "Behold, my servants shall sing for gladness of heart, but you shall cry out for pain of heart, and shall wail for anguish of spirit. You shall leave your name to my chosen for a curse, and the Lord God will slay you; but his servants he will call by a different name." And in the same chapter we read [v. 1]: "I was ready to be sought by those who did not ask for me; I was ready to be found by those who did not seek me. I said, 'Here am I, here am I,' to a nation that did not call on my name (that is, who were not my people). I spread out my hands all the day to a rebellious people."

We, indeed, have such a Messiah, who says to us (John 11:25): "I am the resurrection and the life; he who believes in me, though he die, yet shall he live, and whoever lives and believes in me shall never die." And John 8:51: "Truly, truly, I say to you, if any one keeps my word, he will never see death." The Jews and the Turks care nothing for such a Messiah. And why should they? They must have a Messiah from the fool's paradise, who will satisfy their stinking belly, and who will die together with them like a cow or dog.

Nor do they need him in the face of death, for they themselves are holy enough with their penitence and piety to step before God and attain this and everything. Only the Christians are such fools and timid cowards who stand in such awe of God, who regard their sin and his wrath so highly that they don't venture to appear before the eyes of his divine Majesty without a mediator or Messiah to represent them and to sacrifice himself for them. The Jews, however, are holy and valiant heroes and knights who dare to approach God themselves without mediator or Messiah, and ask for and receive all they desire. Obviously the angels and God himself must rejoice whenever a Jew condescends to pray; then the angels must take this prayer and place it as a crown on God's divine head. We have witnessed this for 1,500 years. So highly does God esteem the noble blood and circumcised saints, because they can call his son *Hebel Vorik!*

Part V

Furthermore, not only do we foolish, craven Christians and accursed Goyim regard our Messiah as so indispensable for delivering us from death through himself and without our holiness, but we wretched people are also afflicted with such great and terrible blindness as to believe that he needs no sword or worldly power to accomplish this. We cannot comprehend how God's wrath, sin, death, and hell can be banished with the sword, since we observe that, from the beginning of the world to the present day, death hasn't cared a fig for the sword; it has overcome all emperors, kings, and whoever wields a sword as easily as it overcomes the weakest infant in the cradle.

In this respect, the great seducers Isaiah, Jeremiah, and all the other prophets do us great harm. They beguile us mad Goyim with their false doctrine, saying that the kingdom of the Messiah will not bear the sword. Oh, that the holy rabbis and the chivalrous, bold heroes of the Jews would come to our rescue here and extricate us from these abominable errors! When Isaiah 2:2 prophesies concerning the Messiah that the Gentiles shall come to the house and mountain of the Lord and let themselves be taught—for undoubtedly they don't expect to be murdered with the sword; in this case, they would surely not approach but would stay away—he says [v. 4]: "He (the Messiah) shall judge between the nations, and shall decide for many peoples; and they shall beat their swords into plowshares, and their spears into pruning hooks; nation shall not lift up sword against nation, neither shall they learn war anymore."

Similar sorcery is also practiced upon us poor Goyim in Isaiah 11:9: "They shall not hurt or destroy in all my holy mountain; for the earth shall be full of the knowledge of the Lord." We poor blind Goyim cannot conceive of this "knowledge of the Lord" as a sword, but as the instruction by which one learns to know God; our understanding agrees with Isaiah 2, cited above, which also speaks of the knowledge which the Gentiles shall pursue. Knowledge doesn't come by the sword, but by teaching and hearing, as we stupid Goyim assume. Likewise Isaiah 53:11: "By his knowledge shall the righteous one, my servant, make many to be accounted righteous"; that is, by teaching them and by their hearing him and believing in him. What else might "his knowledge" mean? In brief, the knowledge of the Messiah must come by preaching.

The proof of this is before your eyes, namely, that the apostles used no spear or sword but solely their tongues. And their example has been followed in all the world now for 1,500 years by all the bishops, pastors, and preachers, and is still being followed. Just see whether the pastor wields sword or spear when he enters the church, preaches, baptizes, administers the sacrament, when he retains and remits sin, restrains evildoers, comforts the godly, and teaches, helps, and nurtures everyone's soul. Does he not do all of this exclusively with the tongue or with words? And the congregation, likewise, brings no sword or spear to such a ministry, but only its ears.

And consider the miracles. The Roman Empire and the whole world abounded with idols to which the Gentiles adhered; the devil was mighty and defended himself vigorously. All swords were against it, and yet the tongue alone purged the entire world of all these idols without a sword. It also exorcised innumerable devils, raised the dead, healed all types of diseases, and snowed and rained down sheer miracles. Thereafter it swept away all heresy and error, as it still does daily before our eyes. And further—this is the greatest miracle—it forgives and blots out all sin, creates happy, peaceful, patient hearts, devours death, locks the doors of hell and opens the gate of heaven, and gives eternal life. Who can enumerate all the blessings effected by God's word? In brief, it makes all who hear and believe it children of God and heirs of the kingdom of heaven. Do you not call this a kingdom, power, might, dominion, glory? Yes, most certainly, this is a comforting kingdom and the true *chemdath* of all Gentiles. And should I, in company with the Jews, desire or accept bloodthirsty Kokhba in place of such a kingdom? As I said, in such circumstances I would rather be a pig than a man.

«««—»»»

PART V

All the writings of the prophets agree fully with this interpretation, that the nations, both Jews and Gentiles, flocked to Shiloh after the scepter had been wrested from Judah (as Jacob says in Genesis 49); likewise, that the 70 weeks of Daniel are fulfilled; that the temple of Haggai is destroyed, but the house and throne of David have remained until the present time and will endure forever. On the other hand, according to the mischievous denial, lying, and cursing of the Jews, whom God has rejected, this is not the meaning, much less has it been fulfilled.

To speak first of the saying of Jacob in Genesis 49, we heard before what idle and senseless foolishness the Jews have invented regarding it, yet without hitting upon any definite meaning. But if we confess our Lord Jesus and let him be the "Shiloh" or Messiah, all agrees, coincides, rhymes, and harmonizes beautifully and delightfully. He appeared promptly on the scene at the time of Herod, after the scepter had departed from Judah. He initiated his rule of peace without a sword, as Isaiah and Zechariah had prophesied, and all the nations gathered about him—both Jews and Gentiles—so that on one day in Jerusalem 3,000 souls became believers, and many members of the priesthood and of the princes of the people also flocked to him, as Luke records in Acts 3 and 4.

For more than 100 years after Jesus' resurrection—that is, from the 18th year of the reign of Emperor Tiberius until the 18th year of the reign of Emperor Hadrian, who inflicted the second and last bloodbath of the Jews, who defeated Kokhba, and drove the Jews utterly and completely from their country—there were always bishops in Jerusalem from the tribe of the children of Israel, all of whom our Eusebius mentions by name (*Eccl. Hist.*, Bk. 4, ch. 5). He begins with St. James the apostle and enumerates about 15 of them, all of whom preached the gospel with great diligence, performed miracles and lived a holy life, converting many thousands of Jews and children of Israel to their promised Messiah who had now appeared, Jesus of Nazareth; apart from these, there were the Jews living in the Diaspora who were converted together with the Gentiles by St. Paul, other apostles, and their disciples. This was accomplished despite that fact that the other faction, the blind, impenitent Jews—the fathers of the present-day Jews—raved, raged, and ranted against it without letup and without ceasing, and shed much blood of members of their own race both within their own country and abroad among the Gentiles, as was related earlier also of Kokhba.

After Hadrian had expelled the Jews from their country, however, it was necessary to choose the bishops in Jerusalem from the Gentiles who had become Christians, for the Jews were no longer found or tolerated in the country because of Kokhba and his rebellious followers, who gave the Romans no rest. Yet the other, pious, converted Jews who lived dispersed among the Gentiles converted many of the children of Israel, as we gather from the Epistles of St. Paul and from the histories. But these always and everywhere suffered persecution at the hands of the Kokhbaites, so that the pious children of Israel had no worse enemies than their own people. This is true today in the instance of converted Jews.

The Gentiles all over the world now also gathered about these pious, converted children of Israel. This they did in great numbers and with such zeal that they gave up not only their idols and their own wisdom but also forsook wife and child, friends, goods and honor, life and limb for the sake of it. They suffered everything that the devil and all the other Gentiles, as well as the mad Jews, could contrive. For all of that, they didn't seek a Kokhba, nor the Gentiles' gold, silver, possessions, dominion, land, or people; they sought eternal life, a life other than this temporal one. They were poor and wretched voluntarily, and yet were happy and content. They were not embittered or vindictive, but kind and merciful. They prayed for their enemies, and, in addition, performed many and great miracles. That has lasted uninterruptedly from that time on down to the present day, and it will endure to the end of the world.

«««—»»»

Part V

It's a great, extraordinary, and wonderful thing that the Gentiles in all the world accepted, without sword or coercion, with no temporal benefits accruing to them, gladly and freely, a poor Man of the Jews as the true Messiah, one whom his own people had crucified, condemned, cursed, and persecuted without end. They did and suffered so much for his sake, and forsook all idolatry, just so that they might live with him eternally. This has been going on now for 1,500 years. No worship of a false god ever endured so long, nor did all the world suffer so much because of it or cling so firmly to it. And I suppose one of the strongest proofs is found in the fact that no other god ever withstood such hard opposition as the Messiah, against whom alone all other gods and peoples have raged and against whom they all acted in concert, no matter how varied they were or how they otherwise disagreed.

Whoever is not moved by this miraculous spectacle quite deserves to remain blind or to become an accursed Jew. We Christians perceive that these events are in agreement with the statement of Jacob found in Genesis 49: "To the Shiloh or Messiah (after the scepter has dropped from the hands of Judah) shall be the obedience of the peoples." We have the fulfillment of this before our eyes: The peoples, that is, not only the Jews but also the Gentiles, are in perfect accord in their obedience to this Shiloh; they have become one people, that is, Christians. One cannot mention or think of anyone to whom this verse of Jacob applies and refers so fittingly as to our dear Lord Jesus. It would have had to be someone who appeared just after the loss of the scepter, or else the Holy Spirit lied through the mouth of the holy patriarch Jacob, and God forgot his promise. May the devil say that, or anyone who wishes to be an accursed Jew!

Likewise, the verse regarding the everlasting house and throne of David fits no other than this our Messiah, Jesus of Nazareth [2 Sam 23:5]. Subsequent to the rule of the kings from the tribe of Judah and since the days of Herod, we cannot think of any son of David who might have sat on his throne or still occupies it today "to preserve his throne eternally." Yet that's what had to take place and still must take place, since God promised it with an oath. But when this Son of David arose from the dead, many, many thousands of children of Israel rallied about him, both in Jerusalem and throughout the world, accepting him as their King and Messiah, as the true Seed of Abraham and of their lineage. These were and still are the house, the kingdom, the throne of David. For they are the descendants of the children of Israel and the seed of Abraham, over whom David was king.

That they have now died and lie buried doesn't matter; they are nonetheless his kingdom and his people before him. They are dead to us and to the world, but to him they are alive and not dead. It's natural that the blind Jews are unaware of this; for he who is blind sees nothing at all. We Christians, however, know that he says in John 8:58 and in Matthew 22:32: "Abraham lives." Also, in John 11:25: "He who believes in me, though he die, yet shall he live." Thus, David's house and throne are firmly established. There is a Son occupying it eternally, who never dies, nor does he ever let die those who are of his kingdom or who accept him in true faith as King. That marks the true fulfillment of this verse that declares that David's throne shall be eternal. Now let all the devils and Jews, Turks and whoever wants to concern himself with it also, name one or more sons of David to whom this verse regarding the house of David applies so precisely and beautifully, since the time of Herod, and we shall be ready to praise them.

To such kingdom and throne of David we Gentiles belong, along with all who have accepted this Messiah and Son of David as King with the same faith, and who continue to accept him to the end of the world and in eternity. Jacob's saying in Genesis 49:10 states: "To him shall be the obedience of the peoples." This means not only one nation, such as the children of Israel, but also whatever others are called nations. And earlier we read in Genesis 22:18: "In thy seed shall all the nations of the earth bless themselves." In this verse we find the term "Goyim," which in the Bible commonly means the Gentiles, except where the prophets also call the Jews this, in a strong tone of contempt. To summarize, the blessing of God through the seed of Abraham shall not be confined to

Part V

his physical descendants but shall be disseminated among all the Gentiles. That's why God himself calls Abraham "father of a multitude of nations" [Gen 17:5]. There are many more such sayings in Scripture.

The reason that Scripture calls this kingdom "David's throne" and that it calls the King Messiah "David's Seed" is found in the fact that this kingdom of David and the King Messiah didn't come from we Gentiles to the children of Abraham and Israel, but came from the children of Abraham and Israel, as the Lord himself says in John 4:22: "Salvation is from the Jews." Even if we are all descended from Adam and partake of the same birth and blood, nevertheless all other nations were shunted aside and solely Abraham's seed was selected as the nation from which the Messiah would come. After Abraham only Isaac, after Isaac only Jacob, after Jacob only Judah, after Judah only David were chosen, and the other brothers, each in his turn, were pushed aside and not chosen as the lineage from which the Messiah was to come. But everything, all things, happened for the sake of the Messiah. Therefore, the whole seed of Abraham, especially those who believed in this Messiah, were highly honored by God, as St. Paul says in Acts 13:17: "God made the people great." It surely is a great honor and distinction to be able to boast of being the Messiah's relative and kin. The closer the relationship, the greater the honor.

However, this boasting must not stem from the idea that Abraham's and his descendants' lineage is worthy of such honor; for that would nullify everything. It must be based rather on the fact that God chose Abraham's flesh and blood for this purpose out of sheer grace and mercy, although it surely deserved a far different lot. We Gentiles, too, have been honored very highly by being made partakers of the Messiah and the kingdom and by enjoying the blessing promised to Abraham's seed. But if we should boast as though we were deserving of this, and not acknowledge that we owe it to sheer, pure mercy, giving God alone the glory, all would also be spoiled and lost. It is as said in 1 Corinthians 4:7: "What have you that you did not receive? If then you received it, why do you boast as if it were not a gift?"

Thus, the dear Son of David, Jesus Christ, is also our King and Messiah, and we glory in being his kingdom and people, just as much as David himself and all children of Israel and Abraham. We know that he has been instated as Lord, King, and Judge over the living and the dead. "If we live, we live to the Lord, and if we die, we die to the Lord"; that is, we will also live after death, as we just heard, and as St. Paul preaches in Romans 14:8. We look for no bloodthirsty Kokhba in him, but the true Messiah who can give life and salvation. That's what is meant by a son of David sitting on his throne eternally. The blind Jews and Turks know nothing at all of this. May God have mercy on them, as he has had and will have on us. Amen.

«««—»»»

Neither can one produce a Messiah to whom the statement in Daniel 9 applies other than this Jesus of Nazareth, even if this drives the devil with all his angels and Jews to madness. We heard before how lame are the lies of the Jews regarding King Cyrus and King Agrippa. However, things did come to pass in accord with the words of the angel Gabriel, and we see the fulfillment before our eyes. "Seventy weeks of years," he says, "are decreed concerning your people and your holy city." He doesn't mention the city by name, Jerusalem, but he simply says "your holy city"; nor does he say, "God's people," but simply "your people." This people's and this city's holiness are to terminate after the expiration of the 70 weeks. In its place, a new people, a new Jerusalem, and a different holiness would arise in which one would no longer have to propitiate sin annually by sacrifice, worship and holiness in the temple and yet never become righteous and perfectly holy, because the atonement had to be repeated and sought anew by sacrifice every year.

Rather the Messiah would bring eternal righteousness, make misdeeds of no effect, check transgressions, atone for sin, fulfill prophecies and visions, etc. Where sin has been forever removed and eternal righteousness is found, there sacrifice for sin or for righteousness is no

Part V

longer required. Why should one sacrifice for sin if it no longer exists? Why should one seek righteousness by service to God if this righteousness is already at hand? But if sacrifice and worship are no longer necessary, of what use are priests and temple? If priests and temple are no longer necessary, why a people and a city who are served by them? It must develop into a new people and city that no longer needs such priests, temple, sacrifice, and worship, or it must be laid low and destroyed together with the useless temple and worship, priests and sacrifice. The 70 weeks pronounce the final judgment and put an end to them, together with city and temple, priests, sacrifice, and worship.

The Christian church, composed of Jews and Gentiles, is just such a new people and a new Jerusalem. This people knows that sin has been removed entirely by Jesus Christ, that all prophecy has been fulfilled, and eternal righteousness established. He who believes in him is eternally righteous, and all his sins are forever made of no effect, they are atoned for and forgiven, as the New Testament, especially St. Peter and St. Paul, strongly emphasizes. We no longer hear it said: Whoever offers guilt-offerings or sin-offerings or other offerings in Jerusalem becomes righteous or has atoned for his sin; but now we hear: "He who believes and is baptized will be saved; but he who does not believe will be condemned" [Mark 16:16], no matter where in the wide world he may be. He need not travel to Jerusalem; no, Jerusalem has to come to him.

David, too, proclaimed this in Psalm 40:6: "Sacrifice and offering thou dost not desire; but thou hast given me an open ear"—that is, the ears of the world, that they might hear and believe and thus be saved without sacrifice, temple, and priests. "Burnt offering and sin offering thou hast not required. Then I said, 'Lo, I come; in the roll of the book it is written of me; I delight to do thy will, O God'." Indeed, this is the Messiah who brought righteousness through his will and obedience. This is the message of the books of Moses and of all the prophets. Thus also Gabriel says that the sacrifice will not be adequate; he declares that the Messiah "shall be cut off and have nothing" [Dan 9:28]. Of what will he have nothing? Find out what he's talking about. He's speaking to Daniel about his people and his holy city. He will have none of these, so that their holiness will no longer be with him and in him. Thus Psalm 18:4 says: "I do not want their libations of blood, nor will I take their names upon my lips."

So also we read in Isaiah 33: "The people who will dwell in the new Jerusalem will be called *Nesu awon, levatus peccato*: a people forgiven of all sin." And Jeremiah also promises another, a new, covenant in which not Moses with his covenant shall reign, but rather, as he says: "I will forgive their iniquity, and I will remember their sin no more" [Jer 31:34]. This is, indeed, a covenant of grace, of forgiveness, of remission of all sins eternally. That cannot, of course, be effected by the sword, as the bloodthirsty Kokhbaites aspire to do. No, this was brought into the unworthy world by pure grace through the crucified Messiah, for eternal righteousness and salvation, as Gabriel here declares.

As was said before, this saying is too rich; the whole New Testament is summed up in it. Consequently, more time and space would be needed to expound it fully. At present it will suffice if we are convinced that it's impossible to understand this statement as referring to any other Messiah or King than our Lord Jesus of Nazareth. This is true also for the reason that at that time, in the last week, no other Messiah than this was killed; for as Daniel's words clearly indicate, there must be a Messiah who was killed at that time.

And, finally, also Haggai's saying fits no one else. From Haggai's time on, there was no one who might with the slightest plausibility be called "the *chemdath* of all the Gentiles," their delight and consolation, except this Jesus Christ alone. For 1,500 years, the Gentiles have found their comfort, joy, and delight in him, as we perceive clearly and as the Jews themselves confirm with their cursing to the present day. Why do they curse us? Solely because we confess, praise, and laud this Jesus, the true Messiah, as our consolation, joy, and delight, from whom we will not be parted or separated by weal or woe, in whom and for whom we will confidently and willingly live and die. And the more the Jews,

Part V

Turks, and all other foes revile and defame him, the more firmly will we cling to him and the dearer we will be to him, as he says [Matt 5:11]: "Blessed are you when men revile you and persecute you on my account. Rejoice and be glad, for your reward is great in heaven." All praise and thanks, glory and honor be to him, together with the Father and the Holy Spirit, the one true and veritable God. Amen.

So long an essay, dear sir and good friend, you have elicited from me with your booklet in which a Jew demonstrates his skill in a debate with an absent Christian. He would not, thank God, do this in my presence! My essay, I hope, will furnish a Christian—who in any case has no desire to become a Jew—with enough material not only to defend himself against the blind, venomous Jews, but also to become the foe of the Jews' malice, lying, and cursing, and to understand not only that their belief is false but that they are surely possessed by all devils. May Christ, our dear Lord, convert them mercifully and preserve us steadfastly and immovably in the knowledge of him, which is eternal life. Amen.

AFTERWORD

THOMAS DALTON

Martin Luther died in February 1546, at the age of 62. By that time he had become the most well-known figure in Christendom, on par with the pope himself. Luther's "reformation"—the Protestant movement within the Church—not only made him famous, but it also inaugurated a gradual decline in Catholic authority within Europe. But it was a slow process. In the year 1600, the Church still had the power to burn heretics at the stake, with Giordano Bruno being the most notable example. In 1633 it confined the famous scientist Galileo to house arrest for the remaining portion of his life, simply because his astronomical theories posed a threat to Church ideology. But with the coming of the Enlightenment around 1650, the papacy suffered a steady erosion of political power.

The decline of the Church, and Christian theology generally, had an effect on how people responded to the Jewish Question. Critiques shifted from Lutheran-type attacks based on the Bible to more secular ones grounded in Jewish attitudes, values, and actions. Significantly, the substance of later criticisms was similar or identical to Luther, but they were cast in a new, non-religious light.

Let me, therefore, continue the brief historical recount that I presented in the Introduction, now in the period after Luther's death, to show the continuity of criticisms over time. I will then close with a look at some present-day implications of Luther's views.

ON THE JEWS AND THEIR LIES

POST-LUTHER ATTACKS

Standard accounts of Luther's ideas on the Jews frequently claim that his writings marked a 'low-point' in Christian-Jewish relations, and that afterward, they suggest, criticism of the Jews and their actions gradually faded away, as Europe and Western civilization became more 'civilized.' This, however, is not the case. Critiques in fact became harsher than ever, even as they shifted from theological figures to men more secular in orientation: philosophers, writers, sociologists, and politicians.

Consider Shakespeare, for example. Born about two decades after Luther's death, he employed anti-Jewish themes of the day in one of his greatest plays, *The Merchant of Venice* (circa 1598). A central character is Shylock, a Jewish money-lender who ruthlessly demands his payment of interest. Launcelot falls into his debt and finds himself virtually enslaved by this financial "master": "Certainly the Jew is the very devil incarnal" (Act II, sc. II). When Launcelot later defaults on his debt, Shylock demands payment nonetheless: his infamous "pound of flesh," to be cut from the debtor's chest. Though metaphorical, such ruthlessness would have resonated with European audiences of that time.[1]

By the 1700s, the rise of secular monarchies and nascent democracies throughout Europe and the West gave wealthy Jews new access to power, something they had lacked with the former rigid Christian hierarchy. But with the same negative qualities that they exhibited over the centuries, Jews now were causing visibly greater damage to society. Consequently, criticisms grew harsher than ever. In France, several notable critics emerged. Montesquieu wrote the following remark in a 1721 letter: "Know that wherever there is money, there are Jews".[2] Somewhat later, Mirabaud published a booklet, *Ancient Opinions on the Jews*, in which he said:

---

[1] Another such literary example, predating *Merchant of Venice*, is Christopher Marlowe's play *The Famous Tragedy of the Rich Jew of Malta* (1590).

[2] Unless noted otherwise, sources of all quotations in this Afterword are cited in my book *Eternal Strangers* (2020); interested readers are invited to check details there.

Afterword

You will therefore see from this that, a long time before they had brought down upon themselves this curse, which is now regarded as the cause of their wretchedness, [the Jews] were generally hated and generally despised in every country which knew them: after which you will agree that there is no mention of them in the old books except in connection with this contempt, and in relation to the general aversion felt for them...

Not only did all the nations despise the Jews; they even hated them and believed that they were as justified in hating as in despising them. They were hated because they were known to hate other men...

The philosopher Denis Diderot was likewise extremely critical. The Jews were taught by the Talmud, he said, "to steal the goods of Christians, to regard them as savage beasts, to push them in a precipice...to kill them with impunity and to utter every morning the most horrible imprecations against them... This people should be kept separate from others." Later, Diderot attacked both the Old Testament and present-day Jews who sustained that mythology: "And you, angry and brutish people, vile and vulgar men, slaves worthy of the yoke which you bear...go, take back your books and remove yourselves from me." In his famous *Encyclopédie*, he added that, among the Jews,

> [one does not find] any rightness of thought, any exactness in reasoning or precision of style, in a word, any of that which ought to characterize a healthy philosophy. One finds among them, on the contrary, only a confused mélange of the principles of reason and revelation, a pretentious and often impenetrable obscurity, principles that lead to fanaticism, blind respect for the authority of the rabbis and for antiquity, in a word, all the faults that mark an ignorant and superstitious people.

On the Jews and Their Lies

Around the same time, Rousseau described the Jews as "the vilest of peoples"; one is aghast at "the baseness of this people, incapable of any virtue," a race that constituted "the vilest people perhaps who existed then." To maintain their identity, Moses gave the Hebrew tribe "customs and practices which are incompatible with those of other nations...to render it always a foreigner amongst other men."

The harshest French critic, though, was surely Voltaire, who condemned the Jews at every point of his long writing career. In an early 1722 letter, he asked: "A Jew belongs to no land other than the one where he makes money; can he not just as easily betray the king for the emperor as the emperor for the king?" His famous *Philosophical Dictionary* of 1745 contains lengthy passages on the Jews, such as this:

> It is certain that the Jewish nation is the most singular that the world has ever seen, and...in a political view, the most contemptible of all... [T]he Hebrews have ever been vagrants, or robbers, or slaves, or seditious. They are still vagabonds upon the earth, and abhorred by men, yet affirming that heaven and earth and all mankind were created for them alone. ... You ask, what was the philosophy of the Hebrews? The answer will be a very short one—they had none. Their legislator [Moses] himself does not anywhere speak expressly of the immortality of the soul, nor of the rewards of another life. ...
>
> It is commonly said that the abhorrence in which the Jews held other nations proceeded from their horror of idolatry; but it is much more likely that the manner in which they, at the first, exterminated some of the tribes of Canaan, and the hatred which the neighboring nations conceived for them, were the cause of this invincible aversion. As they knew no nations but their neighbors, they thought that in abhorring them they detested the whole earth, and thus accustomed themselves to be the enemies of all men. ...

AFTERWORD

> [The ancient Jews'] stay in Babylon and Alexandria… formed the people to no art, save that of usury. In short, we find in them only an ignorant and barbarous people, who have long united the most sordid avarice with the most detestable superstition and the most invincible hatred for every people by whom they are tolerated and enriched.

A 1756 piece, *Essay on Morals*, includes this memorable passage: "The Jewish nation dares to display an irreconcilable hatred against all nations, and revolts against all masters; always superstitious, always greedy for the good of others, always barbarous—cringing in misfortune, and insolent in prosperity." But perhaps Voltaire's most ominous remark was the following, from 1771: "[The Jews] are, all of them, born with raging fanaticism in their hearts, just as the Bretons and Germans are born with blond hair. I would not be in the least bit surprised if these people would not some day become deadly to the human race."

By the late 1700s, Germans critics began speaking up as well. Johann Herder remarked, in 1791, on the "intolerant spirit of the Jewish religion," noting in particular the Jews' "antipathy to other nations." When they reached Europe, he said, "this widely-diffused republic of cunning usurers" managed to overpower local financial systems, primarily through trickery and deception: "[this] people of God…have been for thousands of years, nay almost from their beginning, parasitical plants on the trunks of other nations; a race of cunning brokers, almost throughout the whole world." We see here the first apparent use of the term 'parasite' with respect to the Jews; we can well imagine the impression given of a people who grew wealthy by doing little more than drawing interest—that is, wealth—from the indigenous German populace. And through numerous debt defaults, the Jews certainly extracted their "pound of flesh" from the German people. Hence, seeing Jews as parasites would again have struck a chord with the people of that time.

On the Jews and Their Lies

Another prominent intellectual, Johann Fichte, was concerned that Jews, through their wealth and notorious insularity, were creating a functional state of their own within the larger German nation. This "state within a state" critique would prove of increasing concern over time. In 1793, Fichte wrote:

> Throughout almost all the countries of Europe, a mighty hostile state is spreading that is at perpetual war with all other states, and in many of them imposes fearful burdens on the citizens; it is the Jews. I don't think, as I hope to show subsequently, that this state is fearful—not because it forms a separate and solidly united state but because this state is *founded on the hatred of the whole human race*... In a state where the absolute monarch cannot take from me my paternal hut and where I can defend my rights against the all-powerful minister, the first Jew who likes can plunder me with impunity. This you see and cannot deny, and you utter sugary words of tolerance and of the rights of man and civil rights...
>
> Don't you remember the state within the State? Does the thought not occur to you that if you give civil rights to the Jews, who are citizens of a state more solid and more powerful than any of yours, they will utterly crush the remainder of your citizens? ... To protect ourselves against them, I see no other way than to conquer for them their promised land [i.e. Palestine] and send them all there.

As we can see, this is very much aligned with Luther's view: that the Jews have an inbred hatred of the rest of humanity, and therefore that they must be physically—and perhaps forcibly—removed from civil society.

In 1796, Georg Hegel composed a text on the past and future of Christianity which included some biting remarks. Judaism, he said, was "rooted in contempt for the whole world," recognizing only "the most destructive, invincible, irresistible hostility" in humanity. As a result, "the only act Moses reserved for the Israelites was...to borrow

Afterword

with deceit and repay confidence with theft." Fellow philosopher Immanuel Kant had similar observations, ones that explicitly recall Luther's concern with "Jewish lies." In his work *Anthropology* (1798) he made the following comment:

> [The Jews], living among us, or at least the greatest number of them, have, through their usurious spirit since their exile, received the not-unfounded reputation of deceivers. It seems strange to think of a nation of deceivers; but it's just as strange to think of a nation made up of nothing but merchants, which are united for the most part by an old superstition that's recognized by the government under which they live. They don't seek any civil honor, but rather wish to compensate their loss by profitably outwitting the very people among whom they find protection, and even to make profit from their own kind. It cannot be otherwise with a whole nation of merchants, who are nonproductive members of society (for example, the Jews in Poland).
>
> Their condition, sanctioned by ancient precepts and recognized even by us, cannot be altered by us without serious consequences, even though they have made the saying "buyer beware" the supreme principle of morality in their dealings with us. ...
>
> [T]hese merchants, after the destruction of their city [Jerusalem], were able to migrate gradually into far-distant lands (in Europe) taking language and religion with them... [W]e may suppose that their dispersion throughout the world, with their unity in religion and language, must not be attributed to a *curse* that had been inflicted upon this people, [but rather] must be considered as a *blessing* [to them]—especially since the wealth of the Jews, if we think of them as individuals, apparently exceeds per capita that of any other nation at the present time.

Again we see echoes of Luther: Jews as a "nation of merchants and deceivers," whose "usurious spirit" exploits their host population.

On the Jews and Their Lies

19th Century Critiques

Into the 1800s, more condemnation from prominent quarters around Europe and even America. In the US, then-senator (and future president) John Quincey Adams gave a speech of 1804 decrying the sorry state of German Jews in Frankfurt; he said, "the word 'filth' conveys an ideal of spotless purity in comparison with Jewish nastiness." Some years later, in his diary, he concurred with the idea that "[the Jews'] hatred of all Christians is rancorous beyond conception." Meanwhile across the Atlantic, French Emperor Napoleon had his share of troubles with the Hebrews, as he remarked in an 1808 letter to his brother: "I have undertaken to reform the Jews, but I haven't endeavored to draw more of them into my realm. Far from that, I have avoided doing anything that could show any esteem for the most despicable of mankind." In England, the poet Lord Byron penned a work, "The Age of Bronze" (1823), that made several cutting remarks on Jewish influence in his nation:

> Not without Abraham's seed can Russia march;
> 'Tis gold, not steel, that rears the conqueror's arch.
>
> Two Jews, a chosen people, can command
> In every realm their scripture-promised land—
>
> Two Jews keep down the Romans, and uphold
> The accursed Hun, more brutal than of old;
>
> Two Jews—but not Samaritans—direct
> The world, with all the spirit of their sect.

Byron is undoubtedly referring to the rising power in England of the Jewish banking family, the Rothschilds; it was their dominant financial influence, both in Britain and the Continent, that allowed them and their co-religionists to "direct the world."

Afterword

Back in Germany, the philosopher Schopenhauer had his own complaints. In his *Parerga and Paralipomena* (1851), he made extended remarks:

> The real religion of the Jews, as presented and taught in Genesis and all the historical books up to the end of Chronicles, is the crudest of all religions because it's the only one that has absolutely no doctrine of immortality, not even a trace thereof. ... It is, therefore, the crudest and poorest of all religions and consists merely in an absurd and revolting theism. ... While all other religions endeavor to explain the metaphysical significance of life to the people by symbols and parables, the Jews' religion is entirely immanent and furnishes nothing but a mere war-cry in the struggle with other nations.
>
> Also we should not forget God's chosen people who, after they had stolen by Jehovah's express command the gold and silver vessels lent to them by their old and trusty friends in Egypt, now made their murderous and predatory attack on the 'Promised Land,' with the murderer Moses at their head, in order to tear away from the rightful owners, by the same Jehovah's express and constantly repeated command, showing no mercy and ruthlessly murdering and exterminating all the inhabitants, even the women and children.
>
> Tacitus and Justinus have handed down to us the historical basis of the Exodus... We see from the two Roman authors how much the Jews were at all times and by all nations loathed and despised. This may be partly due to the fact that they were the only people on earth who did not credit man with any existence beyond this life and were, therefore, regarded as beasts... Scum of humanity—but great master of lies [*grosse Meister im Lügen*].

ON THE JEWS AND THEIR LIES

The ultimate tragedy, for Schopenhauer, is that the pathetic *Judeo-Christian* culture dominated the history of Europe, rather than the nobler Greco-Roman: "The religion of the Greeks and Romans, those world-powers, has perished. The religion of the contemptible little Jewish race (*verachteten Judenvölkchens*), on the other hand, has been preserved…" The Jews are a "*gens extorris*" (refugee race), eternally uprooted, always searching for but never finding a homeland: "Till then, it lives parasitically on other nations and their soil; but yet it is inspired with the liveliest patriotism for its own nation. This is seen in the very firm way in which Jews stick together…and no community on earth sticks so firmly together as does this."

Schopenhauer's compatriot, the composer Richard Wagner, was likewise incensed at the role of Jews in his country. In an 1881 letter, he wrote, "I regard the Jewish race as the born enemy of pure humanity and everything that is noble in it; it is certain that we Germans will go under before them, and perhaps I am the last German who knows how to stand up as an art-loving man against the Judaism that is already getting control of everything." The same year he penned an essay that included this observation:

> The Jew, on the other hand, is the most astonishing example of race consistency ever produced by world history. … Even racial mixing fails to harm him; he mixes male or female with the most foreign of races, and a Jew always comes to light. … A wonderful, incomparable phenomenon: the *plastic demon of decay of humanity*, in triumphant security…

Also in 1881, Friedrich Nietzsche began his long series of negative comments on the Jews. In his book *Daybreak* (sec. 377) he observed that "The command 'love your enemies' had to be invented by the Jews, the best haters there have ever been." This is a fascinating remark, especially given that, today, Jews lead the charge when it comes to condemnations of "hate speech." The master haters, it seems, are the best

Afterword

at accusing others of their own vice. In *The Gay Science* (1882), Nietzsche sarcastically notes that the Jews are indeed 'chosen' people, precisely because "they had a *more profound contempt* for the human being in themselves than any other people" (sec. 136). Then in a notebook entry of the same year, he states that if one thing is certain, it's that the Jews are, in some sense, deeply untrustworthy:

> People of the basest origin, in part rabble, outcasts not only from good but also from respectable society, raised away from even the smell of culture, without discipline, without knowledge, without the remotest suspicion that there is such a thing as conscience in spiritual matters; simply— Jews: with an instinctive ability to create an advantage, a means of seduction out of every superstitious supposition... When Jews step forward as innocence itself, then the danger is great. (*Will to Power*, sec. 199)

And in truth, they have never moved beyond their historical role as subverters of society and culture. As Nietzsche writes in one of his final works, *Antichrist* (1888):

> [T]he Jews are the *most catastrophic* people of world history... The Jewish nation...took the side of all *decadence* instincts...because it divined in them a power by means of which one can prevail against 'the world.' The Jews...have a life-interest in making mankind *sick*, and in inverting the concepts of 'good' and 'evil,' 'true' and 'false' in a mortally dangerous and world-maligning sense. (sec. 24)

"In short," adds Nietzsche, "everything that contains its value *in itself* is made altogether valueless, *anti*-valuable, by the parasitism of the priest." This holds true, above all, in that very religion that sprang from Jewish roots: Christianity. He writes,

ON THE JEWS AND THEIR LIES

In Christianity, all of Judaism, a several-century-old Jewish preparatory training and technique of the most serious kind, attains its ultimate mastery as the art of lying in a holy manner. The Christian, the *ultima ratio* of the lie, is the Jew once more—even *three times* a Jew. (sec. 44)

Christianity is a "lie," says Nietzsche, because it is a Jewish construction (Paul, the disciples, and all the New Testament writers were Jews) that was based on a whole host of falsehoods, such as a God that loves everyone, a happy afterlife in heaven, a miracle working God-man called Jesus who came to earth, etc. From the perspective of Martin Luther, this is perhaps the ultimate irony: Luther, a man who decried Jewish lies, even as he fell for the biggest lie of them all. Of all people—Martin Luther, the famed author of *On the Jews and Their Lies*.

There are many more prominent critics that I could cite here: Robert Louis Stevenson, Mark Twain, Henry Adams, H. G. Wells, Martin Heidegger, H. L. Mencken, Henry Ford…the list goes on. And I emphasize, these are not obscure commentators; the people I quoted above and in the Introduction are all major thinkers—among the brightest and most insightful men in history. Their opinions are not offered lightly. Their opinions *count*. It's no coincidence that we see the same complaints, repeated across nations and centuries. There is, as Martin Luther saw, something highly objectionable, highly repugnant, and highly dangerous about the Jewish people. Not all of them, of course. There are always individual exceptions. But *en masse*, somehow their worst characteristics come to the fore, and their most objectionable individuals rise to positions of power. This seems to be a universal constant, suggesting that it is something genetic, something embedded in and intrinsic to the Jewish race.

Afterword

To the Present Day

To close, let me recap and paraphrase Luther's position, in light of the modern day. The Jews, he said, are inveterate liars and misanthropes. They lie repeatedly, on even the most serious of topics, and therefore we can never really trust what they say about anything. They hate others—*all* others—and they have no concern about using lies and deceit, with impunity, to achieve their goals. Human well-being matters not to them; they are willing to harm, injure, or even kill, if it serves their ends. And their extensive wealth affords them considerable sway within society, and therefore much opportunity for damage.

Hence, Luther might say, we need both short-term and long-term actions. Short-term, synagogues must be dismantled or sold off, and all Jewish schools and centers closed; their homes must be seized and sold off, and them placed in low-income public housing; we must abolish their freedom of movement, which means tracking all physical movement (such as via electronic tagging, ankle bracelets, etc); Jews must be terminated immediately from all financial positions (banking, finance, investment, corporate management, etc); all Jewish wealth must be immediately confiscated, and held by the government for the use of various social services; and all able-bodied young Jews must be put to hard physical labor in government-monitored labor camps, on projects serving the public interest.

The only long-term solution is to completely remove them from our midst; they must be deported, expelled, or otherwise banished. In practice, this would mean sending them to Israel, where all Jews are already granted citizenship. Those who refuse to leave, given sufficient warning, would be imprisoned for life, or sentenced to death; after all, "we are at fault in not slaying them," said Luther. Harsh, perhaps, and brutal. And yet we are dealing with a group that is potentially "deadly to the human race," as Voltaire said. We can imagine Luther saying to us, No actions are too severe, for this devilish brood.

Given the Jewish propensity to accumulate vast wealth, to use that wealth in malicious ways, and to go as far as fomenting international chaos and war to achieve their ends, their cost to humanity and overall human well-being is incalculable. I have documented the extensive Jewish role in global wars elsewhere, and it's an appalling story indeed.[3] Jews (and their Gentile supporters) who have forced war and mass death on the world should be put on trial for war crimes and crimes against humanity. But in modern democratic nations, mass media bears some responsibility as well. Jews (and their Gentile supporters) in the media who have misled, deceived, and lied to the public should be put on trial for gross and malicious abuse of the public interest, and as virtual enemies of the state.

On the financial front, the truly immense Jewish accumulation of wealth is breath-taking. An historical point of note: All the way back in 1885, French journalist Edouard Drumont estimated that "Jews possess half of the capital in the world".[4] We are initially taken aback at such a claim, and yet, amazingly, this figure is not as outrageous as it might appear. Recent analysis in the US shows, for example, that five of the ten richest individuals, and at least 54% of the top 50, are Jews. Of the top 35 highest-paid corporate CEOs, again, around 54% are Jews. Of the 585 American billionaires, around half—some 290—are Jews.[5] Just how much money is this, exactly? The 290 Jewish billionaires likely own or control around $1.5 trillion. Note: this is just *290 individual people*. Just imagine the combined wealth of some 6 million American Jews.

From the above, we can infer that Jews indeed own or control about half of the total private wealth in the US. The US total was recently estimated by the *Wall Street Journal* to be around $100 trillion. Therefore, total Jewish wealth likely comes to an astonishing *$50 trillion*. This is a truly stunning figure. Most of us can scarcely conceive of what it would mean to own $1 million. American Jews own, in total, not 50 times or 500 times, but *50,000,000 times* $1 million.

---

[3] See Dalton (2019).

[4] In Mendes-Flohr and Reinharz (2011: 315).

[5] See T. Dalton, "A brief look at Jewish wealth" (www.theoccidentalobserver.net). Ginsberg (1993: 1) also confirms this fact: "Today, though barely 2% of [America's] population is Jewish, close to half its billionaires are Jews."

Afterword

If the American government was to follow Luther's suggestion and confiscate this wealth—much of it, unquestionably, having been acquired by illegal or unethical means—then we can hardly imagine the benefits to ordinary Americans. Simply distributing this money among the roughly 325 million US citizens would mean a colossal payout of over $150,000 per person; every family of four would get around $600,000 in a lump sum. This would go a long way toward righting past wrongs. And it would deprive the American Jewish Lobby from doing further harm, for many years to come.

Of course, such an action is utterly inconceivable in present-day America. But why is this? Something comparable has happened many times in the past in Europe; why is it so unimaginable today? When the British expelled their Jews in 1290, it set the stage for the greatness of Shakespeare, the Elizabethan Age, and the British Empire. When the many nations of Continental Europe banished their Jews in the 14th and 15th centuries, it inaugurated the stellar accomplishments in the arts and culture of the Renaissance. When Germany deported their Jews in the 1930s, it allowed a broken and bankrupt nation to become a leading world power in just five or six years. These are not coincidences. The many brutal criticisms leveled at Jews, by Luther and others for centuries, are not coincidences. There is a causal relationship here. The lesson of history is this: expel the Jews, and greatness ensues.

So once again, we ask: Why is such a thing so unimaginable today? Why can it not even be discussed? Are we too 'civilized'? For what—our own self-defense? Are we too humane?—that we allow countless Jewish-inspired atrocities, in the realms of warfare, economics, and politics, to continue? Are we too weak? Too ignorant? Too confused? Who has convinced us that such a thing is impossible today? In whose interest is it, that we are not even allowed to contemplate such things today?

We can imagine the very reverend Martin Luther lecturing us from afar: *Awake, my dear and good friends! Fight the devils. Confront the evil. Save yourselves—your present and future lives hang in the balance.*

BIBLIOGRAPHY

Burnett, S. 2018. "Jews and Judaism." In *Martin Luther in Context* (D. Whitford, ed.). Cambridge University Press.
Carroll, J. 2001. *Constantine's Sword*. Houghton Mifflin.
Dalton, T. 2015. *Debating the Holocaust*. Castle Hill.
Dalton, T. 2019. *The Jewish Hand in the World Wars*. Castle Hill.
Dalton, T. 2020. *Eternal Strangers: A Critical History of Jews and Judaism*. Castle Hill.
Gabba, E. 1984. "The growth of anti-Judaism or the Greek attitude toward the Jews," in W. Davies and L. Finkelstein, (eds.), *Cambridge History of Judaism*, vol. 2. Cambridge University Press.
Ginsberg, B. 1993. *The Fatal Embrace*. University of Chicago Press.
Goshen-Gottstein, A. 2018. *Luther the Anti-Semite*. Fortress.
Gritsch, E. 2012. *Martin Luther's Anti-Semitism*. Eerdmans.
Hillerbrand, H. 1990. "Martin Luther and the Jews." In *Jews and Christians* (J. Charlesworth, ed.). Crossroad Publishing.
Hitler, A. 2019. *Hitler on the Jews* (T. Dalton, ed). Castle Hill.
Hood, J. 1995. *Aquinas and the Jews*. University of Pennsylvania Press.
Jaher, F. 1994. *A Scapegoat in the New Wilderness*. Harvard University Press.
Joyce, A. 2019. "Crypto-Jews, German guilt, and the Wittenberg Jew-pig." www.theoccidentalobserver.net.
Kaufmann, T. 2006. "Luther and the Jews." In *Jews, Judaism, and the Reformation in 16th Century Germany* (D. Bell and S. Burnett, eds.). Brill.
Kaufmann, T. 2017. *Luther's Jews*. Oxford University Press.
Lindberg, C. 1994. "Tainted greatness: Luther's attitudes toward Judaism and their historical reception." In *Tainted Greatness* (N. Harrowitz, ed.). Temple University Press.

Lohse, B. 1999. *Martin Luther's Theology*. Fortress Press.

Luther, M. 1902. *The Table Talk of Martin Luther* (W. Hazlitt, trans.). G. Bell and Sons.

Luther, M. 1955. *Luther's Works*, vol. 55. Concordia.

Mendes-Flohr, P. and Reinharz, J. (eds.). 2011. *The Jew in the Modern World*. Oxford University Press.

Miller, G. 2014. "Luther's views of the Jews and Turks." In *The Oxford Handbook of Martin Luther's Theology* (R. Kolb et al, eds.). Oxford University Press.

Rupp, G. 1972. *Martin Luther and the Jews*. Council of Christians and Jews.

Schramm, B. 2012. "Introduction." In *Martin Luther, the Bible, and the Jewish People*. Fortress Press.

Simon, M. 1996. *Verus Israel*. Vallentine Mitchell.

Stern, M. 1974. *Greek and Latin Authors on Jews and Judaism*, vol. 1. Israel Academy of Sciences and Humanities.

Wallmann, J. 1990. "The reception of Luther's writings on the Jews." In *Stepping-Stones to Further Jewish-Lutheran Relationships* (H. Ditmanson, ed.). Augsburg.

Wiener, P. 1945. *Martin Luther: Hitler's Spiritual Ancestor*. Hutchinson & Co.

Wistrich, R. 2010. *A Lethal Obsession*. Random House.

Yuval, I. 2006/2000. *Two Nations in Your Womb*. University of California Press.

GENERAL INDEX

"70 weeks" of Daniel 114, 140-142, 149-152, 156-157, 222-223

Adam 52, 187
Aesop's fables 138
Agrippa *see* Herod Agrippa I
Akiba (Akiva) ben Yosef 145,146
Alexander the Great 118, 132, 159
Antioch 143
Antiochus IV Epiphanes 131-132, 136, 140, 159
ark of the covenant 97, 134-135

Babylon 81, 105, 114-116, 120, 136, 139, 151, 178
Bethlehem 142
Bible, Chaldean 90, 94
Burgensis *see* Burgos, Paul of
Burgos, Paul of ("Burgensis") 45, 87n24, 101, 125, 128, 134, 139, 149, 198

Calf of Aaron *see* calf, golden
calf, golden 69
Cato 138
Charles V (emperor) 133, 178
Cicero, Marcus 138
circumcision 50, 57-72, 82
Conrad of Weissensee 127
Cyrus, King of Persia 65, 153, 156-158, 160, 222

Darius, King of Persia 65, 159
Dionysius 212

Epicureans 138
Eusebius 147, 217

Gabriel (angel) 140, 149-151, 156, 161-163, 171, 222-223
Gog and Magog 162

Hadrian (emperor) 148, 217-218
Hebel Vorik 169, 200-202, 214
Henry V, Duke 167n77
Herod Agrippa I 154, 160, 222
Herod I 92, 94, 106, 116, 132, 135, 142
Homer 90, 160
Hyrcanus, John 132

Jews
  abolish safe travel of 185
  and usury 76-77, 128-129, 137, 139, 153, 168, 179, 185-191, 198-199, 203
  blood libel 128n59, 177
  deserve to be slain 180
  desire to rule the world 212
  expelled by Hadrian 218
  expelled from France 178
  expelled from Magdeburg 179
  expelled from Prague 179
  expelled from Regensburg 179
  expelled from Spain 178
  forbidden to speak God's name 201
  hatred of mankind 53, 56-57, 72, 78, 127
  houses to be destroyed 184
  Luther's meeting with 102
  must expel 187, 191, 203
  must burn synagogues 183, 201
  prayer books to be taken 184, 201
  prohibit their usury 185
  put to hard labor 187
  rabbis forbidden to teach 184, 201
  seize their silver and gold 185
  would slaughter Gentiles 203
John the Baptist, Saint 49, 142, 167
Josephus 135, 144, 161
Judensau ('Jew pig') 123

Kokhba, Simon bar 145-147, 185, 211-212, 216-218, 222

Lyra, Nicholas of 45, 101, 125, 128, 136, 139, 149, 198

Maccabees 118, 120, 133, 140
Margaritha, Anthony 139n57, 169
Mary, Jewishness of 173
Muhammad, prophet 69, 131, 163, 183, 212
Münster, Sebastian 174
Muslims *see* Turks

Nebuchadnezzar II, King of Babylon 65, 98
Nero (emperor) 160

Paul of Tarsus, Saint 47, 51, 67, 84, 102, 163, 183, 207, 217, 221-223
Peter, Saint 70, 223
pharaoh, Egyptian 47, 119
Philo 142
Pilate, Pontius 143
Plato 48
pope 69-70, 91, 101, 131, 163, 183
Ptolemy II Philadelphus, King 134

Raymund Martini 101

Sabbatarians 66, 99, 117
Sadducees 138, 139
Saracens *see* Turks
Saul, King 97

Schem Hamphoras see Von Schem Hamphoras
Sennacherib, King of Assyria 81n19, 114
"sharp mercy" 183, 187, 211
Shiloh 89, 94, 97-101, 107, 125, 131, 142, 160, 217, 219
Simon of Trent 127

Tacitus 53n6
Targumim *see* Bible, Chaldean
Ten Commandments 77-78, 137
Terence, Publius 138
Tiberius (emperor) 217
Titus (emperor) 46
Trajan (emperor) 145
Trinity, doctrine of 204-206
Turks ("Saracens") 72, 84, 88, 91, 193, 214, 220

usury *see* Jews, usury

Vespasian (emperor) 46, 148
Von Schem Hamphoras 123n47, 169

Wittenberg 102, 155, 156
Wolfenbüttel 167

INDEX OF BIBLICAL PASSAGES

Note: only book and chapter are indexed

Acts 2	115
Acts 3	217
Acts 4	217
Acts 13	221
1 Chronicles 17	108
1 Chronicles 28	108-109
1 Chronicles 29	108-109
2 Chronicles 6	134
2 Chronicles 21	104
2 Chronicles 22	133
2 Chronicles 30	114
2 Chronicles 31	114
2 Chronicles 36	157
1 Corinthians 2	84
1 Corinthians 4	221
1 Corinthians 15	154
Daniel 7	117
Daniel 9	134, 136, 140-158, 161-162, 198, 222-223
Daniel 11	133, 136
Deuteronomy 4	61, 150, 184
Deuteronomy 6	205
Deuteronomy 9	96, 152
Deuteronomy 10	61
Deuteronomy 12	61, 184
Deuteronomy 13	184
Deuteronomy 17	185
Deuteronomy 23	177, 186
Deuteronomy 28	175
Deuteronomy 30	150
Deuteronomy 31	74
Deuteronomy 32	83, 100, 129, 144
Esther 9	64-65
Exodus 1	107
Exodus 20	79, 201
Exodus 21	117
Exodus 30	161
Exodus 33	68
Ezra 1	157
Ezra 2	114
Ezra 6	159
Genesis 1	95
Genesis 3	52, 187
Genesis 5	158
Genesis 10	55
Genesis 11	158-159
Genesis 15	52
Genesis 17	50, 58, 60, 67, 68, 70, 221
Genesis 18	52
Genesis 22	220
Genesis 25	54, 59, 159
Genesis 49	89-102, 106, 117, 120, 125, 129, 131, 145, 147, 149, 217, 219-220
Haggai 2	99, 120-140, 147
Hosea 1	46, 129, 144
Hosea 2	78, 83, 129, 144
Hosea 11	152
Isaiah 2	125, 215
Isaiah 6	84
Isaiah 8	72, 148
Isaiah 9	92, 113, 117
Isaiah 11	215
Isaiah 28	102
Isaiah 33	224
Isaiah 40	197
Isaiah 48	74, 81

On the Jews and Their Lies

Isaiah 52	198	1 Maccabees 1	136
Isaiah 53	79, 125, 198, 215		
Isaiah 65	214	Mark 16	223
Isaiah 66	107		
		Matthew 3	49
Jeremiah 4	61, 176	Matthew 5	137, 225
Jeremiah 6	62	Matthew 10	130, 192, 194
Jeremiah 9	62	Matthew 11	49
Jeremiah 29	139, 157, 178	Matthew 12	192
Jeremiah 31	224	Matthew 15	137
Jeremiah 33	111-112, 116	Matthew 18	185
		Matthew 22	220
John 3	51	Matthew 23	137
John 4	47, 221	Matthew 27	186, 197
John 5	194	Matthew 28	213
John 7	197		
John 8	49, 214, 220	Micah 4	125
John 11	197, 214, 220		
John 15	194, 200	Numbers 16	74
John 19	186	Numbers 24	145, 152
Joshua 24	52	Obadiah 20	178
Judges 3	98	2 Peter 2	70
Judges 8	97		
Judges 21	97	Proverbs 11	78
1 Kings 1	108	Psalms 2	131, 196
1 Kings 3	92	Psalms 5	64
1 Kings 9	82, 96-97	Psalms 18	207, 224
1 Kings 12	98, 114	Psalms 19	131
1 Kings 20	192	Psalms 32	79, 151
		Psalms 34	75
2 Kings 8	104, 118	Psalms 40	223
		Psalms 50	75
Leviticus 20	173	Psalms 51	56, 80
Leviticus 26	61, 150	Psalms 74	94
		Psalms 81	70
Luke 1	133	Psalms 89	109, 117
Luke 3	176	Psalms 95	74
Luke 10	194	Psalms 103	73
Luke 11	130, 168	Psalms 105	66
Luke 21	46	Psalms 109	127
		Psalms 110	117

Index of Biblical Passages

Psalms 111	104	1 Samuel 10	98
Psalms 130	96	1 Samuel 15	184
Psalms 132	117		
Psalms 143	79, 96	2 Samuel 7	105, 107-109
Psalms 145	75	2 Samuel 12	151
Psalms 147	73	2 Samuel 23	102-120, 219
Romans 3	51, 67	Zechariah 5	137
Romans 9	47, 207	Zechariah 9	197
Romans 10	83	Zechariah 11	137
Romans 11	163, 183	Zechariah 12	137
Romans 14	222	Zechariah 14	162